Discrete Choice Experiments in Marketing

Contributions to Management Science

Ulrich A. W. Tetzlaff
Optimal Design of Flexible Manufacturing Systems
1990, 190 pp. ISBN 3-7908-0516-5

Fred von Gunten
Competition in the Swiss Plastics Manufacturing Industry
1991, 408 pp. ISBN 3-7908-0541-6

Harald Dyckhoff/Ute Finke
Cutting and Packing in Production and Distribution
1992, 248 pp. ISBN 3-7908-0630-7

Hagen K. C. Pfeiffer
The Diffusion of Electronic Data Interchange
1992, 257 pp. ISBN 3-7908-0631-5

Evert Jan Stokking/Giovanni Zambruno (Eds.)
Recent Research in Financial Modelling
1993, 174 pp. ISBN 3-7908-0683-8

Richard Flavell (Ed.)
Modelling Reality and Personal Modelling
1993, 407 pp. ISBN 3-7908-0682-X

Lorenzo Peccati/Matti Virén (Eds.)
Financial Modelling
1994, 364 pp. ISBN 3-7908-0765-6

Michael Hofmann/Monika List (Eds.)
Psychoanalysis and Management
1994, 392 pp. ISBN 3-7908-0795-8

Rita L. D'Ecclesia/Stavros A. Zenios (Eds.)
Operations Research Models in Quantitative Finance
1994, 364 pp. ISBN 3-7908-0803-2

Mario S. Catalani/Giuseppe F. Clerico
Decision Making Structures
1996, 175 pp. ISBN 3-7908-0895-4

M. Bertocchi/E. Cavalli/S. Komlósi (Eds.)
Modelling Techniques for Financial Markets and Bank Management
1996, 296 pp. ISBN 3-7908-0928-4

Holger Herbst
Business Rule-Oriented Conceptual Modeling
1997, 246 pp. ISBN 3-7908-1004-5

Constantin Zopounidis
New Operational Approaches for Financial Modelling
1997, 466 pp. ISBN 3-7908-1043-6

Klaus Zwerina

Discrete Choice Experiments in Marketing

Use of Priors in Efficient Choice Designs
and Their Application to
Individual Preference Measurement

With 8 Figures
and 12 Tables

Springer-Verlag Berlin Heidelberg GmbH

Series Editors
Werner A. Müller
Peter Schuster

Author
Dr. Klaus Zwerina
Wilhelmine-Fliedner-Str. 14
D-40723 Hilden, Germany

ISBN 978-3-7908-1045-5   ISBN 978-3-642-50013-8 (eBook)
DOI 10.1007/978-3-642-50013-8

Cataloging-in-Publication Data applied for
Die Deutsche Bibliothek – CIP-Einheitsaufnahme
Zwerina, Klaus: Discrete choice experiments in marketing: use of priors in efficient choice designs and their application to individual preference measurement; with 12 tables / Klaus Zwerina. – Heidelberg: Physica-Verl., 1997
 (Contributions to management science)
 Zugl.: Kaiserslautern, Univ.; Diss.

This work is subject to copyright. All rights are reserved, whether the whole or part of the material is concerned, specifically the rights of translation, reprinting, reuse of illustrations, recitation, broadcasting, reproduction on microfilm or in any other way, and storage in data banks. Duplication of this publication or parts thereof is permitted only under the provisions of the German Copyright Law of September 9, 1965, in its current version, and permission for use must always be obtained from Physica-Verlag. Violations are liable for prosecution under the German Copyright Law.

© Springer-Verlag Berlin Heidelberg 1997
Originally published by Physica-Verlag Heidelberg in 1997.

The use of general descriptive names, registered names, trademarks, etc. in this publication does not imply, even in the absence of a specific statement, that such names are exempt from the relevant protective laws and regulations and therefore free for general use.

Softcover Design: Erich Kirchner, Heidelberg
SPIN 10636413   88/2202-5 4 3 2 1 0 – Printed on acid-free paper

To my wife Eva

Acknowledgments

This dissertation arose from a very positive cross-national interchange of research between the University of Kaiserslautern (Germany) and Duke University (USA). I would like to express my gratitude to the following people and organizations which importantly supported and contributed to this research.

I wish to express my appreciation to my first co-chair Friedhelm Bliemel who gave me the opportunity to join the doctoral program in Germany and always supported the idea of pursuing my dissertation research abroad. Thanks are extended to the other members of my dissertation committee, Jürgen Ensthaler and Michael von Hauff. I wish to thank the University of Kaiserslautern for awarding my doctoral scholarship, which was based on a competitive dissertation proposal, and the German Academic Exchange Program (DAAD) for granting supplement funds that allowed me to conduct my dissertation research abroad.

I would like to thank the faculty of the Fuqua School of Business (Duke University) for giving me the opportunity to conduct my research at this great place; they treated me not just as a "visiting scholar," but truly as one of them. Additional travel funds from Fuqua are gratefully acknowledged. I also wish to thank Steve Hoeffler who helped debugging the thesis. I was very glad to meet Rick Staelin at Fuqua. He is not only an outstanding researcher, but also the best teacher I have ever had, a combination that is unique. I would like to thank him for his valuable feedback and research insights. Further, I owe many helpful and inspiring discussions to Mark An (Economics, Duke University), Richard Johnson (Sawtooth Software), Warren Kuhfeld (SAS Institutes), and Jordan Louviere (University of Sydney).

I have been extremely fortunate to have Joel Huber as my second co-chair. He has been a major influence on me *both* personally and professionally. He invited me to Duke to work with him on my thesis. Mere words cannot express my gratitude to Joel. He had always time when I needed a piece of advice. He inspired, encouraged, and guided me in every stage of my thesis. He is a true scholar and friend.

I am indebted to my parents who believed in and supported me for over two decades of study. Finally and foremost, I wish to express my appreciation and affection to my wonderful wife Eva. Together, we dared the step over the "big pond." During the years that I prepared this thesis, she was always patient and had a word of encouragement for me. With her love and support, she turned the long and arduous course of a dissertation into an enjoyable journey.

KLAUS ZWERINA

Table of Contents

LIST OF TABLES AND FIGURES	XIII
1. INTRODUCTION	1
1.1 Positioning of the Dissertation	1
1.2 Conjoint Analysis vs. Discrete Choice Experiments	5
1.3 Context of Discrete Choice Experiments	7
1.4 Research Problems and Objectives of the Dissertation	8
1.5 Outline of the Dissertation	9
2. REVIEW OF LINEAR DESIGN AND DISCRETE CHOICE MODELS	11
2.1 Linear Design Theory	11
2.1.1 Terminology	11
2.1.2 Confounding and Resolution in Fractional Factorials	12
2.1.3 Linear Models	15
2.1.4 Design Efficiency	19
2.1.5 Summary and Discussion	24
2.2 Discrete Choice Models	25
2.2.1 Derivation and Assumptions of the Multinomial Logit Model	25
2.2.2 Properties of the Logit Model	33
2.2.3 Choice Models Not Subject to the IIA Assumption	38
2.2.4 Summary and Discussion	42
3. DESIGNS FOR DISCRETE CHOICE MODELS	45
3.1 Review of Previous Design Strategies	45
3.1.1 Strategies for Identifiable Choice Designs	45
3.1.2 A Strategy for Efficient Generic Designs	50
3.2 Efficiency in Choice Designs	50
3.2.1 Measure of Choice Design Efficiency	51
3.2.2 Principles of Efficient Choice Designs	54
3.3 Summary and Discussion	56

4. USING PRIORS IN CHOICE DESIGNS — 59

   4.1 Generating Efficient Choice Designs — 59
      4.1.1 Swapping Attribute Levels — 61
      4.1.2 Relabeling Attribute Levels — 64
      4.1.3 Swapping and Relabeling to More Complex Choice Designs — 66

   4.2 Sensitivity to Misspecification of Priors — 69
      4.2.1 Defining Misspecifications — 69
      4.2.2 Investigating Efficiency Losses — 70

   4.3 Ways to Gather Priors — 72

   4.4 Summary and Discussion — 72

5. INDIVIDUAL CHOICE MODELS — 75

   5.1 An Approach to Building an Individual Choice Model — 77
      5.1.1 Self-Explicated Stage — 78
      5.1.2 Choice Design Generation Stage — 78
      5.1.3 Model Estimation Stage — 82

   5.2 Empirical Test of the Individual Choice Model — 82
      5.2.1 Study Design — 83
      5.2.2 Results — 84
      5.2.3 Predictive Validity — 85
      5.2.4 Heterogeneity Problem in Logit — 87
      5.2.5 Direct Use of Prior Information — 90
      5.2.6 Differences between Partworths in Different Models — 91

   5.3 Summary and Discussion — 94

6. CONCLUSION — 97

   6.1 Summary — 97

   6.2 Limitations and Future Research — 100
      6.2.1 Behavioral Areas — 101
      6.2.2 Methodological Areas — 102

Table of Contents

APPENDIX A: Derivation of Probability-Centered Estimation Error   105
APPENDIX B: Example Screens of Self-Explicated Task   106
APPENDIX C: Example Screen of Conjoint Task   108
APPENDIX D: Example Screen of Choice Task   109
APPENDIX E: Holdout Choice Sets   110
APPENDIX F: Experimental Conjoint Design   111
APPENDIX G: Experimental Choice Designs and Partworth Values   112

REFERENCES   163

List of Tables and Figures

TABLES

Table 2.1	Relation between responses and effects in a 1/2-fraction of a 2^4 factorial	13
Table 2.2a	3^{3-1} Main-effects-only design	18
Table 2.2b	Different types of coding and corresponding covariance matrices	20
Table 2.3	$3^2 2$ Orthogonal unbalanced design and covariance matrix	23
Table 4.1	Comparison of original and swapped $3^3/3/9$ choice design	60
Table 4.2	Gains in expected errors due to utility balance from relabeling and swapping	63
Table 4.3	Comparison of original and relabeled $3^4/2/15$ choice design	65
Table 4.4	Relative efficiencies given misspecifications of priors	71
Table 5.1	Laptop attributes and levels	77
Table 5.2	Comparison of predictive validity	86
Table 5.3	Predictive validity of constrained model estimation	91
Table 5.4	Comparison of partworths for individually most and second most important attributes	93

FIGURES

Figure 1.1	Overview of models and measurement of consumer preferences	2
Figure 2.1	Common probability density of two random utilities	28
Figure 2.2	Comparison of normal and Gumbel probability density function	29
Figure 2.3	Choice probabilities for different values of μ	36
Figure 3.1	Principles of efficient choice designs	55
Figure 4.1	Comparison between true priors and distorted priors by weights and skewness	70
Figure 5.1	Number of choice sets needed to equal 18 conjoint judgments	81
Figure 5.2	Comparison between pooled choice estimate and average of individual choice estimates	88

1. Introduction

The chapter starts with a positioning of this dissertation in the marketing discipline. It then provides a comparison of the two most popular methods for studying consumer preferences/choices, namely conjoint analysis and discrete choice experiments. Chapter 1 continues with a description of the context of discrete choice experiments. Subsequently, the research problems and the objectives of this dissertation are discussed. The chapter concludes with an outline of the organization of this dissertation.

1.1 Positioning of the Dissertation

During this century, increasing globalization and technological progress has forced companies to undergo rapid and dramatic changes—for some a threat, for others it offers new opportunities. Companies have to survive in a Darwinian marketplace where the principle of natural selection applies. Marketplace success goes to those companies that are able to produce *marketable value*, i.e., products and services that others are willing to purchase (Kotler 1997). Every company must be engaged in new-product development to create the new products customers want because competitors will do their best to supply them. Besides offering competitive advantages, new products usually lead to sales growth and stability. As household incomes increase and consumers become more selective, firms need to know how consumers respond to different features and appeals. Successful products and services begin with a thorough understanding of consumer needs and wants. Stated otherwise, companies need to know about consumer preferences to manufacture tailor-made products, consumers are willing to buy.

For at least the last two decades, analyzing and measuring consumer preferences has been one of the most heavily researched areas in marketing. There are two important aspects of consumer preferences: modeling and measurement. *Modeling* of consumer preferences is concerned with specifications of the process by which a product is evaluated and finally chosen. In contrast, *measurement* emphasizes scaling aspects, i.e., finding specific numerical scale values (estimates), assuming that a particular decision rule applies, possibly with some error (Green and Srinivasan 1978). Figure 1.1 provides an overview of models and measurement techniques of consumer preferences.

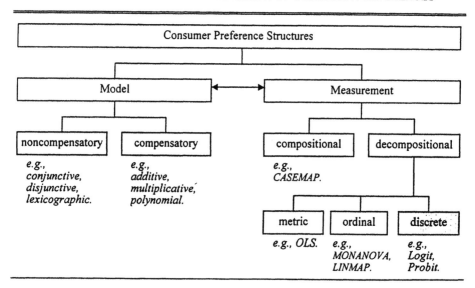

Figure 1.1
OVERVIEW OF MODELS AND MEASUREMENT OF CONSUMER PREFERENCES

Products are characterized by different attributes, such as brand name or price, and different attribute levels, for example, IBM, HP, and NEC. We can distinguish between compensatory and noncompensatory models or decision rules (e.g., Bettman 1979). The key to this distinction is the ability of a good value on one attribute to make up for bad values on other attributes. Strategies that make trade-offs among attributes are called *compensatory*, whereas strategies that do not make trade-offs are called *noncompensatory*. The three most important noncompensatory approaches are the conjunctive, the disjunctive, and the lexicographic model (e.g., Eliashberg and Lilien 1993, Kotler and Bliemel 1996).

In a *conjunctive model*, a consumer considers a product only if it meets certain minimum, acceptable standards on all attributes. If any one attribute is deficient, the product is eliminated from consideration. In a *disjunctive model*, instead of preferred products having to satisfy all attribute values, they have to satisfy at least one superior attribute, disregarding other attributes. For example, under the conjunctive model, the consumer may insist on a computer that has lots of memory *and* high speed. Under the disjunctive model, the consumer may settle for a computer with either lots of memory *or* high speed. A *lexicographic model* assumes that all attributes are used, but in a stepwise manner. Products are evaluated on the most important attribute first; then the second most important attribute is used only if there are ties, and so on.

Compensatory models can be characterized by the way information about attributes is transformed into an overall evaluation (utility or preference) of the product. In an *additive model*, for example, each attribute is weighted according to its relative importance and the weighted attribute values are added to form an overall evaluation. Similarly, in a *multiplicative model*, weighted attribute values are combined in a multiplicative fashion to form the overall evaluation. The *polynomial model* results as a mixture of both models.

Measurement techniques of consumer preferences can be divided into compositional and decompositional approaches. *Compositional* or build-up approaches go back to the expectancy-value class of attitude models (Fishbein 1967, Rosenberg 1956), where the overall utility for a multiattribute product is found as a weighted sum of the product's perceived attribute levels and associated value ratings which are separately judged by the respondent. In the same spirit, self-explicated models are used in marketing to form consumer preference structures. In a self-explicated model, the respondent first evaluates attribute levels on, say, a 10-point desirability scale. Next, the respondent indicates the relative importances of the attributes by, for example, allocating 100 points across the attributes, reflecting the relative importances. The overall utility of the product is calculated as a weighted sum of the attribute values (desirability ratings), where the weights are the relative importances. A particular version of an implemented self-explicated model is, for example, CASEMAP (Srinivasan 1988).

With self-explicated models come several problems (see Green and Srinivasan 1990). Perhaps the most important problem is the inability of subjects to appraise their "true" preference structures. For example, in judging the importance of attributes, respondents tend to underestimate more important attributes and overestimate less important attributes (e.g., Einhorn 1970). Decompositional models, on the other hand, overcome this problem.

Decompositional methods estimate the structure of a consumer's preference based on his or her overall evaluations of a set of different product descriptions rather than asking the respondent directly about his or her preference structure. Respondents react to, say, 16 product descriptions, which attribute levels are systematically varied according to statistical rules. Traditionally, respondents are asked to rank the product descriptions reflecting their perceived preferences, or rate them on, say, a 100-point likelihood-of-purchase scale. Then, statistical methods are applied to derive preference structures. In the case of ratings (metric measure), ordinary least squared (OLS) regression is applied; in the case of rankings (ordinal measure), more specialized procedures, such as MONANOVA (Kruskal 1965) or LINMAP (Srinivasan and Shocker 1973), can be used. The literature suggests, however, that OLS applied to rank data yields very similar results compared to the more specialized and complicated methods (e.g., Carmone, Green, and Jain 1978, Cattin and Bliemel 1978, Jain et al. 1979). Further, its ease of use and widespread availability make OLS the most popular estimation procedure (Wittink and Cattin 1989). We refer to the class of methods that rely on rank or rate data as conjoint analysis.

A related method to conjoint analysis are discrete choice experiments, or sometimes called choice-based conjoint analysis. Here, respondents are asked to select their most attractive options among sets of several product descriptions. Probabilistic discrete choice models, such as logit (e.g., McFadden 1974) or probit models (e.g., Daganzo 1979, Currim 1982), are applied to the data. Generally speaking, this thesis is concerned with the question of how to design such choice experiments.

1.2 Conjoint Analysis vs. Discrete Choice Experiments

Currently, conjoint analysis and discrete choice experiments represent the most widely applied methodologies for measuring and analyzing consumer preferences or choices. These methods are mainstream methods in both academia and industry (Carroll and Green 1995). The seminal theoretical contribution to conjoint analysis was made by Luce, a mathematical psychologist, and Tukey, a statistician (Luce and Tukey 1964). Since its introduction in marketing (Green and Rao 1971), conjoint analysis has been heavily researched and used in many applications (reviews by Green and Srinivasan 1990, Wittink and Cattin 1989, and Wittink, Vriens, and Burhenne 1994). Although most theoretical and empirical analyses have been conducted in the United States, numerous contributions to conjoint have been made in other countries, such as Germany (e.g., Bauer, Herrmann, and Mengen 1994, Gaul, Aust, and Baier 1995, Schweikl 1985, Simon 1992, Simon and Kucher 1988, and Thomas 1979).

In a conjoint task, respondents sort, rank, or rate a set of full-profiles on, for example, a likelihood of purchase scale. These full-profiles are experimentally designed, hypothetical products or services described by multiple factors (or attributes) and levels. Typically, ordinary least squares is applied to the data and parameters, known as partworths, are estimated. These partworths reflect weights, respondents put on the experimentally controlled product attributes and levels, when making an overall evaluation of that hypothetical product. The results from conjoint provide insights into how consumers perceive and evaluate certain products, and are useful in, for example, developing of new products, predicting market shares or segmenting markets.

Discrete choice experiments, sometimes called choice-based conjoint, represent a relatively new technique and was introduced in the marketing literature by Louviere and Woodworth (1983). In recent years, this technique has increased in popularity among marketing practitioners as a way to more directly study consumer choice (Batsell and Louviere 1991, Carson et al. 1994). An experimental design for a choice model (choice design) consists of choice sets composed of several alternatives, each defined as combinations of different attribute levels. In this technique, respondents are shown sets of two or more explicitly defined competitive profiles that are often identified by brand name. The respondent is asked to select his or her most preferred offering in each choice set and probabilistic choice models (e.g., multinomial logit or probit models) are applied to such choice data.

Discrete choice experiments hold several important advantages over traditional conjoint analysis. First, data collection involves simulated purchase decisions (hypothetical choices), generally providing a more realistic, simpler, and less ambiguous task for respondents than rankings or ratings. Second, choice models directly estimate market shares instead of requiring a two-stage process, that is, estimation followed by choice simulation. Third, alternative- or brand-specific attributes and levels, such as unique price effects for Coke versus Pepsi, can easily be accommodated. Finally, a no-choice option (or constant alternative) can be incorporated to estimate demand volume rather than just market shares.

However, a disadvantage in choice experiments comes from the fact that choices are less informative than corresponding ratings. Choice experiments usually require large numbers of observations (choices) to obtain reliable parameter estimates. Therefore, choice experiments are typically carried out at aggregate level (or latent segment level, DeSarbo, Ramaswamy, and Cohen 1995) rather than at the individual level.

1.3 Context of Discrete Choice Experiments

Analyzing how consumers make choices among multiattribute alternatives has been a major activity in marketing research (see, e.g., Meyer and Johnson 1995). Knowing about that process enables companies to predict market shares as the cumulative effect of individual choices across different consumers and provides critical measures of market share elasticities with respect to price, product features, and other marketing mix variables.

From an analyst's point of view, a consumer is an optimizing "black box" with, for example, product attributes as input, and purchase decisions as output. Economic choice theory is an approach to modeling the "black box" that is designed to provide quantitative forecasts with well-defined statistical properties (McFadden 1986). Economic choice theory has primarily used field data (e.g., scanner data). In field data, however, the inability to control the choice circumstances can create undesirable statistical properties. In contrast, data collected from experiments with hypothetical, but realistic choice problems offer some important advantages. First, the circumstances of choice can be precisely specified with a proper choice design, avoiding the need to untangle effects from the "natural experiment." In field data, identification of the effects is often a problem due to lack of variability, limited range, or confoundment of explanatory variables. Second, specifically constructed choice designs allow one to estimate effects of interest with maximum precision. Third, experiments are particularly useful in situations where field data just do not exist; for example, in developing and testing of new products and services. In sum, choice experiments overcome many of the problems that can occur with data obtained from field surveys.

However, external validity of the results obtained from experiments remains an issue, i.e., is experimental (laboratory) behavior a good predictor of actual (field) behavior. In general, the closer an experiment mimics real market decisions, the more valid the obtained results will be.

1.4 Research Problems and Objectives of the Dissertation

Providing Principles of Efficient Choice Designs. Building designs for choice models is more complex than for linear (conjoint) models. A number of methods have been suggested in the marketing literature for building choice designs. Most of these methods use extensions of standard linear experimental designs focusing on identification issues rather than on (statistical) efficiency issues. However, efficiency is an important concept in experimental designs. A more efficient design produces more precise estimates, or equivalently, requires less responses to achieve a certain level of precision in the estimates. Consequently, efficiency is beneficial in the sense that it produces either higher quality surveys or saves expenses in the data collection. The first goal of this thesis is therefore to develop principles that characterize efficient choice designs.

Developing Methods for Constructing Efficient Choice Designs. After providing principles of choice design efficiency, the next task is to use this knowledge to develop methods to construct such efficient designs. An important property in probabilistic choice models is that the statistical efficiency of a choice design depends on an (unknown) parameter vector. This property implies the need to bring prior parameter estimates into choice designs. In order to simplify the design problem, previous design strategies have assumed the parameter vector to be zero. While this assumption is justified when there is very little information about the model parameters, the analyst has typically some prior beliefs or information on the relative importance of attributes or the relative value of their levels. Incorrectly assuming that the parameter vector is zero may result in considerable efficiency losses. Therefore, our second goal is to develop ways to incorporate such prior estimates on model parameters in the choice design generation process in order to improve design efficiency.

Building an Individual-Level Choice Model. Due to the lack of information in choices as opposed to ratings or rankings, choice models are usually estimated at aggregate level, assuming homogeneity of consumer preferences, which is a very restrictive assumption. The current approach to alleviate the heterogeneity problem involves the use of latent class models, enabling analysis of choice at segment level as opposed to aggregate level (e.g., DeSarbo et al. 1995, Kamakura and Russell 1989, Wedel and DeSarbo 1993). If segmentation is effective at the group level, it is likely to be even more so at the individual level, avoiding the heterogeneity problem completely. So far, however, individual choice models were infeasible because they required too many choices per respondent. Thus, our final goal is to develop choice designs so efficient that they result in reliable individual-level estimates based on reasonable numbers of choices per respondent. We will present a feasible individual choice model and demonstrate its use for both commercial applications and behavioral research.

1.5 Outline of the Dissertation

Chapter 2 provides a review of statistical methods and models which are useful for the material in later chapters. The chapter discusses basic principles of linear design theory and explains important probabilistic choice models. Chapter 2 is intended to help readers not familiar with these topics to better understand what follows in subsequent chapters.

Chapter 3 discusses the topic of efficiency in choice designs and gives an overview of previous approaches to build choice designs. We introduce four principles of choice design efficiency and highlight why choice designs built from extensions of the general linear design literature are nonoptimal.

Chapter 4 is concerned with the generation of efficient choice designs. We provide methods that build efficient choice designs by using prior estimates on model parameters. We show that by using reasonable priors, the methods can produce important efficiency gains and that these gains are quite robust against misspecifications of priors.

Chapter 5 presents the first practical approach to an individual-level choice model. We show that it is possible to reliably estimate 10 parameters of a choice model from 30 individual choices among three alternatives. We test the predictive validity of the proposed approach and show that it outperforms a conjoint and a self-explicated model. Furthermore, we illustrate how the individual choice model permits the exploration of behavioral differences between judgment and choice without having to aggregate across heterogeneous respondents.

Chapter 6 concludes the dissertation. It summarizes findings of the dissertation, discusses limitations, and suggests directions for future research.

2. Review of Linear Design and Discrete Choice Models

In this chapter, we review some basics of the linear design theory and probabilistic choice models. The purpose of this chapter is not a detailed discussion of the developments that have taken place in these fields; rather, we briefly highlight some selected concepts and introduce notation and terminology used in the subsequent chapters. Chapter 2 is intended to help those who are not familiar with these topics to better understand what follows in the next chapters. The reader who is familiar with these topics can omit this chapter and continue with Chapter 3 of the thesis.

2.1 Linear Design Theory

The basic theory of the design and analysis of factorial experiments was first described by Fisher (1926), and was developed to a great extent initially by Yates (1935, 1937), Bose and Kishen (1940), and Bose (1947). In subsequent years, a host of other researchers have contributed to this field.

In this section, we do not provide a detailed discussion of the linear design theory rather than introduce some important concepts of that theory. This section covers the following selected topics: fractional factorials, confounding, resolution, linear models, coding, and efficiency.

2.1.1 Terminology

A *factorial experiment* investigates the relation between a response (output, yield) variable and several independent (input) variables. These independent variables, known as *factors* (or attributes) are systematically varied and are under control of the experimenter. A factor may be quantitative or qualitative. Typically, a factor is tested at various discrete values or *levels*. For example, the levels of brand in a soft drink experiment may be Coke, Pepsi, and RC Cola. A *treatment combination* (trial, run, profile) is one of the possible combinations of levels of all factors under consideration. A *design* (or plan) is a specified set of treatment combinations. A factorial in which each factor has the same number of levels is called *symmetric*, otherwise *asymmetric* factorial. A factorial design that involves all combinations of levels of factors is called a *full factorial*.

2.1.2 Confounding and Resolution in Fractional Factorials

A full factorial involves a large number of profiles when the number of factors and/or levels increase. For example, with only five factors each at three levels, there exist $3^5 = 243$ possible treatment combinations. Such a large experiment is often too expensive and impractical. Fortunately, these large numbers can be considerably reduced if the interest lies in estimating only lower order effects, namely main effects and two-factor interactions, under the assumption of absence or negligibility of higher order effects. Such subsets of factorials by which useful information can be obtained with a reasonable degree of precision are called *fractional factorials*.

2.1.2.1 Confounding

In a full factorial design with N treatment combinations, all possible N-1 effects are estimable. To see the implications of a fractional factorial instead of a full factorial design, we consider a simple example. Suppose there are four factors A, B, C, and D each at two levels. Out of the possible 16 combination, we use only the following eight in our experiment (cf. Dey 1985): (0000, 0011, 0101, 0110, 1001, 1010, 1100, 1111).

The relation between the responses from these eight treatment combinations and the main effects and interactions is presented in Table 2.1. The pattern of plus

Review of Linear Design and Discrete Choice Models 13

and minus signs in the columns for the four main effects A, B, C, and D represent a specific coding, where -1 is used if the factor in question is at its low level and +1 if the factor is at its high level. The columns for the eleven interactions AB, AC,..., $ABCD$ are simply the appropriate cross products of individual effects (e.g., Green, Carroll, and Carmone 1978).

Table 2.1
RELATION BETWEEN RESPONSES AND EFFECTS IN A 1/2-FRACTION OF A 2^4 FACTORIAL

response	treatment	μ	A	B	C	D	AB	AC	AD	BC	BD	CD	ABC	ABD	ACD	BCD	ABCD
y_1	0000	+	-	-	-	-	+	+	+	+	+	+	-	-	-	-	+
y_2	0011	+	-	-	+	+	+	-	-	-	-	+	+	+	+	-	-	+
y_3	0101	+	-	+	-	+	-	+	-	-	+	-	+	-	+	-	+
y_4	0110	+	-	+	+	-	-	-	+	+	-	-	-	+	+	-	+
y_5	1001	+	+	-	-	+	-	-	+	+	-	-	+	-	-	+	+
y_6	1010	+	+	-	+	-	-	+	-	-	+	-	-	+	-	+	+
y_7	1100	+	+	+	-	-	+	-	-	-	-	+	-	-	+	+	+
y_8	1111	+	+	+	+	+	+	+	+	+	+	+	+	+	+	+	+

The main effect of factor A, for example, can be estimated by subtracting the average response when A is at its low level from the average response when A is at its high level, that is,

$$A = [\,+1(y_5) + 1(y_6) + 1(y_7) + 1(y_8) - 1(y_1) - 1(y_2) - 1(y_3) - 1(y_4)\,]/4.$$

It can be seen, e.g., that the same linear function of responses (contrast) estimates both the grand mean μ and the four-factor interaction $ABCD$. Similarly, the same contrasts estimate both A and BCD, and so on. That is, those pairs of effects cannot be estimated independently from each other and are said to be *confounded* or *aliased*. If μ is represented by I, then the *alias statements* for this one half fractional can be written as $I \equiv ABCD$, $A \equiv BCD$, $B \equiv ACD$, $C \equiv ABD$, $D \equiv ABC$, $AB \equiv CD$, $AC \equiv BD$, $AD \equiv BC$.

In this case, the eight treatments are solutions of the equation

$$x_1 + x_2 + x_3 + x_4 = 0 \pmod{2},$$

where $x_i \in \{0,1\}$ denotes the levels of the *i*th factor for $i=1, 2, 3, 4$. Thus, the interaction *ABCD* is confounded for obtaining the 8-treatment fraction and said to form the *identity group* (or *defining relation*). In general, there can be more than one member in the identity group; for example, in order to create a 1/4 fraction two such members (or equations, respectively) are needed, and so on. A computer program can generate these fractional factorials by solving the type of modulo equation(s) shown previously.

Once the identity group is given, the alias relation(s) of an effect can easily be obtained by taking the generalized interactions of the relevant effect with (each of the members of) the identity group. In a p^n design with p prime (i.e., n factors with p levels each), the *generalized interactions* of two effects U and V are UV, $UV^2,...,UV^{p-1}$. For example, to obtain the alias relation of A we have $p=2$, $U=A$, and $V=ABCD$. Then, based on the relation $A^p = B^p = ... = I$, we obtain $UV = A^2BCD = BCD$, that is, A is aliased with BCD, or in formulas $A \equiv BCD$. The principles can directly be extended to factors with larger numbers of levels (see, e.g., Winer et al. 1991).

In order to obtain unbiased estimates for certain effects, assumptions regarding the absence of other effects are necessary. For example, the main effect A can only be estimated without bias if the *BCD* interaction is zero. This potential bias is the cost of reducing the number of treatment combinations in fractional factorials.

2.1.2.2 Resolution

Resolution is a means of classifying (orthogonal) fractional factorial designs. The resolution identifies which effects, possibly including interactions, are estimable. The most commonly used designs are of resolution III, IV, and V. *Resolution III* or main-effects-only designs are those that permit the estimation of all main effects, unaliased with any other main effect but potentially aliased with two-factor interactions. *Resolution IV* designs are those in which no main effect is aliased with any other main effect or two-factor interaction, but where the two-factor interactions are potentially aliased among themselves. *Resolution V* designs are those where no main effect or two-factor interaction is aliased with any other main effect or two-factor interaction. Generally, higher resolutions require larger designs. In all three cases, the designs produce uncorrelated (orthogonal) estimates of the (unaliased) effects. Resolution III designs are very popular because they handle relatively many factors in a minimal number of treatment combinations, however, they offer no protection against interactions.

2.1.3 Linear Models

The designs discussed are based on the theory of linear models. We will review some basics of linear models and their application to experimental designs.

2.1.3.1 Formulation

The term *linear model* is used to refer to an equation

(2.1) $$y = \beta_0 + \beta_1 x_1 + \ldots + \beta_m x_m + \varepsilon,$$

that relates the behavior of a dependent variable y to a linear (in the β's) function of the set of independent variables $x_1, x_2, \ldots, x_m$. The β_j are the parameters that specify the nature of the relationship, and ε is the random error that takes into account the fact that the model does not describe exactly the behavior of the data. The principle of least squares is applied to a set of n observed values of y and the associated x_j to obtain estimates $\hat{\beta}_0, \hat{\beta}_1, \ldots, \hat{\beta}_m$ of the respective (true) parameters

$\beta_0, \beta_1, \ldots, \beta_m$. Letting y_i, x_{ij}, and ε_i denote respectively the values of y, x_j, and ε in the ith observation, we define the $\mathbf{y}$ vector, the $\mathbf{X}$ matrix, and the $\boldsymbol{\varepsilon}$ vector as

$$\mathbf{y} = \begin{bmatrix} y_1 \\ \vdots \\ y_n \end{bmatrix}, \quad \mathbf{X} = \begin{bmatrix} 1 & x_{11} & \cdots & x_{1m} \\ \vdots & \vdots & & \vdots \\ 1 & x_{n1} & \cdots & x_{nm} \end{bmatrix}, \quad \boldsymbol{\varepsilon} = \begin{bmatrix} \varepsilon_1 \\ \vdots \\ \varepsilon_n \end{bmatrix}.$$

Then the model in matrix notation is

(2.2) $$\mathbf{y} = \mathbf{X}\boldsymbol{\beta} + \boldsymbol{\varepsilon},$$

where $\boldsymbol{\beta}' = (\beta_0, \beta_1, \ldots, \beta_m)$ is the parameter vector. The $n \times (m+1)$ $\mathbf{X}$ matrix is called the *design matrix*. For estimating this parameter vector one requires the minimization of the quadratic form

$$\mathbf{e}'\mathbf{e} = (\mathbf{y} - \mathbf{X}\boldsymbol{\beta})'(\mathbf{y} - \mathbf{X}\boldsymbol{\beta}).$$

On differentiating this expression and equating the derivative to zero, we obtain the following system of linear equations, known as *normal equations*:

$$\mathbf{X}'\mathbf{X}\boldsymbol{\beta} = \mathbf{X}'\mathbf{y}.$$

If the *information matrix* $X'X$ is of full rank or nonsingular, then there exists an unique solution that is given by

(2.3) $$\hat{\boldsymbol{\beta}} = (\mathbf{X}'\mathbf{X})^{-1}\mathbf{X}'\mathbf{y}$$

and the covariance matrix of $\hat{\boldsymbol{\beta}}$ is given by

(2.4) $$\boldsymbol{\Sigma} = (\mathbf{X}'\mathbf{X})^{-1}\sigma^2,$$

Review of Linear Design and Discrete Choice Models   17

where σ^2 is the (true) variance of the observations y_i. An unbiased estimator of σ^2 is

$$s_e^2 = (\mathbf{y'y} - \hat{\boldsymbol{\beta}}'\mathbf{X'y})/(n-m-1).$$

2.1.3.2 Coding of the Design

The design matrix for a factorial is constructed from the design and a proper type of coding. There are a number of different coding types. The most commonly used are dummy coding, effects coding, and orthogonal coding. Generally, each factor with p levels, a_p, requires exactly $p-1$ independent (indicator) variables. The use of the coding scheme 0, 1 for the indicator variable is referred to as *dummy coding*. The coding of the indicator variables, x, is as follows:

$$x_{i1} = \begin{cases} 1, \text{ if a treatment } i \text{ appears in } a_1 \\ 0, \text{ otherwise} \end{cases}$$

$$\vdots$$

$$x_{i,p-1} = \begin{cases} 1, \text{ if a treatment } i \text{ appears in } a_{p-1} \\ 0, \text{ otherwise} \end{cases}$$

Instead of dummy coding, a similar scheme called *effects coding* can be used:

$$x_{i1} = \begin{cases} 1, \text{ if treatment } i \text{ appears in } a_1 \\ -1, \text{ if treatment } i \text{ appears in } a_p \\ 0, \text{ otherwise} \end{cases}$$

$$\vdots$$

$$x_{i,p-1} = \begin{cases} 1, \text{ if treatment } i \text{ appears in } a_{p-1} \\ -1, \text{ if treatment } i \text{ appears in } a_p \\ 0, \text{ otherwise} \end{cases}$$

This coding type looks slightly more complicated, but the resulting design matrix is the same as for dummy coding except for the last level a_p, where a row of minus ones replaces a row of zeros. In dummy coded designs, the β's can be interpreted as differences between the treatment mean of a particular level and the treatment mean of the last level. Instead, in effects coded designs, the β's can be interpreted as differences between the treatment means of a particular level and the grand mean; that is, the regression parameters are equal to the treatment effects in an ANOVA model.

A third coding type called *orthogonal coding* is sometimes used. There is not just one orthogonal coding scheme but rather a variety of schemes with the only restriction being that column sums in a design matrix (of a full factorial) are zero and the columns are mutually orthogonal. A special case of orthogonal coding are *orthogonal polynomial coefficients*, which are typically used to perform a trend analysis in ANOVA models (see, e.g., Winer et al. 1991). Using the latter coding in regression models, the resulting estimates of β's reflect the contributions of the error sums of squares of the linear, quadratic, and so on, trend components (see Kirk 1995). In general, the β parameters do not have a simple interpretation using orthogonal codings. One advantage, however, of orthogonal coding is that the information matrix, X'X, of an (orthogonal) design is diagonal. This simplifies determining its inverse, since the inverse of a diagonal matrix is obtained replacing each diagonal element by its reciprocal. Today, where linear design model software is widely available, such computational advantages no longer play an important role.

Table 2.2a
3^{3-1} MAIN-EFFECTS-ONLY DESIGN

\multicolumn{3}{c}{Factors}
A	B	C
1	1	1
1	2	2
1	3	3
2	1	2
2	2	3
2	3	1
3	1	3
3	2	1
3	3	2

To illustrate the different types of codings, let us consider the following design depicted in Table 2.2a. This design represents an orthogonal 1/3-fraction of a 3^3 factorial design, where all main effects can be estimated on an uncorrelated basis (with a suitably coded X). Table 2.2b shows the design matrices of three different kinds of codings (dummy coding, effects coding, and orthogonal polynomials) and the corresponding covariance matrices $(X'X)^{-1}$

assuming that $\sigma^2 = 1$. The coefficients for the orthogonal polynomials can be obtained from tables in textbooks of experimental designs (e.g., Kirk 1995, Winer et al. 1991).

As one can see, in the dummy-coded and effects-coded design, the covariance matrix contains some off-diagonal elements, whereas in the orthogonal polynomial-coded design, the covariance matrix is diagonal, that is, the effects can be estimated on an uncorrelated (i.e. orthogonal) basis.

The choice of a certain type of coding is largely a matter of personal preference and depends on the interpretability of the parameters (coefficients). A particular type of coding does not affect the interpretability of the overall model, i.e., the model fit, the predicted y's, or the F-statistics. However, the t-statistics for the single parameters depend on the type of coding used since the parameters are interpreted as contrasts between the different levels. For example, in dummy coding, a parameter of a factor level is interpreted as the mean difference between a particular level and the level that is omitted (usually the last level of a factor).

So far we have seen how fractional factorial designs can be used to reduce the large numbers of treatment combinations and we know that these designs produce unbiased estimates of relevant effects, namely main effects and lower order interactions, if we can assume that higher order interactions are negligible. In the next section we will discuss properties of fractional factorials that allow one to estimate relevant parameters with maximum precision.

2.1.4 Design Efficiency

In a full factorial design, all main effects, two-way interactions, and higher-order interactions are estimable and uncorrelated (for an orthogonally-coded **X**). Since for most practical situations, the number of treatment combinations is too large, fractional factorial designs are used. The question is then how to create a fractional factorial that produces "good" parameter estimates.

Table 2.2b
DIFFERENT TYPES OF CODING AND CORRESPONDING COVARIANCE MATRICES

Dummy-Coded Design (X)

m	A x_1 x_2	B x_3 x_4	C x_5 x_6
x_0			
1	1 1	0 0	0 0
1	1 0	1 0	0 0
1	1 0	0 1	0 0
1	0 1	0 0	1 0
1	0 0	1 0	0 1
1	0 0	0 1	0 0
1	0 0	0 0	1 0
1	0 0	0 0	0 1

Dummy-Coded Covariance Matrix $(X'X)^{-1}$

	x_0	x_1	x_2	x_3	x_4	x_5	x_6
x_0	.778	-.333	-.333	-.333	-.333	-.333	-.333
x_1	-.333	.667	.333	0	0	0	0
x_2	-.333	.333	.667	0	0	0	0
x_3	-.333	0	0	.667	.333	0	0
x_4	-.333	0	0	.333	.667	0	0
x_5	-.333	0	0	0	0	.667	.333
x_6	-.333	0	0	0	0	.333	.667

Effects-Coded Design (X)

m	A x_1 x_2	B x_3 x_4	C x_5 x_6
x_0			
1	1 0	0 0	0 0
1	0 1	0 0	0 0
1	-1 -1	0 0	0 0
1	0 0	1 0	0 0
1	0 0	0 1	0 0
1	0 0	-1 -1	0 0
1	0 0	0 0	1 0
1	0 0	0 0	0 1
1	0 0	0 0	-1 -1

Effects-Coded Covariance Matrix $(X'X)^{-1}$

	x_0	x_1	x_2	x_3	x_4	x_5	x_6
x_0	.111	0	0	0	0	0	0
x_1	0	.222	-.111	0	0	0	0
x_2	0	-.111	.222	0	0	0	0
x_3	0	0	0	.222	-.111	0	0
x_4	0	0	0	-.111	.222	0	0
x_5	0	0	0	0	0	.222	-.111
x_6	0	0	0	0	0	-.111	.222

Orthog. Polyn.-Coded Design (X)

m	A x_1 x_2	B x_3 x_4	C x_5 x_6
x_0			
1	-1 1	0 0	0 0
1	0 -2	0 0	0 0
1	1 1	0 0	0 0
1	0 0	-1 1	0 0
1	0 0	0 -2	0 0
1	0 0	1 1	0 0
1	0 0	0 0	-1 1
1	0 0	0 0	0 -2
1	0 0	0 0	1 1

Orthog. Polyn.-Coded Cov. Matrix $(X'X)^{-1}$

	x_0	x_1	x_2	x_3	x_4	x_5	x_6
x_0	.111	0	0	0	0	0	0
x_1	0	.167	0	0	0	0	0
x_2	0	0	.056	0	0	0	0
x_3	0	0	0	.167	0	0	0
x_4	0	0	0	0	.056	0	0
x_5	0	0	0	0	0	.167	0
x_6	0	0	0	0	0	0	.056

2.1.4.1 Efficiency Measures

Efficiencies are measures of design goodness. Common measures of the efficiency of a design matrix **X** are based on the information matrix **X'X**. We have seen that the covariance matrix of the vector of parameter estimates $\hat{\beta}$ in a regression model is proportional to $(\mathbf{X'X})^{-1}$. An efficient design will have a "small" covariance matrix, i.e., it will produce *precise* parameter estimates. There are various summary measures of error size that can be derived from the covariance matrix (see, e.g., Raktoe, Hedayat and Federer 1981). Perhaps the most intuitive summary measure is the average variance around the estimated parameters of a model. This measure is referred to in the literature as A-efficiency or

(2.5) $$A - error = trace(\Sigma) / (m+1),$$

where $m+1$ is the total number of parameters. Two problems with this measure limit the suitability as an overall measure of design efficiency. First, relative A-error is not invariant to (nonsingular) recodings of the design matrix, i.e., design efficiency depends on the type of coding. Second, it is computationally expensive to update. A related measure,

(2.6) $$D - error = \det(\Sigma)^{1/(m+1)},$$

is based on the determinant as opposed to the trace of the covariance matrix. Applying Equations (2.5) and (2.6) to the orthogonally-coded design in Table 2.2b yields $A - error = .780/7 = .111$ and $D - error = (9.079 \times 10^{-8})^{1/7} = .099$.

Minimizing D-error is the most common criterion for evaluating designs. D-error is computationally efficient to update and the ratios of D-errors are invariant under different codings of the design matrix. Since A-error is the arithmetic mean and D-error is the geometric mean of the eigenvalues of Σ, they are generally highly correlated. D-error thereby provides a reasonable way to find designs that are good on alternative criteria. For example, if A-error is the ultimate criterion, we can first minimize D-error and then select the design with minimum A-error rather than minimizing A-error directly.

2.1.4.2 Orthogonality and Balance

There are two principles in linear models that affect design efficiency—orthogonality and balance. A special type of fractional factorial designs is the *orthogonal array*, in which all estimable effects are uncorrelated. A design is *balanced* when each level occurs with equal frequency within each factor. A balanced and orthogonal design has minimum D-error (or maximum efficiency), i.e., the parameter estimates have smallest variances (Kuhfeld et al. 1994). Conversely, the more efficient a design is, the more it tends toward balance and orthogonality.

A design is balanced and orthogonal when $(\mathbf{X'X})^{-1}$ is diagonal (for an orthogonally-coded $\mathbf{X}$). A design is orthogonal when the submatrix of $(\mathbf{X'X})^{-1}$, excluding the row and the column for the intercept, is diagonal. A design is balanced when all off-diagonal elements in the intercept row and column are zero.

To illustrate, let us reconsider the symmetrical 3^{3-1} design from Table 2.2a. This design is in fact orthogonal and balanced—the orthogonal polynomials-coded matrix $(\mathbf{X'X})^{-1}$ is diagonal. Suppose, instead of the three levels for factor C, we needed only two levels. Addelman (1962) suggests a technique known as *collapsing levels* to build asymmetrical (orthogonal) designs. Designs are created using factors that have numbers of levels equal to the largest number required in the design. Factors that have fewer levels are created by recoding. In our example, the three-level factor C with {1, 2, 3} can be recoded into a two-level factor by duplicating levels {1, 2, 1}. Table 2.3 shows the results.

Table 2.3
$3^2 2$ ORTHOGONAL UNBALANCED DESIGN AND COVARIANCE MATRIX

			\multicolumn{6}{c}{Orthog. Polyn.-Coded Design (X)}						
\multicolumn{3}{c}{$3^2 2$ Orthogonal Design}	m	\multicolumn{2}{c}{A}	\multicolumn{2}{c}{B}	C	\multicolumn{6}{c}{Covariance Matrix $(X'X)^{-1}$}
A	B	C	x_0	x_1	x_2	x_3	x_4	x_5	x_0	x_1	x_2	x_3	x_4	x_5
1	1	1	1	-1	1	-1	1	1	.125	0	0	0	0	-.042
1	2	2	1	-1	1	0	-2	-1	0	.167	0	0	0	0
1	3	1	1	-1	1	1	1	1	0	0	.056	0	0	0
2	1	2	1	0	-2	-1	1	-1	0	0	0	.167	0	0
2	2	1	1	0	-2	0	-2	1	0	0	0	0	.056	0
2	3	1	1	0	-2	1	1	1	-.042	0	0	0	0	.125
3	1	1	1	1	1	-1	1	1						
3	2	1	1	1	1	0	-2	1						
3	3	2	1	1	1	1	1	-1						

Note that this technique preserves orthogonality, but violates balance. The design on the left hand panel shows that the first level of factor C occurs twice as often as the second level. Unbalance is also reflected in the none-zero off diagonal elements between the intercept, x_0, and the two-level factor x_5.

Kuhfeld et al. (1994) point out that orthogonal (and unbalanced) designs are not always more efficient than nonorthogonal (and more balanced) designs. Orthogonality was important in the days before general linear design model software became widely available. Today, it is more important to consider efficiency when choosing a design. The authors suggest the use of computerized search routines to build efficient designs. In optimizing efficiency, the search algorithms optimize both balance and orthogonality. In contrast, in tabled orthogonal designs, balance and efficiency may be sacrificed to preserve orthogonality.

Orthogonal designs are available for only a relatively small number of specific problems, with specific numbers of treatment combinations for specific numbers of factors with specific numbers of levels (see. e.g., Addelman 1962 for a catalog of such designs). Often in practical problems, orthogonal designs are not available, for example, when a nonstandard number of treatment combination is desired, or a nonstandard model (say, with specific interactions) is being used. The only general way to find efficient nonorthogonal designs is by using computers.

2.1.5 Summary and Discussion

We introduced basic terminology and notation for linear designs and models. A full factorial design consists of all possible combinations of attribute levels. Full factorials require too many treatment combinations if the number of attributes or levels increase. Instead, fractional factorials can be used to precisely estimate some relevant effects by sacrificing estimability of other effects. Effects that cannot be estimated independently from each other are said to be confounded or aliased. Resolution is a means to classify orthogonal fractional factorials; it identifies which effects are estimable (not confounded). Generally, higher resolutions require larger designs.

There are many ways a design can be coded. The most commonly used coding schemes are dummy coding, effects coding, and orthogonal coding. The type of coding affects the interpretability of the estimated parameters, but does not change the interpretability of the overall model. In the past, orthogonal coding was used because of computational advantages, however, nowadays the choice of coding is largely a matter of personal preference.

Efficiencies are measures of design goodness. An efficient design will have a smaller covariance matrix, i.e., it will produce more precise parameter estimates. The most commonly used measure of size of the covariance matrix is its determinant, known as D-error. It is easy to update and relative D-error is invariant to recodings of a design. There are two principles affecting linear design efficiency: orthogonality and balance. Except for special cases, these two principles compete with each other. Orthogonality is not the primary goal in design creation. The primary goal is efficiency, i.e., minimizing the variances of the parameter estimates. Nonorthogonal balanced designs can be more efficient than orthogonal unbalanced designs. Computer searches optimally trade off balance against orthogonality in generating efficient designs.

2.2 Discrete Choice Models

Marketing researchers have modeled consumer choice behavior by applying theoretical frameworks primarily from two basic disciplines—psychology (e.g., Luce 1959, Thurstone 1927, Tversky 1972) and economics (e.g., Amemiya 1981, McFadden 1981). Probabilistic choice models have been extensively used in marketing, psychology, civil engineering, and geography.

This section introduces the reader to a class of models of probabilistic choice, discrete (or quantal) choice models. The most popular discrete choice model, the multinomial logit (MNL) model, will be discussed in detail because it plays an important role in this thesis. We will first derive the MNL model, discuss properties of the model, and finally provide an overview of other important discrete choice models.

2.2.1 Derivation and Assumptions of the Multinomial Logit Model

Probabilistic discrete choice models go back to Thurstone's (1927) work in psychometrics. He proposed a random utility model of choice in which a random variable is associated with each alternative in a choice set, and the alternative with the greatest realization is the one selected. This approach was later taken as the basis for the theory underlying the econometric formulation of discrete choice models. Discrete choice models start with the assumption that each consumer chooses the single option that yields the greatest random utility. The term "random utility" does not mean that consumers' behavior is necessarily stochastic (like in the Thurstone model). Each individual could well be perfectly consistent in his or her choice of an option, but the modeler cannot observe and measure *all* the factors that determine consumer preferences for different options (lack of information). Following Manski (1977), there are four different sources of uncertainty:

1. *Nonobservable characteristics*: The vector of characteristics affecting the choice of the individual is only partially known by the modeler. Choice may also be affected by factors of which the consumer is not fully aware (the role of the subconscious in choice).
2. *Nonobservable variations in individual utilities*: Any population of consumers will have an associated variance in preferences, and the random term will therefore have a variance that increases with increasing preference heterogeneity.
3. *Measurement errors*: The amount of the observable characteristics is not perfectly known.
4. *Functional misspecification*: The utility function is not known with certainty. The modeler must assume a particular functional relationship and this may be a potential source of error.

It is worth noting that "intra-individual and inter-individual variations in tastes are indistinguishable in their effect on the observed distribution of demand" (McFadden 1981, p. 205). Note also that in an individual-level choice experiment (as opposed to aggregate field data) all of the above error sources except (4) are eliminated.

Discrete choice models start with the assumption that an individual has a utility u_i for a choice alternative i which is (additive) separable into two components: first, a deterministic component, v_i, measured in terms of expressed preference toward the alternative and second, a random component, ε_i, which is not observable by the modeler, that is

$$(2.7) \qquad u_i = v_i + \varepsilon_i.$$

Further we assume that an individual chooses the alternative perceived to have the greatest utility (*principle of random utility maximization*). The probability of choosing the alternative i among a set of J alternatives is given by

(2.8)
$$P_i = P(u_i \geq u_j, \quad j = 1,....,J) \quad \text{or}$$
$$P_i = P(\varepsilon_j \leq v_i - v_j + \varepsilon_i, \quad j = 1,....,J).$$

To keep the notation simple, we assume that an individual chooses the first alternative. We then can write the corresponding choice probability as

$$P_1 = P(\varepsilon_2 \leq v_1 - v_2 + \varepsilon_1, \varepsilon_3 \leq v_1 - v_3 + \varepsilon_1,..., \varepsilon_J \leq v_1 - v_J + \varepsilon_1).$$

For any given realization ε_1^* of ε_1 alternative I will be chosen with probability

$$P_1 = \int_{-\infty}^{v_1-v_2+\varepsilon_1^*} \cdots \int_{-\infty}^{v_1-v_J+\varepsilon_1^*} f(\varepsilon_1^*, \varepsilon_2,..., \varepsilon_J) \, d\varepsilon_J \cdots d\varepsilon_2,$$

where f denotes the corresponding probability density function. Accounting for all possible realizations, we have

$$P_1 = \int_{-\infty}^{\infty} \int_{-\infty}^{v_1-v_2+\varepsilon_1} \cdots \int_{-\infty}^{v_1-v_J+\varepsilon_1} f(\varepsilon_1, \varepsilon_2,..., \varepsilon_J) \, d\varepsilon_J \cdots d\varepsilon_1.$$

This process can geometrically be portrayed for two alternatives. The cut off volume beneath the common probability density f in Figure 2.1 represents the probability that the utility of alternative I is greater than the utility of alternative 2, denoted by u_1 and u_2, respectively.

Figure 2.1
COMMON PROBABILITY DENSITY OF TWO RANDOM UTILITIES

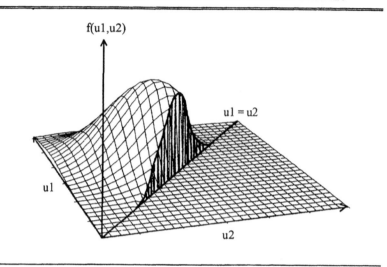

All probabilistic choice models share this derivation of specific choice probabilities. The difference in the various choice models lies in the different assumptions of the error distribution. Perhaps the most natural approach would be to assume that the errors follow a multivariate normal distribution. In fact, we will see at the end of this chapter that this assumption leads to the well-known multinomial probit (MNP) model. However, one difficulty with the probit model is that the choice probabilities cannot be expressed in an analytically closed form. A function which resembles the Normal distribution and produces a closed form of choice probabilities is the Gumbel or extreme-value distribution. If we assume that the random errors in the underlying utility function of Equation (2.7) are i.i.d. Gumbel, then the popular MNL model results (McFadden 1974).

The cumulative distribution function and the probability density function of a random variable that is Gumbel distributed has the form

(2.9) $$F(\varepsilon) = e^{-e^{-\mu(\varepsilon-\eta)}}, \quad \mu > 0$$

and

$$\text{(2.10)} \qquad f(\varepsilon) = \mu e^{-\mu(\varepsilon-\eta)} e^{-e^{-\mu(\varepsilon-\eta)}},$$

respectively, where η is a location parameter and μ is a positive scale parameter. The variance is $\pi^2/6\mu^2$. Figure 2.2 displays the probability density function of a standard Normal and a standard Gumbel random variable.

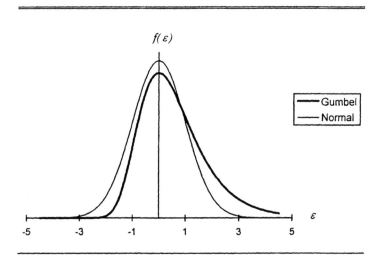

Figure 2.2
COMPARISON OF NORMAL AND GUMBEL PROBABILITY DENSITY FUNCTION

As one can see, both functions have quite similar shapes, that is, a unimodal density. The only difference being that the Gumbel density is positively skewed rather than symmetrical. In fact, if the alternatives have equal variances and there are no correlations across alternatives (independent probit) then the probit model and the logit model produce very similar results (see Maddala 1983).

Since the errors in the MNL model are assumed to be independent from each other, we can write the common probability density function, $f(\varepsilon_1,...,\varepsilon_J)$, as the product of univariate probability density functions. It then follows

$$P_1 = \int_{-\infty}^{\infty} \int_{-\infty}^{v_1-v_2+\varepsilon_1} \cdots \int_{-\infty}^{v_1-v_J+\varepsilon_1} f(\varepsilon_1)f(\varepsilon_2)\cdots f(\varepsilon_J)\,d\varepsilon_J\cdots d\varepsilon_1$$

$$= \int_{-\infty}^{\infty} f(\varepsilon_1) \int_{-\infty}^{v_1-v_2+\varepsilon_1} f(\varepsilon_2)\cdots \int_{-\infty}^{v_1-v_J+\varepsilon_1} f(\varepsilon_J)\,d\varepsilon_J\cdots d\varepsilon_1$$

$$= \int_{-\infty}^{\infty} f(\varepsilon_1) \prod_{j=2}^{J} F(v_1 - v_j + \varepsilon_1)\,d\varepsilon_1.$$

Using Equations (2.9) and (2.10) with $\eta=0$ and $\mu=1$ (i.e., standard Gumbel) we have

$$P_1 = \int_{-\infty}^{\infty} e^{-\varepsilon_1} e^{-e^{-\varepsilon_1}} \prod_{j=2}^{J} e^{-e^{(-v_1+v_j-\varepsilon_1)}}\,d\varepsilon_1$$

$$= \int_{-\infty}^{\infty} e^{-\varepsilon_1} e^{\left(-e^{-\varepsilon_1} \sum_{j=1}^{J} e^{(v_j-v_1)}\right)}\,d\varepsilon_1.$$

Let us write the constant term $a = \sum_{j=1}^{J} e^{(v_j-v_1)}$ and apply the substitution $z = e^{-\varepsilon_1}$. Since $\varepsilon_1 = -\ln(z)$ and $\dfrac{d\varepsilon_1}{dz} = -\dfrac{1}{z}$ we have

$$P_1 = \int_{\infty}^{0} -ze^{-az}\frac{1}{z}\,dz = \int_{0}^{\infty} e^{-az}\,dz.$$

It then follows that

$$P_1 = \int_0^\infty e^{-az} \, dz = -\frac{1}{a} e^{-az} \Big|_0^\infty = 0 - (-\frac{1}{a}) = \frac{1}{a}$$

and resubstituting a, we finally obtain the well-known MNL formulation

$$P_1 = \frac{1}{\sum_{j=1}^{J} e^{(v_j - v_1)}} = \frac{e^{v_1}}{\sum_{j=1}^{J} e^{v_j}}$$

or more generally for an alternative i and a choice set C_n comprised of J_n alternatives,

$$P_{in} = \frac{e^{v_{in}}}{\sum_{j=1}^{J_n} e^{v_{jn}}} .$$

Typically, we assume that the deterministic component of an utility function can be represented by a linear additive combination of the attributes of an alternative and the unknown parameters, so that the probability that an individual chooses the alternative i from choice set number n is

(2.9) $$P_{in} = \frac{e^{\beta' x_{in}}}{\sum_{j=1}^{J_n} e^{\beta' x_{jn}}},$$

where x_{in} is a vector of characteristics describing the alternative i in choice set C_n and β is a vector of weights associated with the characteristics. In this form, the model has a compensatory or trade-off interpretation between the x's. This is a very general model and, depending on the construction of the x's, can capture a wide variety of different choice patterns (see, e.g., McFadden 1986). For example, interactions of product attributes can be easily accommodated by entering corresponding products of the x's. The task of the modeler is to estimate a parameter vector β for the model in Equation (2.9), based on the choice data collected in the experiment. The estimation procedure is usually carried out by formulating the log-likelihood function of the sample and searching for the parameter vector β that maximizes this function.[1]

In order to formulate the log-likelihood function, we introduce the vector y_n, describing how often the alternative i in choice set C_n was selected. This vector has the form $y_n = (y_{1n}, y_{2n}, \ldots, y_{J_n n})$, where y_{in} denotes the corresponding frequencies. If we assume that the choices are independent from each other, then the vector y_n follows a multinomial distribution given by

$$P(y_n) = c_n \cdot \prod_{j=1}^{J_n} (P_{jn})^{y_{jn}} \quad \text{with} \quad c_n = \frac{(\sum_{j=1}^{J_n} y_{jn})!}{y_{1n}! \, y_{2n}! \cdots y_{J_n n}!}.$$

If we further assume, the choices across N individuals are independent from each other, then the likelihood function can be written as

(2.10)
$$L(\beta) = \prod_{n=1}^{N} c_n \cdot \prod_{j=1}^{J_n} (P_{jn}(\beta))^{y_{jn}}.$$

Instead of maximizing (2.10) directly, it is computationally easier to maximize the corresponding log-likelihood function. In addition, c_n can be omitted because it is constant, and we obtain

---

[1] Bunch and Batsell (1989) compared different estimation techniques and found that the maximum likelihood estimator generally outperformed alternative estimation techniques. Furthermore, maximum likelihood is feasible if there is only one observation per choice set.

$$(2.11) \quad l(\beta) = \sum_{n=1}^{N} \sum_{j=1}^{J_n} y_{jn} \ln(P_{jn}(\beta)),$$

with the P_{jn}'s from Equation (2.9). McFadden (1974) shows that Equation (2.11) is concave under very general conditions and has therefore a unique maximum in β. Since maximizing (2.11) results in a system of nonlinear equations, numerical procedures, such as the Newton-Raphson-algorithm, are required to solve this problem.

To summarize, probabilistic discrete choice models are derived from the random utility theory. What distinguishes the different model formulations from each other is the assumption of the error distribution. The logit model, in particular, assumes that the error components in the utilities are identically and independently Gumbel distributed.

2.2.2 Properties of the Logit Model

In the next section, we address three important properties of the logit model. First, we explain the independence from irrelevant alternatives property. Second, we portray the relation between the scale factor in the logit model and its choice probabilities. Third, we derive and discuss direct and cross elasticities from the logit model.

2.2.2.1 Independence from Irrelevant Alternatives Property

The logit model can be derived in various ways (cf. Ben-Akiva and Lerman 1985). Its original formulation is due to Luce (1959), a mathematical psychologist, who proposed an axiomatic approach. Luce's derivation starts with the assumption that utilities are fixed (strict utility model) rather than random and imposes a relation between choice probabilities known as the *choice axiom*. The probability of choosing an alternative is given by the ratio of its scale value (which measures its attractiveness) to the sum of the scale values of all alternatives in a choice set. This implies that the ratio of two choice probabilities is independent of whatever other alternatives are available. Luce calls this property the *independence from irrelevant alternatives (IIA)*. The term is somewhat misleading and Block and Marschak (1960) suggest instead the term "irrelevance of added alternatives."

One can show that the choice axiom (Luce model) and the aggregate logit model are mathematically indistinguishable. Further, we can easily show that the logit model is subject to the IIA property:

$$(2.12) \qquad \frac{P_i}{P_j} = \frac{e^{V_i}}{\sum_{k \in A} e^{V_k}} \bigg/ \frac{e^{V_j}}{\sum_{k \in A} e^{V_k}} = e^{(v_i - v_j)}.$$

The last term in (2.12) does not depend on the other alternatives in the choice set A. Consequently, the logit model cannot account for choice situations where a newly introduced alternative draws proportionally more choice probabilities from similar alternatives than from dissimilar ones. Thus, no allowance is made for different degrees of substitutability or complementarity among the choice alternatives.

The IIA assumption is clearly false in many applied contexts. Consider the example of the "blue bus/red bus paradox" (Debreu 1960). Suppose an individual wants to reach a certain destination and has the choice between traveling by car or by a blue bus. Assume that both alternatives have the same utility so that $P_{car} = P_{blue\ bus} = 1/2$. Then another bus becomes available which is identical to the blue bus except that it is red. The Luce model would predict the postintroduction probabilities to be $P_{car} = P_{blue\ bus} = P_{red\ bus} = 1/3$. This outcome seems implausible; we rather would expect the probabilities to be closer to $P_{car} = 1/2$ and $P_{blue\ bus} = P_{red\ bus} = 1/4$.

Review of Linear Design and Discrete Choice Models 35

It is important to note that the IIA property in the logit model holding for a specific individual (or for a homogeneous group), generally does not apply for the population as a whole—the logit model does not predict that the ratio of market shares in a *heterogeneous* population will be invariant with the introduction of a new alternative (see, e.g., McFadden et al. 1977). This suggests that one way to alleviate the IIA restriction in practice is to account for heterogeneity in choice models, for example, by properly segmenting respondents (cf. McAlister et al. 1991, Swait et al. 1993).

Statistical tests have been proposed to determine when the IIA property is violated. A test suggested by Hausman and McFadden (1984) compares the logit model with the more general, nested logit model. McFadden (1987) suggests a regression-based specification test for the logit model.

2.2.2.2 Role of the Scale Factor

In deriving the logit model, we assumed that the errors in Equation (2.7) follow a Gumbel distribution with the location parameter $\eta=0$ and the scale parameter $\mu=1$. In general, the logit model has the form (assuming linear-in-parameters logit)

$$(2.13) \quad P_{in} = \frac{e^{\mu\beta' x_{in}}}{\sum_{j=1}^{J_n} e^{\mu\beta' x_{jn}}} = \frac{1}{1 + \sum_{j=1, j\neq i}^{J_n} e^{\mu\beta'(x_{jn} - x_{in})}}.$$

Logit produces an estimate of the product $\mu\beta$ instead of β alone, that is, the parameter vector β and the scale parameter μ are confounded with each other. The scale parameter μ has to be fixed a priori in order to render the parameter vector, β, identifiable (typically $\mu=1$). The assumption of a constant η for all alternatives is not in any sense restrictive as long as each systematic utility has a common constant term—adding a constant term in the utility function in Equation (2.13) does not change the resultant choice probabilities. The latter term in Equation

(2.13) also emphasizes that what drives the choice probabilities are *differences* in utilities, scaled by μ. The impact of a change in μ on (binary) choice probabilities is illustrated in Figure 2.3.

The S-shape of the curve is more pronounced for greater values of μ. The curve has an inflexion point at $v_1=v_2$, where $P_1=P_2=1/2$. Note that P_1 is increasing in μ when $v_1>v_2$ and vice versa.

Figure 2.3
CHOICE PROBABILITIES FOR DIFFERENT VALUES OF μ

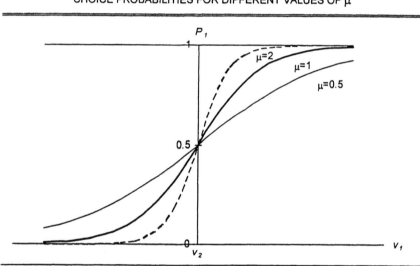

For $\mu \to \infty$, the variance of the errors approaches zero and the logit model reduces to the neoclassical deterministic model

$$P_i = \begin{cases} 1 & \text{if } v_i > \max_{j \neq i} v_j \\ 0 & \text{if not.} \end{cases}$$

All the information about preferences is contained in the systematic utilities and the random impact vanishes.

Review of Linear Design and Discrete Choice Models 37

For $\mu \to 0$, the variance approaches infinity and the impact of the systematic utilities vanishes. The decision process becomes purely random and all alternatives become equally probable, thus,

$$P_i = \frac{1}{J}, \quad i = 1,\ldots,J.$$

The scale factor plays an important role when one wants to compare the results from different data sets. Since the estimated parameter vectors are confounded with constant factors, µ, only ratios of coefficients can be compared across data sets, canceling out the effect of that constant (see Swait and Louviere 1993). This also implies that when separate sources of data are equivalent up to a scaling constant, they can be rescaled and combined to obtain more precise estimates (Ben-Akiva and Morikawa 1990).

2.2.2.3 Elasticities of Logit

A useful measure in demand models is the marginal choice probability. A disadvantage of this measure is that it is not invariant to different scales (e.g., miles vs. yards) of the independent variables. Instead, one uses a similar measure, known as elasticity, that overcomes this disadvantage. We distinguish between the *direct elasticity* of probabilities and the *cross elasticity* of probabilities. If we assume a linear-additive utility function, then the direct elasticity measures the percentage change of the probability of choosing the alternative *i* with respect to the percentage change in the independent variable (attribute) x_{ik}, and is given by

$$E_{x_{ik}}^{P_i} = \frac{\partial P_i}{\partial x_{ik}} \cdot \frac{x_{ik}}{P_i} = (1 - P_i) x_{ik} \beta_k, \quad i = 1,\ldots,J.$$

The cross elasticity measures the percentage change of the probability of choosing the alternative *i* with respect to the percentage change in the variable x_{jk} of the alternative *j*, and is given by

$$E^{P_i}_{x_{jk}} = \frac{\partial P_i}{\partial x_{jk}} \cdot \frac{x_{jk}}{P_i} = -P_j x_{jk} \beta_k, \quad i,j = 1,\ldots,J, i \neq j.$$

Increasing the systematic utility of an alternative (by increasing x_{ik}) increases its choice probability and decreases the choice probabilities of the other alternatives. Note that the cross elasticities with respect to a change in x_{jk} are identical for all alternatives $i \neq j$. This aspect of the logit model is another manifestation of the IIA property. It should be noted that elasticity measures are generally different from those above if calculated for a heterogeneous population. It can be shown that for a uniform percentage change in x_{ik} across all individuals, the aggregate elasticities are a weighted average of the individual elasticities using the choice probabilities as weights (see Ben-Akiva and Lerman 1985, pp. 111).

2.2.3 Choice Models Not Subject to the IIA Assumption

One of the most widely discussed aspects of the logit model is the IIA property. Several researchers have suggested different discrete choice models that allow for richer patterns of substitution of alternatives. In this section, we briefly discuss the most important approaches. For a more comprehensive discussion of the different choice models see, e.g., Ben-Akiva and Lerman (1985).

2.2.3.1 The Tversky Model (EBA)

Similar to the Luce model, Tversky (1972) proposed a choice model in which the decision rule is stochastic, while the utility is deterministic. The choice of an alternative involves a stochastic process successively eliminating alternatives until a single alternative remains (known as the *model of elimination by aspects*, EBA). Tversky assumes that each alternative can be characterized by a list of binary attributes ("aspects"), so that an alternative possesses a certain attribute or not. Each attribute is assigned a positive scale value (strict utility) expressing the importance of that attribute to the individual.

The choice process of an alternative works then as follows: First, an attribute is selected with a probability depending on its scale value. The alternatives not possessing this attribute are eliminated from the choice set. Then, a second attribute is selected in the same manner to determine which of the remaining alternatives to eliminate. This process continues until no elimination is possible. If a single alternative remains, this is the alternative chosen by an individual, otherwise, an alternative is selected at random. This process is similar to the lexicographic decision rule except that the order selecting the attributes is stochastic. Since different sequences of elimination are possible, the choice probability of a particular alternative is the sum of the probabilities of all sequences ending with this alternative.

Tversky shows that the EBA model is not subject to the IIA property and it is consistent with random utility maximization. However, the EBA model also has important weaknesses. First, since attributes are assumed to be binary, descriptions of alternatives may be unrealistic. Second, the total number of parameters increases exponentially in the number of choice sets. Consequently, for large number of choice sets, the model becomes computationally infeasible, so that heuristic choice procedures are needed (see Tversky and Sattath 1979, Rotondo 1986). Perhaps because of this difficulties, the EBA model has not enjoyed widespread application in marketing.

2.2.3.2 Generalizations of the Logit Model

The multinomial logit model is by far the most widely applied discrete choice model. A popular extension of the logit model is the *nested logit model* due to McFadden (1978). This model avoids the IIA problem by formulating choice as a hierarchical decision process. The choice set C is partitioned into subsets C_k that group together alternatives having several observable characteristics in common. Let's denote the set of the K subsets $\Theta = \{C_k; k = 1,...,K\}$. For example, C could be a set of four different dishes $C = \{beef, pork, grouper, trout\}$ that could then be subdivided into the two groups $C_{meat} = \{beef, pork\}$ and $C_{fish} = \{grouper, trout\}$. It is assumed that an individual first selects with a certain probability the subset C_k, from which then a particular alternative is chosen according to a probability depending on the utility of that alternative. In order to determine the probability of selecting the subset $C_k \in \Theta$ in the first stage, the expected value of the maximum of the utilities in that subset is calculated. The probability of choosing the *beef*, for example, can then be written as $P(beef) = P(C_{meat}) \cdot P(beef | C_{meat})$.

The nested logit model involves the sequential use (for each stage) of the logit model, starting from the bottom of the decision tree. The IIA property no longer holds when two alternatives belong in different subsets, allowing for more general pattern of dependence among alternatives than the logit model. McFadden (1978) showed that the nested logit model is consistent with random utility maximization.

If a decision process can be reasonably characterized by a tree-like structure, a priori, then the nested logit model seems to be a very appealing alternative to the logit model. However, in real markets, it is not always clear how to partition C and the choice probabilities may be quite sensitive to the grouping of the alternatives into subsets C_k (Anderson et al. 1992b). It can happen that different tree structures provide indistinguishable fits to the data and yet produce different estimates of market shares for new products (Batsell and Polking 1985).

McFadden (1978) shows that there is a more general discrete choice model known as the *generalized extreme-value (GEV)* model that includes the logit model and the nested logit model as special cases. Further, all choice models belonging to this class are consistent with random utility maximization. However, as noted by Ben-Akiva and Lerman (1985) "having a definition for a class of models and actually formulating realizations from that class are two different things."

Review of Linear Design and Discrete Choice Models 41

Another way around the IIA problem is to formulate the deterministic utility of an alternative as a function that will not only depend on its own attributes, but also on the attributes of other alternatives (cross effects) in a choice set. This approach holds the advantage of staying within the computationally attractive logit family, while avoiding the IIA restriction. This model goes back to McFadden (1975) and is known as *universal* or *mother logit*. The author noted that this model is useful for testing different model specifications, but is generally inconsistent with random utility maximization (McFadden 1981, p. 282).[2] Nevertheless, several researchers estimated this model in marketing contexts providing useful insights into the competitive structure of markets (e.g., Batsell and Polking 1985, Lazari and Anderson 1994).

2.2.3.3 The Multinomial Probit Model

Of all discrete choice models, the multinomial probit model allows for the most flexible error structure in the utility functions (Daganzo 1979, Currim 1982). The probit model results if we assume that the errors $\varepsilon_n = (\varepsilon_{1n},\ldots,\varepsilon_{J_n n})$ are J_n-variate normally distributed with expected values equal to zero and covariance matrix

$$\Sigma_n = \begin{bmatrix} \sigma_{11}^n & \cdots & \sigma_{1J_1}^n \\ & \ddots & \vdots \\ & & \sigma_{J_n J_n}^n \end{bmatrix},$$

where σ_{ii}^n denotes the variance of the error component of the alternative i and σ_{ij}^n denotes the covariance between alternative i and j in choice set C_n. Unlike the logit model, the error components can have different variances (not identically distributed) and can be correlated (not independent), allowing one to consider general configurations of substitution across alternatives. Hausman and Wise

---

[2] McFadden et al. (1977) show how to use this model in order to test IIA violations of the logit model.

(1978), for example, have shown how to properly specify the covariance matrix Σ_n in order to obtain intuitive results of the "blue bus/red bus paradox."

Nevertheless, the probit model has an important disadvantage. To obtain the choice probabilities one has to calculate a (J_n-1)-dimensional integral, which makes direct calculation in iterative statistical analysis computationally intractable for sets of more than four alternatives (Maddala 1983, McFadden 1986). Thus the primary difficulty in the probit model was the lack of practical, accurate procedures for approximating the choice probabilities (McFadden 1981). However, McFadden (1989) has more recently developed a new estimation technique for the probit model (called the *method of simulated moments*) that is practical for high-dimensional problems. Increasing use of this new technique suggests that many of these problems can now be overcome (in marketing see, e.g., Chintagunta 1992, Elrod and Keane 1995).

2.2.4 Summary and Discussion

We derived the multinomial logit model, discussed its properties, and provided a brief overview of the most discussed choice models that overcome the independence from irrelevant alternatives (IIA) property. Probabilistic discrete choice models can be derived from a common framework, the random utility theory. What distinguishes the different model formulations from each other is the assumption of the error distribution. The logit model, in particular, assumes that the error components in the utilities are identically and independently Gumbel distributed.

The logit model is by far the most widely used choice model, but there are other models that have been developed and applied. The logit model is particular appealing in applications because of computational advantages, that is, choice probabilities can be calculated analytically (closed form) rather than numerically. The primary drawback of this model, on the other hand, is that it underlies the IIA property which "may not be a realistic assumption in many consumer behavior contexts (Green and Srinivasan 1978)." The IIA property implies that when a new brand or alternative is introduced, it draws choice probabilities proportionally from all other alternatives, regardless of substitutability among the alternatives. To overcome this limitation, several alternative choice models have been suggested. Whereas these models alleviate the IIA problem in one way or another, they generally involve greater computational difficulty and cost. In addition, the multinomial probit and nested logit model guarantee no global optimum (Currim 1982, McFadden 1986).

Tversky (1972) showed that the IIA property applies to any model based on simple scalability. Simple scalability means that any alternative can be characterized by a scale value ("utility") and the choice probability is proportional to its scale value. Such models, in which the choice probabilities do not depend on the orientation or similarity of alternatives in attribute space, are termed "simple scaleable" or "simple models." Consequently, no model which evaluates alternatives in terms of scale values without accounting for similarities in *unobserved* attributes can avoid the IIA property (McFadden 1976). In particular, the independent probit model shares the basic drawback of the logit model. The approaches to overcome the IIA property discussed so far allow for different correlations between the unobserved attributes (error terms) and different variances of these attributes.

It is obviously controversial in what respect the random utility maximization paradigm provides a necessary condition for the "appropriateness" of choice models. One positive property of the universal logit model is, for example, that it can capture violations of regularity, whereas models consistent with random utility maximization cannot (Batsell and Polking 1985, Anderson et al. 1992b, p. 53). Regularity implies that the probability of choosing a certain alternative can never increase as the number of alternatives increases. However, there are practical circumstances, where this regularity assumption does not hold. Consider, for example, the uniqueness of an orange in a bowl of many apples making it a more conspicuous alternative than in a situation involving one orange and one apple;

thus, the probability of choosing the orange could increase with the number of apples (example borrowed from Anderson et al. 1992b).

3. Designs for Discrete Choice Models

In this chapter, we first provide an overview of various strategies that have been used to build choice designs and discuss their limitations. Then, we derive a measure of efficiency in choice designs, and finally, introduce four design principles that when jointly satisfied, result in optimal choice designs, i.e., designs that minimize the variance of the estimated parameters.

3.1 Review of Previous Design Strategies

Today most choice designs have been built as extensions of concepts and results from the general linear design literature. Emphasis was put on model *identification (or estimability)* rather than on *statistical efficiency*. One reason for this was that most researchers who worked in the choice area were primarily interested in modeling and only secondarily in design issues. Moreover, researchers used the term "efficient" in the context of choice designs to indicate that a subset of many possible choice sets was sufficient for model identification. The use of the term in this way can be misleading. In this thesis, we will use the term efficiency in a statistical sense, i.e., the precision of parameter estimates. We will first describe design strategies that have been used in choice experiments ordered by the degree of model complexity. Subsequently, we will discuss a pioneer approach in marketing to generate designs which are statistically efficient for a specific class of choice models.

3.1.1 Strategies for Identifiable Choice Designs

In this section, we describe design strategies which were typically used in commercial choice experiments. These strategies focus on identification issues. We start with simple generic models, and move on to more complex models, such as availability and attribute cross effects models.

3.1.1.1 Generic Models

The simplest form of choice models involve alternatives characterized by generic attributes. The utility functions of these models consist of attribute parameters which are constant for all alternatives, e.g., a common price slope across all alternatives. Louviere and Woodworth (1983) suggest the following two-stage approach for building generic choice designs. In stage one, an orthogonal main-effect plan is used to generate "conjoint" profiles, i.e., each row of that plan represents a single profile. In stage two, an additional fractional factorial plan (two to the power of the number of profiles) is used to assign the profiles into choice sets. A zero level of those two-level factors indicates absence, a one level indicates presence of a profile in a particular choice set, respectively. A disadvantage of this strategy might be that the choice sets have different sizes. Moreover, the number of choice sets is dependent on the number of profiles.

3.1.1.2 Alternative-Specific Models

In contrast to generic models, the utility functions of alternative-specific models involve parameters which differ among alternatives. Often, brands are characterized by specific attributes and attribute levels. For example, price levels for Coke are usually higher than those for Pepsi. Conceptually, an alternative-specific attribute is equivalent to modeling an interaction between two generic attributes. Louviere (Louviere and Woodworth 1983, Louviere 1988) suggests the use of orthogonal main effect plans in order to define alternatives and choice sets at once. Here, a column represents an alternative-specific attribute and a row represents a choice set.

3.1.1.3 Attribute Cross Effects Models

Applications of choice models to estimate market share which rely on Luce's choice axiom (IIA, Luce 1959), such as the MNL models, have been widely criticized because they cannot account for the effects of differential product substitutability and product dominance. Modeling attribute cross effects models is a way to account for violations of IIA. Here, the utility of an alternative depends on both its own attributes and the attributes of other alternatives in a choice set. Technically, additional constants and attribute effects are incorporated in the specification of the utility function. This generalization of the conventional MNL model in known as the universal logit (UL) model (McFadden 1975). UL models were initially used to diagnose the validity of the IIA property of the MNL models (McFadden et al. 1977) and has later been used to estimate more complex choice models (e.g., Timmermans et al. 1992).

Louviere (1986) indicates that an orthogonal fraction from a $L^{N \times M}$ factorial can be used to estimate attribute cross effects, where N is the number of choice sets, and M is the number of attributes each consisting of L levels. The principle is applicable to the more general case of varying number of levels and varying number of attributes per alternative. A row of the factorial plan represents a choice set and a column represents an alternative-specific attribute. In addition, each choice set contains a constant alternative.

3.1.1.4 Availability Effects Models

Batsell and Polking (1985) suggest a "new" class of choice models that overcome the IIA property by estimating the effects competing alternatives have on each other's market share or choice probability. In fact, the authors' choice models can be viewed as a special case of the universal logit model (McFadden 1975) in that the utility of an alternative depends on the availability (presence or absence) of other alternatives in the same choice set as opposed to attribute cross effects. The models proposed by Batsell and Polking can be used to *describe* the competitive structure within a market, however, they cannot *explain* what causes that—the models are based on "empty" or nonattribute alternatives, making it impossible to predict the differential impact of certain characteristics of existing products, such as price and quality, and of new products on market shares. To accommodate this, a model's parameters must be linked to the product attributes which govern choice. In addition, the choice designs of these models consist of all possible subsets of products under consideration and increase therefore exponentially with the numbers of products. Thus, these designs become infeasible for larger experiments.

More recently, Anderson and Wiley (1992) provide choice designs for this class of availability models which require considerably fewer choice sets. Whereas the availability designs suggested by Batsell and Polking (1985) involve 2^m-m-1 choice sets, the new designs involve only $2m$-1 choice sets, where m is the number of alternatives or brands. It is worth mentioning that in contrast to Batsell and Polking, Anderson and Wiley only focus on such availability effects, where the availability (presence or absence) of *one* available alternative influences the relative probability of choosing another alternative in the choice set. In this case, the availability effects have simple (main effect) ANOVA interpretation. The authors provide a necessary and sufficient condition for the identification of availability effects and demonstrate the use of Hadamard matrices to generate (minimal) availability designs. A Hadamard matrix has orthogonal rows and columns, and each subdesign is an orthogonal main-effect plan. Designs for m alternatives are generated by taking a Hadamard matrix of size m and appending its foldover. Additionally, each choice set must contain a constant alternative.

3.1.1.5 Availability and Attribute Cross Effects Models

Lazari and Anderson (1994) extend the work of Batsell and Polking (1985) and Anderson and Wiley (1992) to the (single-) attribute case, i.e., alternatives have an explicit attribute structure. In the same spirit as before, availability and attribute cross effects are incorporated into the utility function of each alternative under study. The authors give a necessary and sufficient condition for the identification of all model parameters and provide a catalogue of choice designs to estimate both availability and attribute cross effects. The designs have specific numbers of choice sets dependent on the number of alternatives and each set contains a constant alternative. The practical use of these choice designs is, however, rather limited because alternatives or brands are defined on *one* attribute only. The choice designs are represented as collections of treatment combinations from fractional factorial plans, where each row is a choice set and each column is an alternative-specific attribute.

As Lazari and Anderson (1994) indicate, general solutions to the problem of generating choice designs to estimate both availability and attribute cross effects, where there is more than one attribute, are not available. For a particular choice study, Anderson et al. (1992a), for example, construct a choice design for estimating availability and attribute cross effects, where the number of attributes is 24. The process for constructing this particular design is rather complicated. The underlying choice design consists of orthogonal fractional plans arranged in a balanced incomplete block structure (orthogonal fractions for each pair of alternatives) plus another orthogonal plan with all alternatives present. All choice sets contain a constant alternative. Although this particular choice design may prove to render the desired model effects identifiable, it is generally not obvious how to combine different fractions in a way to guarantee identification.

Kuhfeld et al. (1994) suggest the use of computer search routines to generate efficient linear designs and choice designs. Computer search routines offer high flexibility in the process of generating experimental designs. The authors indicate how this process may be used to generate complex choice designs. They directly apply the principles documented by Lazari and Anderson (1994) to choice designs that estimate availability and attribute cross effects, where the number of attributes is *greater* than one. Conceptually, the process seems to be problematic for two reasons. First, it is not clear that these principles can be extended to the multiattribute case (and within-alternative interactions) in a straightforward manner. Second, the process, as carried out by Kuhfeld et al. (1994), may not produce identifiable choice designs because according to Lazari and Anderson (1994), not only the overall design matrix must be of full rank, but also all the submatrices including a particularly available brand. In contrast, Kuhfeld et al. (1994) only operate on the overall (linear) design matrix.

3.1.2 A Strategy for Efficient Generic Designs

Up to this date, research has primarily been motivated by identification issues, using extensions of concepts and results from the general linear models literature. It was noted at two recent workshops on experimental choice analysis (Carson et al. 1994; Batsell and Louviere 1992) that "despite the progress made in understanding *how* to construct identifiable choice designs, the statistical efficiency properties of these design strategies had not been well understood."

As a pioneer work in marketing, Bunch et al. (1996) recently examined statistical efficiency of various design strategies for generic models. The authors find that cyclic or shifted choice designs outperform alternative design strategies over a broad range of different β vectors. In fact, in the special case of $\beta=0$, these designs are (locally) optimal, i.e., the variances of the estimated parameters are minimal.

Cyclic designs start with an orthogonal factorial plan, where each row represents an alternative and each column represents a generic attribute. Subsequent alternatives within each choice sets are constructed by adding cyclically generated alternatives to each set. That is, the attribute levels of the new alternatives add one to the level of the previous alternative until it is at its highest level, at which point the assignment re-cycles to the lowest level. The number of different alternatives in a choice set is limited by the maximum number of levels among all attributes.

3.2 Efficiency in Choice Designs

Efficiency is an important concept in experimental designs. An efficient design produces precise estimates of the model parameters or, vice versa, requires a minimal amount of information (data) to achieve a certain degree of precision in the parameter estimates. In this section, we derive a measure of efficiency in

Designs for Discrete Choice Models 51

choice designs, highlight the important differences between linear and choice designs, and introduce four principles characterizing efficient choice designs.

3.2.1 Measure of Choice Design Efficiency

We derive the measure of efficiency for a choice design given a set of priors on the coefficients. The derivation basically follows the seminal work of McFadden (1974), and is summarized in a variety of sources (Ben-Akiva and Lerman 1985, Madalla 1983). We know from Chapter 2 that in the logit model, the probability of choosing an alternative i from a choice set $C_n = \{\mathbf{x}_{1n},\ldots,\mathbf{x}_{J_n n}\}$ is given by

$$(3.1) \quad P_{in}(\mathbf{X}_n,\beta) = \frac{e^{x_{in}\beta}}{\sum_{j=1}^{J_n} e^{x_{jn}\beta}},$$

where x_{jn} is a row vector of K characteristics describing i, and β is a column vector of weights associated with each of those K characteristics. The $J_n \times K$ matrix $\mathbf{X}_n$ consists of the row vectors $\mathbf{x}_{jn} \in C_n$. If $M = \sum_{n=1}^{N} J_n$ is the total number of alternatives in the choice experiment, then the choice design matrix, $\mathbf{X}$, reflecting the concatenation of all submatrices, $\mathbf{X}_n$, is of size $M \times K$. Further, if $\mathbf{Y}$ is a matrix of choices with elements y_{in}, each of which equals one if alternative i is chosen in C_n, and zero otherwise, and we assume that each choice reflects an independent draw from a multinomial distribution, then the log-likelihood of a given sample, $\mathbf{Y}$, is

$$(3.2) \quad L(\mathbf{Y}|\mathbf{X},\beta) = \sum_{n=1}^{N}\sum_{j=1}^{J_n} y_{jn} \ln(P_{jn}(\mathbf{X}_n,\beta)) + \text{constant}.$$

Here, $P_{jn}(\mathbf{X}_n,\beta)$, calculated from Equation (3.1), is the choice probability of alternative j in set C_n, which depends on the characteristics of the alternatives, $\mathbf{X}_n$, and the true parameter vector β.

Maximizing Equation (3.2) yields the maximum likelihood estimator, $\hat{\beta}$, of a choice model, given a particular choice design. McFadden (1974) showed that the distribution of $\hat{\beta}$ is asymptotically normal with mean β and covariance matrix

(3.3) $$\Sigma_p = (\mathbf{Z'PZ})^{-1} = [\sum_{n=1}^{N} \sum_{j=1}^{J_n} \mathbf{z}'_{jn} P_{jn} \mathbf{z}_{jn}]^{-1},$$

where $\mathbf{P}$ is an $M \times M$ diagonal matrix with elements P_{jn}, and $\mathbf{Z}$ is an $M \times K$ matrix with rows

$$\mathbf{z}_{jn} = \mathbf{x}_{jn} - \sum_{i=1}^{J_n} \mathbf{x}_{in} P_{in}.$$

Equation (3.3) takes a particularly simple form when one's best guess is that the β's are zero. In this case, the choice probabilities of each alternative in a choice set C_n are equal to $1/J_n$ and the covariance matrix simplifies to

(3.4) $$\Sigma_0 = (\mathbf{Z'P_0Z})^{-1} = [\sum_{n=1}^{N} \frac{1}{J_n} \sum_{j=1}^{J_n} \mathbf{z}'_{jn} \mathbf{z}_{jn}]^{-1},$$

where

$$z_{jn} = x_{jn} - \bar{x}_n, \quad \text{with} \quad \bar{x}_n = \frac{1}{J_n}\sum_{j=1}^{J_n} x_{jn}.$$

Thus, the appropriate design matrix with $\beta = 0$ centers each attribute within each choice set. To emphasize the two different ways in which the choice probabilities affect the covariance matrix of $\hat{\beta}$, we denote Equation (3.3) a "probability-centered" estimate of error, and Equation (3.4) a "zero-centered" or "utility-neutral" estimate of error.

Equations (3.3) and (3.4) reveal some important properties of (nonlinear) choice models. In linear models, centering occurs across all profiles, whereas in choice models, centering occurs within choice sets. This shows that in choice designs both the profile selection and the assignment of profiles to choice sets affects the covariance matrix. Moreover, in linear models, the covariance matrix does not depend on the true parameter vector, whereas in choice models the probabilities, P_{jn}, are functions of β and hence the covariance matrix.

While the zero-centered estimate of error derives directly from the original McFadden (1974) article, it has not to our knowledge been put in this form. Indeed, zero centering the design matrix provides a general way to estimate efficiencies of choice designs under the null hypothesis that $\beta = 0$, and thus is an appropriate first step in evaluating any choice design. Equation (3.3) is routinely used in an *ex post* sense to estimate the accuracy of a choice model once one has a set of coefficients, $\hat{\beta}$, and uses these to estimate the P_{in}'s. In Chapter 4, on the other hand, we will demonstrate its usefulness *ex ante* in generating efficient choice designs given prior estimates of β.

For a Fisher information matrix, Σ, several established summary measures of error are useful in comparing designs (cf. section 2.1.4). The most popular measure is D-efficiency or its inversely related counterpart,

(3.5) $$D\text{-}error = \det(\Sigma)^{1/K}.$$

A more efficient design has a smaller D-error, that is, the "size" of the covariance matrix of the parameter estimates is smaller. In keeping with past practice (Bunch et al. 1996, Kuhfeld et al. 1994), we focus in this dissertation on D-error as a measure of design goodness. We denote D_p-error as the *probability-centered* estimate of error, and D_0-error as the *utility-neutral* estimate of error that is appropriate when all β's are zero.

3.2.2 Principles of Efficient Choice Designs

Four principles, illustrated in Figure 3.1, affect efficiency in choice designs. Two of these, level balance and orthogonality, also characterize linear designs. The other two principles, minimal overlap and utility balance, are specific for choice designs and focus on the within-choice-set structure. Minimal overlap becomes relevant for choice designs because each attribute level is only meaningful in comparison to others *within* a choice set. Utility balance refers to the degree of difficulty of making a choice among alternatives in a choice set. A design has maximum efficiency (or minimum D_p-error) if it satisfies all four principles at once. There are only a few special cases where all four principles can be perfectly satisfied; generally, building an efficient choice design requires optimally trading off the four efficiency principles (cf. Chapter 4).

Level balance is often just termed "balance" (Kuhfeld et al. 1994), but we retain the prefix to distinguish it from utility balance. Level balance is the requirement that the levels of an attribute occur with equal frequency. For instance, each level of a three-level attribute should occur in precisely 1/3 of the cases.

Figure 3.1
PRINCIPLES OF EFFICIENT CHOICE DESIGNS

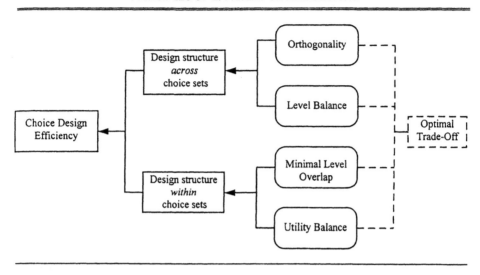

Orthogonality, the second criterion, is satisfied when the joint occurrence of any two levels of different attributes appear in profiles with frequencies equal to the product of their marginal frequencies (Addelman 1962). Thus, the joint occurrence of any combination of a three and a four level attribute must occur in exactly 1/12 of the cases, if there is level balance. However, for many design specifications, level balance and orthogonality conflict, so that one cannot be satisfied without degrading the other. Consider, for example, a design with one three-level and one four-level attribute in which the number of alternatives is not a multiple of twelve. To create such a design with say, 16 profiles, Addelman (1962) recommends taking a 4^{4-2} design and creating a three-level attribute by collapsing two of its four levels into one; for example, by making all level 4's be level 3. Collapsing levels preserves orthogonality, but violates level balance in that the collapsed level occurs eight times, while the others occur only four times. Kuhfeld et al. (1994) show how the OPTEX procedure (SAS Institute 1995) can produce more efficient designs while achieving neither perfect level balance nor orthogonality. Note that, except for special cases, efficiency for linear designs involves trading off incompatible criteria of level balance and orthogonality.

Minimal level overlap becomes important for choice designs because the contrasts between attribute levels are only meaningful as differences *within* a choice set. The impact of this requirement is expressed in the centering of attributes within each choice set found in Equations (3.3) and (3.4). Minimal overlap means the probability that an attribute level repeats itself in each choice set should be as small as possible. The cost of violating this criterion can be seen most clearly in the case where the levels of one attribute are the same across all alternatives within a choice set. Here, the choice set provides **no** information on the attribute's value. We will use the criteria of level balance, orthogonality, and minimal overlap to generate efficient utility-neutral choice designs—designs that minimize D_0-error.

Utility balance is satisfied when the utilities of alternatives within choice sets are as close as possible, i.e., the design will be more efficient as the expected probabilities within a choice set C_n among J_n alternatives approaches $1/J_n$. In order to make a design "utility balanced", the values of the model parameters must be known. If we knew these values with certainty, the experiment would be superfluous. Instead, we use prior estimates as our best guess for the true parameter values. To generate utility-balanced choice designs we minimize D_p-error, capturing all four efficiency principles.

3.3 Summary and Discussion

In this chapter, we provided a review of previous choice design strategies, derived a measure of choice design efficiency, and identified four principles characterizing efficient choice designs.

We first described different methods that have been suggested for building choice designs, which rely on extensions of standard linear design theory. We showed that the use of linear designs in choice experiments may be nonoptimal due to two differences between linear and choice models. First, probabilistic choice models are nonlinear in the parameters, implying that the statistical efficiency of a choice design depends on an (unknown) parameter vector. This property implies the need to bring prior estimates on model parameters into choice designs. Second, choice design efficiency depends both on the creation of appropriate profiles and properly placing them into several choice sets. Despite its limitations, linear design theory has been used to produce satisfactory choice designs for many years, drawing on readily available tables and processes. Such carefully selected linear designs are reasonable, general-purpose choice designs, but are generally not optimal in a statistical sense.

Building on the work by Bunch et al. (1996) to address efficiency issues in choice designs, we identified four principles of choice design efficiency: orthogonality, level balance, minimal overlap, and utility balance. Orthogonality is satisfied when the levels of each attribute vary independently of one another. Level balance is satisfied when the levels of each attribute appear with equal frequency. Minimal overlap is satisfied when the alternatives within each choice set have nonoverlapping attribute levels. Utility balance is satisfied when the utilities of alternatives within choice sets are the same. If these principles are jointly satisfied, then a design indicates maximum efficiency (or minimal D_p-error). In general, building an efficient choice design requires prior estimates of model parameters and optimally trading off all four efficiency principles.

In the next chapter we will demonstrate how to generate efficient choice designs using reasonable priors on model parameters and show how the proposed methods trade off the four efficiency principles.

4. Using Priors in Choice Designs

In the previous chapter we saw that the efficiency in choice designs depends on an (unknown) parameter vector. Therefore, generating an *efficient* choice design requires bringing in prior estimates of that parameter vector. In this chapter, we develop methods incorporating prior estimates of β in order to generate more efficient designs. Our prior β's are point estimates of the true β's and the resultant designs will be more efficient in the region of those priors. We show that our methods produce designs that are 10-50% more efficient than corresponding designs falsely assuming that β=0, and that these efficiency gains are quite robust against misspecifications of priors. The efficiency gains come from making alternatives within choice sets closer in utility, i.e., the choice becomes more difficult to make. We therefore call these designs *utility-balanced* choice designs (cf. Huber and Zwerina 1996).

4.1 Generating Efficient Choice Designs

We denote a choice design which is characterized by, say, three attributes each at two levels, and four alternatives in each of nine choice sets, by $2^3/4/9$. More complex design families can also be described: $3^2 \times 4^3/2/16 + 2^2 \times 4^3/3/15$ is a mixed design with 16 pairs and 15 triples in which attributes have different number of levels in the different subdesigns.

Our methods of generating utility-balanced choice designs start with an efficient utility-neutral design. While there are a number of ways to generate D_0-efficient designs, we will focus on shifted or cyclic designs, first developed for choice designs by Bunch et al. (1996). Cyclic designs are easily generated and have perfect level balance, orthogonality, and minimal overlap. We will consider five families of designs, beginning with simple designs to illustrate the principles, and then moving to more complex, but more managerially useful designs.

The first design we consider is the $3^3/3/9$ design shown in the left-hand panel of Table 4.1. It has three attributes, each defined with three levels, and nine choice sets comprised of three alternatives. The first alternatives within each choice set represent a classic 9-profile, 3^{3-1} orthogonal array (Addelman 1962). Subsequent alternatives are constructed by cyclic permutation (cf. section 3.1.2).

Table 4.1
COMPARISON OF ORIGINAL AND SWAPPED $3^3/3/9$ CHOICE DESIGN

		Original $3^3/3/9$ Design					Swapped $3^3/3/9$ Design				
Set	Altern.	Attr. A	Attr. B	Attr. C	Sum	Prob	Attr. A	Attr. B	Attr. C	Sum	Prob
1	I	1	1	1	3	0.002	3	1	3	7	0.665
	II	2	2	2	6	0.047	2	2	2	6	0.245
	III	3	3	3	9	0.951	1	3	1	5	0.090
2	I	1	2	2	5	0.045	3	1	2	6	0.333
	II	2	3	3	8	0.910	2	3	1	6	0.333
	III	3	1	1	5	0.045	1	2	3	6	0.333
3	I	1	3	3	7	0.488	3	2	1	6	0.333
	II	2	1	1	4	0.024	2	1	3	6	0.333
	III	3	2	2	7	0.488	1	3	2	6	0.333
4	I	2	1	3	6	0.333	3	1	1	5	0.090
	II	3	2	1	6	0.333	1	3	3	7	0.665
	III	1	3	2	6	0.333	2	2	2	6	0.245
5	I	2	2	1	5	0.045	2	1	3	6	0.245
	II	3	3	2	8	0.910	3	3	1	7	0.665
	III	1	1	3	5	0.045	1	2	2	5	0.090
6	I	2	3	2	7	0.488	2	3	1	6	0.245
	II	3	1	3	7	0.488	3	2	2	7	0.665
	III	1	2	1	4	0.024	1	1	3	5	0.090
7	I	3	1	2	6	0.333	1	3	2	6	0.245
	II	1	2	3	6	0.333	3	1	1	5	0.090
	III	2	3	1	6	0.333	2	2	3	7	0.665
8	I	3	2	3	8	0.910	2	3	2	7	0.665
	II	1	3	1	5	0.045	3	2	1	6	0.245
	III	2	1	2	5	0.045	1	1	3	5	0.090
9	I	3	3	1	7	0.488	1	2	3	6	0.333
	II	1	1	2	4	0.024	3	1	2	6	0.333
	III	2	2	3	7	0.488	2	3	1	6	0.333
Dp-Error						0.381					0.280

These cyclically generated alternatives are beneficial in that they mirror perfect level balance and orthogonality of the seed array. That is, the frequency of

Using Priors in Choice Designs 61

occurrence of each pair of attribute levels is equivalent to the product of their marginal frequencies. In the design shown, each level occurs in 1/3 of the profiles, and any pair of levels occurs in precisely 1/9 of the profiles. Finally, due to the symmetry of the design, there is minimal overlap—each level occurs only once for each attribute within a choice set.

The three properties of level balance, orthogonality, and minimal overlap mean that the original $3^3/3/9$ design is optimal with respect to the criterion of D_0-error. The application of Equations (3.3) and (3.4) result in a D_0-error of .19, which assumes $\beta = 0$. To illustrate the impact of nonzero βs, we initially set the partworths for each of the attributes to be evenly spaced between -1 and 1. This equal spacing is convenient in that the partworths become a translation of the level labels. Thus, a partworth of -1 corresponds to level 1, 0 to level 2, and 1 to level 3. Given this scaling, a measure for the utilities of each alternative is the *sum* measure shown in Table 4.1. The logit probabilities that follow are evaluated using Equation (3.1) in which the β's are the original partworth levels. Appendix A shows some intermediate results in calculating D_p-error. Note that the D_p-error of .38 is not directly comparable with the D_0-error of .19 since the former reflects errors around partworths -1,0,1, while the latter reflects errors around the partworths 0,0,0.

4.1.1 Swapping Attribute Levels

The second panel of Table 4.1 shows that D_p-error can be improved by what we call a *swap*. A swap involves switching one level of an attribute within a choice set. Note that in the original design the first choice set is out of balance; alternative III dominates the first two, garnering 95% of the expected choices. The swaps shown switch the first and third levels of attributes A and C, resulting in more equal choice probabilities. A computer program generated the design shown in Table 4.1 by evaluating all possible swaps for a given choice set, and then executing that swap if it could improve D_p-error. The program then examined subsequent choice sets in the same way and continued to make swaps until no more improvement was possible. While this sequential method did not guarantee the optimal design, one iteration consistently provided designs with efficiencies within 98% of the optimal swapped design.

The first column of Table 4.2 shows the net gain from these swaps. Given the prior coefficients, D_p-error decreases from .38 to .28. Thus the swapped design can use 27% fewer respondents and still have the same expected error around the parameters as the original design. Note, however, that while D_p-error improves with swaps, D_0-error becomes 18% worse, implying that if β is zero, that swapping could reduce efficiency. Thus the analyst must decide whether to set β to some non-zero prior vector. Any value, including zero, entails costs if wrong. Later we will show that one can have quite broad errors in one's non-zero priors and still gain from their use, implying that there is generally a net benefit from using priors.

The analysis of the $3^3/3/9$ family is predicated on a particular set of coefficients with partworths arbitrarily ranging from -1 to 1. How big are the efficiency gains from utility balance if this range is increased or decreased? In general, the logit coefficients increase if respondents are more internally consistent, more homogeneous with each other, or if the model better specifies their choices. In any of these cases the "scale" of the solution increases (cf. Ben-Akiva and Lerman, 1985, Swait and Louviere 1993). Looking horizontally across Table 4.2 shows what happens to the gain from utility balance if the coefficients are made larger or smaller by 25%. Enlarging the coefficients increases the efficiency gains from utility balance, while making them smaller has the opposite effect. This result makes intuitive sense. The large coefficients generate extreme choice probabilities, thus exacerbating any initial imbalance within choice sets. By contrast, where coefficients are close to zero, the choice probabilities are close to equivalent, and the choice design has less need for utility balancing.

Table 4.2
GAINS IN EXPECTED ERRORS DUE TO UTILITY BALANCE FROM RELABELING AND SWAPPING

Design Family	Original Values ($\beta = \beta_0$) Dp-err [SD]	Do-err	Less Noise ($\beta = \beta_0 \times 1.25$) Dp-err [SD]	Do-err	Greater Noise ($\beta = \beta_0 \times .75$) Dp-err [SD]	Do-err
$3^3/3/9$						
Original	0.381 [.002]	0.192	0.475 [.012]	0.192	0.305 [.000]	0.192
Swapped	0.280	0.227	0.311	0.223	0.259	0.223
Total % Gains	27%	-18%	34%	-16%	15%	-16%
$3^4/2/15$						
Average relabeled[a]	0.447 [.072]	0.163	0.611 [.140]	0.163	0.325 [.033]	0.163
Best relabeled[b]	0.297	—[d]	0.335	—	0.256	—
Swapped[c]	0.253	0.215	0.265	0.224	0.231	0.185
Total % Gains	43%	-32%	57%	-37%	29%	-14%
$4^4/4/16$						
Average relabeled	0.307 [.024]	0.157	0.384 [.044]	0.157	0.244 [.012]	0.157
Best relabeled	0.263	—	0.301	—	0.222	—
Swapped	0.198	0.178	0.208	0.180	0.188	0.178
Total % Gains	36%	-13%	46%	-14%	23%	-13%
$4 \times 3^3/3/48$						
Average relabeled	0.231 [.013]	0.102	0.295 [.024]	0.102	0.178 [.006]	0.102
Best relabeled	0.199	—	0.238	—	0.163	—
Swapped	0.142	0.112	0.146	0.116	0.133	0.113
Total % Gains	39%	-9%	50%	-13%	25%	-11%
$9 \times 8 \times 4 \times 3^4 2^3/3/63$						
Average relabeled	0.227 [.025]	0.068	0.302 [.043]	0.068	0.165 [.013]	0.068
Best relabeled	0.161	—	0.196	—	0.130	—
Swapped	0.084	0.071	0.089	0.071	0.075	0.075
Total % Gains	63%	-5%	71%	-5%	55%	-11%

[a] Average Dp-err of 1000 randomly relabeled designs. Standard deviations in brackets.
[b] Best design from relabeling.
[c] Best design from relabeling and subsequent swapping.
[d] Relabeling has no affect on expected errors when $\beta = 0$.

To summarize, we have shown that swapping to balance utilities produces an efficiency gain even for this small design with three attributes and nine choice sets, and that this gain increases with the scale of the coefficients. However, the benefit from swaps is not without risk. If the coefficients are zero, then the lack of orthogonality engendered by the swapping produces a less efficient design. The next method we consider to increase utility balance is relabeling. It is less risky because it alters utility balance without affecting orthogonality.

4.1.2 Relabeling Attribute Levels

Relabeling involves reassigning labels to the levels of a design, for example, replacing attribute levels 1, 2 and 3 with 3, 1, and 2 (Krieger and Green 1991, Kuhfeld et al. 1994). Relabeling can improve utility balance without degrading D_0-error. Unfortunately, relabeling does not work for some small designs such as the $3^3/3/9$ family, where it results in virtually the same choice sets in a different order. However, it is very effective for larger designs, as illustrated on a design of 15 pairs with 4 attributes each at 3 levels ($3^4/2/15$) shown in Table 4.3.

We generated the 15 core stimuli for this design with a 3^4 main effect design in 15 profiles by using the OPTEX procedure (SAS Institute 1995), and produced the second alternatives within choice sets using cycles, modulo 3. The three levels of each of the four attributes then can be relabeled in $3! = 6$ different ways, resulting in $6^4 = 1296$ possible designs. The design shown to the left of Table 4.3 is one of these designs, with a D_p-error of .45, the same error as the expected error of a design chosen at random from the set of relabeled designs. The best possible relabeled design has a D_p-error of .30, a 33% improvement of efficiency over the "average" design.

The probabilities in Table 4.3 demonstrate the way utility balance improves the efficiency of choice designs. While both designs have some unbalanced choice sets, the original design has far more. The original design has eleven sets with maximum probabilities exceeding .85, while the relabeled design has only four.

Table 4.3
COMPARISON OF ORIGINAL AND RELABELED $3^4/2/15$ CHOICE DESIGN
REASSIGNMENTS: A -> [1-3,2-1,3-2], B -> [1-3,2-1,3-2], C -> [1-3,2-1,3-2], D -> [1-1,2-3,3-2]

		Original $3^4/2/15$ Design						Relabeled $3^4/2/15$ Design					
Set	Altern.	Attr. A	Attr. B	Attr. C	Attr. D	Sum	Prob	Attr. A	Attr. B	Attr. C	Attr. D	Sum	Prob
1	I	1	3	1	3	8	0.731	3	2	3	2	10	0.953
	II	2	1	3	1	7	0.269	1	3	2	1	7	0.047
2	I	1	2	3	1	7	0.119	3	1	2	1	7	0.500
	II	2	3	2	2	9	0.881	1	2	1	3	7	0.500
3	I	1	1	3	2	7	0.119	3	3	2	3	11	0.998
	II	2	2	2	3	9	0.881	1	1	1	2	5	0.002
4	I	1	3	2	1	7	0.731	3	2	1	1	7	0.047
	II	2	1	1	2	6	0.269	1	3	3	3	10	0.953
5	I	1	2	2	3	8	0.731	3	1	1	2	7	0.500
	II	2	3	1	1	7	0.269	1	2	3	1	7	0.500
6	I	2	2	3	3	10	0.731	1	1	2	2	6	0.500
	II	3	3	2	1	9	0.269	2	2	1	1	6	0.500
7	I	2	3	1	2	8	0.119	1	2	3	3	9	0.500
	II	3	1	3	3	10	0.881	2	3	2	2	9	0.500
8	I	2	2	2	1	7	0.119	1	1	1	1	4	0.002
	II	3	3	1	2	9	0.881	2	2	3	3	10	0.998
9	I	2	1	2	2	7	0.119	1	3	1	3	8	0.500
	II	3	2	1	3	9	0.881	2	1	3	2	8	0.500
10	I	2	1	1	1	5	0.007	1	3	3	1	8	0.500
	II	3	2	3	2	10	0.993	2	1	2	3	8	0.500
11	I	3	3	3	3	12	0.999	2	2	2	2	8	0.500
	II	1	1	2	1	5	0.001	3	3	1	1	8	0.500
12	I	3	1	1	1	6	0.119	2	3	3	1	9	0.500
	II	1	2	3	2	8	0.881	3	1	2	3	9	0.500
13	I	3	3	3	2	11	0.982	2	2	2	3	9	0.500
	II	1	1	2	3	7	0.018	3	3	1	2	9	0.500
14	I	3	1	2	3	9	0.982	2	3	1	2	8	0.500
	II	1	2	1	1	5	0.018	3	1	3	1	8	0.500
15	I	3	2	1	2	8	0.119	2	1	3	3	9	0.500
	II	1	3	3	3	10	0.881	3	2	2	2	9	0.500
D_p-Error							0.449						0.297

Relabeling provides the best utility balance design while preserving orthogonality, level balance, and minimal overlap. Swapping can result in an even better design by sacrificing some orthogonality to achieve more utility balance. Table 4.2 shows for the $3^4/2/15$ family that the total efficiency gain grows from 33% to 43% with swapping, although D_0-error degrades by 32%, suggesting that if one were not confident that $\beta \neq 0$, one might choose the best relabeled design over the one that included both relabeling and swapping.

4.1.3 Swapping and Relabeling to More Complex Choice Designs

The purpose of the previous discussion was to introduce, with simple designs and detailed examples, the concepts of swapping and relabeling to achieve utility balance. In this section the same principles are applied to larger and more complex designs where it is shown that the efficiency gains due to utility balance are even greater.

First consider a choice design that might be used for experimental work: four attributes, each at four levels, represented in 16 choice sets with four alternatives ($4^4/4/16$). The design was developed as before with a core design of 16 profiles defined from a 4^{4-2} orthogonal array, supplemented by competitive alternatives generated with modulo 4 cycles. We then assumed a β vector with partworth values for each attribute of $-1, -1/3, +1/3, 1$ and examined the distribution of D_p-error across 1000 randomly relabeled designs. As shown in Table 4.2, the average error is .31 with a standard deviation of .024. The best relabeled design has a D_p-error of .26 resulting in an efficiency improvement of 16%. Swapping increases this improvement to a total of 36%.

Next consider a brand-specific choice design. These are designs with estimable brand-by-attribute interactions. They are important where one is concerned with modeling choices among brands which themselves have different attributes. As an example, one might have four soft drink brands, Coke, Pepsi, RC, and President's Choice, each at three different prices, and possibly having different flavors and containers. Accordingly, we need a choice design in which brand, brand×price, brand×container, and brand×flavor are all estimable. This leads to a 4×3³/3/48 (interaction) design with 27 parameters (9 for main effects and 18 for interactions).

To generate such choice designs with estimable interactions requires a modification of cycling used to build alternatives from a core choice set. In particular, one must assure that, for example, Coke at it's lowest price is in a choice set against Pepsi at its lowest price, a combination that would not normally be built with cycling. To make the interactions estimable, we modified the choice sets to include a number of such contrasts. This design was then further improved by swapping under the condition that β is zero. This process does not appear to generate the optimal (utility-neutral) design with interactions, but it is sufficient to test whether utility balance works in the case of a design with interactions.

Table 4.2 shows that the average relabeled design has a D_p-error of .23 which drops to .20 (a 14% gain) if the best relabeled design is adopted. Subsequent swaps reduce the D_p-error to .14 resulting in a total efficiency gain of 39%. Thus, the application of swapping and relabeling to achieve utility balance also is effective for designs with interactions.

Finally, Table 4.2 shows the efficiency gains from a large design. This complex design (9×8×4×3⁴×2³/3/63) involves 63 choice sets with 10 factors at varying levels, requiring 29 main-effect parameters. The nine-level attribute could be used as a measured factor in its own right or used to define a blocking variable so that each respondent receives seven choices comprising 1/9th of the total design. To build this design we used the OPTEX procedure to create a core design with 63 profiles and completed each choice set by applying cycles with modulo corresponding to the number of levels of each attribute. These 1000 randomly relabeled versions of this design yield an average D_p-error of .23. The best of these relabeled designs shows an efficiency gain of 30% over the average, and subsequent swapping increases the gain to a total of 63%.

To summarize, we have examined the impact of utility balance on five quite different designs. It is important to stress that these results are not unique to the design families shown but are typical of choice designs generally. Relabeling and swapping enable one to generate utility-balanced designs that are just as accurate as utility-neutral designs with 10-50% fewer respondents. An examination of Table 4.2 indicates that these gains appear to be greater for large designs—presumably because designs with more choice sets can be utility balanced without as greatly distorting their orthogonality. This conjecture is supported by the observation that the smallest loss in D_0-error from swapping comes from the designs that have the most excess degrees of freedom.

Notice that the efficiency gains depend significantly on the original utility-neutral design that one takes as the starting design. We took as the base a design with average efficiency—the expected efficiency given a random selection of one of the utility neutral designs. Thus, not using priors subjects the analyst to both a lower expected efficiency and a substantial variation about that measure. Note further that these gains in efficiency occur despite minimal efforts on our part to find the most efficient design. We only sampled 1000 randomly relabeled designs, and swapping as operationalized is unlikely to find the absolute optimum. Indeed, we have found that gains could have been even greater (although not more than 1-2%) if more thorough searches had been performed.

An important determinant of how much gain in efficiency is due to utility balance is the "scale" of the coefficients. Table 4.2 shows that what was true for the $3^3/3/9$ family occurs generally. Multiplying all coefficients by 1.25 results in an increased efficiency gain of about 25%, while multiplying each by .75 reduces the efficiency gains by about 33%. In the extreme case where scale approaches zero, the utility-neutral design is best. While scale has a strong impact on the extent of the efficiency gains possible, as will be clear in the next section, being wrong about scale has relatively little impact on one's ability to find an efficient design.

4.2 Sensitivity to Misspecification of Priors

Since partworths can only be roughly estimated before the choice experiment, the goal of this section is to examine how the gains from utility balance change if one's assumed priors are incorrect. We test the impact of three kinds of monotone misspecifications: skewness within attributes, relative weighting across attributes, and "scale" of the partworths.

4.2.1 Defining Misspecifications

Misspecifications in *skewness* are generated by halving partworths less than zero and doubling those greater than zero (e.g., -1 -.3 .3 ,1 $\Rightarrow$ -.5, -.15, .60, 2.); note that this changes the spacing, but not the ordering of the levels. *Weight* misspecifications are represented by allowing the weights of the attributes to stretch uniformly between 1 and 4 (e.g., 1, 1, 1 $\Rightarrow$ 1, 2.5, 4). These distorted partworths are then normalized so that the sum of the squared βs is held constant, thus controlling for differences in the scale (Bunch et al. 1996). Figure 4.1 illustrates how the skewness and weight distortions greatly modify the partworths.

Finally, the impact of misspecifications in *scale* are produced by multiplying the normalized partworths either by .5 or 1.5. To measure the impact of multiple misspecifications, we generated 12 designs for each design family reflecting all combinations of the three levels of scale, and two levels each of attribute weighting and skewness.

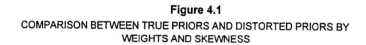

Figure 4.1

COMPARISON BETWEEN TRUE PRIORS AND DISTORTED PRIORS BY WEIGHTS AND SKEWNESS

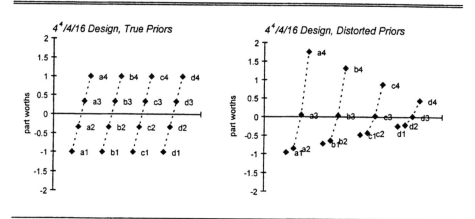

4.2.2 Investigating Efficiency Losses

The loss in efficiency from these misspecifications is gauged relative to the D_p-error of the best utility-balanced design given the true parameter vector β. We created the utility-balanced design, $\tilde{X}^*_{\tilde{\beta}}$, with respect to the misspecified β's, and evaluated this design under the true parameters. The ratio of the D_p-error for the best design, $D_p(\beta, X^*_\beta)$, divided by the D_p-error for the best design given one uses distorted partworths, $D_p(\beta, \tilde{X}^*_{\tilde{\beta}})$, is a measure of the relative efficiency of a design with misspecified prior coefficients.

We ran a descriptive ANOVA using this measure of relative efficiency as the dependent variable and the 5 design families × 3 levels of scale × 2 levels of skewness and weighting, and all two-way interactions as explanatory variables. The model accounted for variation very well; the resulting R^2 was 96%, and all main effects were highly significant (p<.01). Weight and skewness accounted for the largest variation while design and scale were less important (percentage of explained variance = 41%, 21%, 15%, and 3%, respectively). The interactions were significant, accounting for 14% of variation. Given the lack of importance of scale, a good way to display the results is to average over the three values of scale (.5, 1.0, 1.5). The first column of Table 4.4 indicates that misspecifying scale produces designs about 95% as good as knowing scale perfectly. Combining scale with skewness misspecifications results in design efficiencies of about 85%, while scale with weight misspecifications drops efficiencies to about 80%. Finally, combining all three types of misspecifications results in efficiencies of about 70% of the perfectly-known priors condition.

As bad as these losses may be, they are still substantially smaller than the efficiency losses from disregarding priors altogether, shown in the last column of Table 4.4. Thus, the analyst is better off being quite wrong about priors, rather than disregarding them completely.

Table 4.4
RELATIVE EFFICIENCIES GIVEN MISSPECIFICATIONS OF PRIORS

Design Family	Scale only	Scale & Skewness	Scale & Weight	Scale, Weight & Skewness	Relative efficiency of utility-neutral designs ($\beta = 0$)
$3^3/3/9$	95%[a]	89%	86%	83%	73%
$3^4/2/15$	97%	86%	82%	70%	57%
$4^4/4/16$	97%	90%	85%	81%	64%
$4 \times 3^3/3/48$ (interactions)	98%	86%	84%	75%	61%
$9 \times 8 \times 4 \times 3^4 2^3/3/63$	99%	77%	71%	58%	37%

[a]Efficiencies are relative to utility balanced designs using true priors.
The numbers are averages across three scale levels.

It is important to distinguish between the relatively minor impact of scale shown here and its major impact discussed earlier and shown in Table 4.2. In that earlier analysis we showed that scale is important in determining *the potential gain in efficiency* from utility balance. However, Table 4.4 indicates that *identifying a good design* is not importantly dependent on scale. Put differently, making the wrong guess on scale means one could be quite wrong about the extent of gain in efficiency, but this misspecification will have relatively little impact on the relative efficiency of the optimal utility-balanced design.

4.3 Ways to Gather Priors

Prior estimates of the logistic coefficients are required to generate utility-balanced designs. There are a number of ways to generate a coherent and useful set of priors. Perhaps the best way is through a small sample pretest that provides tentative logit coefficients. In this case, these coefficients can be entered directly into the estimate of D_p-error in Equation (3.3). Alternatively, the analyst could subjectively estimate probabilities for a provisional choice experiment, and use the logit coefficients from that pseudo-experiment to provide priors. Finally, one might allow experienced managers to guess the expected partworths for a study, and use these directly as one's estimate for β. The sensitivity analysis clearly shows that using even distorted estimates of β is better than assuming they are zero.

4.4 Summary and Discussion

In this chapter, we showed that utility balance provides substantial improvement in the efficiency of choice designs. Utility-balanced designs can reduce by 10-50% the number of respondents (or choices) required to obtain a specific error level in the parameter estimates. This efficiency gain arises because choices between similarly-valued alternatives provide better information on the coefficients. Thus, when priors are not zero, utility balance joins orthogonality, level balance, and minimal overlap as principles defining efficient choice designs. It is important to stress that while these four principles help us understand what makes a good choice design, in the region of the most efficient designs, they generally conflict with each other. Thus, this chapter portrayed ways to use search routines coupled with design modification strategies to find designs that optimize D_p-error.

We provided two methods, relabeling and swapping, to generate utility-balanced designs. Relabeling attribute levels allows the exploration of designs that reduce D_p-error without altering D_0-error. Particularly for designs with large numbers of attributes or levels, relabeling alone can reduce the number of independent respondents needed to produce a specified error level by 10-40%. Swapping attribute levels within choice sets normally increases overall efficiency drastically, but needs to be more closely monitored. While swapping attribute levels can strongly reduce D_P-error, it can increase colinearity and thereby worsen D_0-error. Thus, swapping is most appropriate when the analyst is confident in the prior β's used to estimate D_p-error. If the priors are inaccurate then a less risky strategy might be to only use relabeling, which has no effect on D_0-error. A sensitivity analysis showed that the efficiency gains from utility balance are diminished, but still substantial, despite quite strong misspecifications of prior parameter estimates.

The idea that the task should mimic marketplace choices as closely as possible (Carson et al. 1994) makes utility balance strategies appealing. To the extent that marketplace dynamics tend to force out competitors with very low shares, market choice sets tend to be utility-balanced. Thus, utility balance may serve a dual role of increasing both the efficiency and the realism of a choice experiment.

We saw that the efficiency gains from utility balance depend (among other things) on the degree of homogeneity in the population under study—efficiency gains increase as the homogeneity increases, reflected in greater "scale" values of the parameter vector. Consequently, we expect that the greatest efficiency gains come from choice designs for a single person. An intriguing question we address in the next chapter is therefore: are these efficiency gains even so great at the individual-level that they result in reliable parameter estimates based on a reasonable number of choices per respondent?

5. Individual Choice Models

Choice models have the important limitation in that the estimation is typically carried out at the aggregate rather than at the individual level. Implicitly, these models assume homogeneity of preference structures, which is a very restrictive assumption. To relax this assumption, several researchers have recently suggested the use of latent class models based on choices to estimate segment-level as opposed to aggregate-level preference structures (e.g., DeSarbo et al. 1995, Kamakura and Russell 1989, Wedel and DeSarbo 1993). While these models significantly limit the problem of preference heterogeneity, it still remains. Taking the idea of segmentation to its logical extreme, the most homogeneous group involves segments of size one, avoiding the heterogeneity problem completely.

One way to derive individual estimates from consumer choices is to stabilize preference functions by combining data from different sources. For example, Allenby, Arora, and Ginter (1995) use Gibbs sampling within a Bayesian framework to incorporate ordinal information on partworths. Huber and his colleagues (1993) use one parameter to adjust ratings-based utilities to choices. Finally, Green and Krieger (1995) adjust conjoint importance weights by incorporating the information of a single choice for each respondent. All of these methods, by combining data of different forms, improve the predictive ability of the model, but may increase bias by predicting choice with non-choice information.

In this chapter, our focus is to develop a practical approach that allows the estimation of individual preference structures based solely upon choices. This goal is not new. In the 1980's, there were several attempts to estimate individual-level choice models. Some researchers modified non-choice data so that it could be analyzed by choice models. For example, Chapman (1984) explodes rankings into choices for input to individual-level logistic estimations. Others have treated a constant-sum allocation directly as a choice probability (Batsell 1980, Moore and

Lehmann 1989). While these approaches avoid the inefficiency of categorical data (choices) by leveraging the power of interval or ratio-scaled inputs, they incur two difficulties. First, by using judgments and translating them into many independent choices, the standard errors become artificially small and the statistical tests invalid. Second, and perhaps more important, as these implied choices are built from ratings or rankings, their validity in predicting actual choice is questionable.

Other early attempts to build individual-level models solely from choices follow the work of Batsell and his colleagues. Batsell and Lodish (1981) require 504 choices per respondent to estimate a six-parameter-model. Later work improves on this ratio, estimating 39 parameters from 312 individual choices (Batsell and Polking 1985). Perhaps with these experiences in mind, Batsell and Louviere (1991) conclude that since "large numbers of observations are needed to achieve asymptotic parameter efficiencies in choice problems of even modest size...it is probably wise to be cautious in design and analysis of individual-level choice experiments..."

To summarize, a growing number of researchers and practitioners have recognized the importance of using choice data in analyzing preference structures and predicting market shares. However, to this date, no *practical* approach has been available that allows for the estimation of individual preference structures, where the data collection *solely relies on choices* made by respondents.

In this chapter, we describe a new approach to building individual choice models that requires few assumptions and can be generated from respondent tasks of moderate size (cf. Zwerina and Huber 1996). The major result is that reliable individual preference structures are feasible if estimated from statistically efficient, customized choice designs. These choice designs use the methods outlined in Chapter 4. Choice sets are utility-balanced using information provided by a series of direct questions about the importance of each attribute and the values of the attribute levels. We show that the gain in efficiency from using this information is so great that it is possible to obtain reliable estimates of 10 parameters from 30 individual choices among three alternatives. To test this process, we compare its predictive validity with well-known benchmarks, that is, a traditional conjoint model and a self-explicated approach.

5.1 An Approach to Building an Individual Choice Model

To motivate and make the discussion more concrete, suppose a researcher needs to model choices of laptop computers defined by the attributes shown in Table 5.1. This is a typical problem in conjoint contexts with five attributes, each at three levels. Clearly, if an individual choice model is not feasible for this simple problem, it will not be feasible for more complex ones.

The proposed approach consists of three stages: a self-explicated stage, a choice design generation stage, and a model estimation stage. The following section describes each of the three stages in detail as we apply them to the laptop study.

Table 5.1
LAPTOP ATTRIBUTES AND LEVELS

	Attributes		*Levels*
I.	Brand name	1.	NEC
		2.	IBM
		3.	Toshiba
II.	Memory size (RAM)	1.	4 MB
		2.	8 MB
		3.	16 MB
III.	Hard drive	1.	250 MB
		2.	340 MB
		3.	510 MB
IV.	Screen type	1.	Passive Display (Monochrome)
		2.	Dual Scan (Color)
		3.	Active Display (Color)
V.	Price	1.	$ 2459.--
		2.	$ 3149.--
		3.	$ 3995.--

5.1.1 Self-Explicated Stage

Our approach begins with an adaptation of the self-explicated model suggested by Srinivasan (1988):

1. Respondents identify the least preferred and the most preferred level of each attribute, and set the desirability ratings for these at 1 and 10, respectively. Then, they rate the remaining attribute levels relative to these anchors. For example, a respondent might give the moderate 340 MB hard drive a desirability rating of "7" compared to a "10" for 510 MB and a "1" for the smallest hard drive, 250 MB.
2. Respondents identify the attribute for which the improvement from the least preferred to the most preferred level is most valuable and set its importance weight at 10. Then, the other attributes are given importance weights (1 to 10) relative to it. Thus, a respondent might give screen type a weight of "3" compared to a weight of "10" for price.

Self-explicated partworths are obtained by multiplying the importance weights with the desirability ratings, normalized so that the partworths within an attribute sum to zero, and the attribute weights sum to one.

5.1.2 Choice Design Generation Stage

We know from Chapter 3 that the efficiency of a choice design depends on the value of the (unknown) model parameters. We use the swapping method outlined in Chapter 4 to generate utility-balanced choice designs. Here, we use the self-explicated partworths as estimates for these unknown parameters to generate customized choice designs.

Before the self-explicated partworths can be submitted in the choice design generation process, one has to transform them to correspond to logit coefficients. As an approximation, we first assume that the ratio of the partworths would be the same for a logit model and a self-explicated model. Second, we assume that the error variance in choice are comparable to what we found in a conjoint pretest. Following these assumptions, we transform the self-explicated model into an approximate choice model by multiplying each partworth by a constant that produces a norm (the square root of the sum of the squared coefficients) of 5.0.[3] The process then follows the three steps of the choice design generation procedure (cf. Chapter 4):

1. We create a fractional factorial plan where each row represents a choice set consisting of an alternative, and each column represents a factor associated with the alternative.
2. We construct additional alternatives by adding cyclically generated alternatives to each choice set. The attribute levels of these new alternatives add one to the level of the previous alternative until it is at the highest level, at which point the assignment re-cycles to the lowest level. For example, if there are five attributes each at three levels and the first alternative is given by (1, 2, 1, 3, 2), then the cyclically constructed second alternative would be (2, 3, 2, 1, 3).
3. We modify the choice design by swapping attribute levels within choice sets to increase design efficiency. This swapping process continues until there is no further gain in design efficiency. Efficiency gains are achieved by making the alternatives within choice sets closer in utility ("utility balance") or probability.

---

[3] Norms of individual choice coefficients cannot be obtained directly because they are artificially high due to model overfitting. As an approximation, we indirectly derived individual logit-norms from corresponding conjoint models in a pretest by using the transformation $\|\hat{\beta}_{logit}\| = \frac{\pi}{\sqrt{6} \cdot \hat{\sigma}_{regr}} \|\hat{\beta}_{regr}\|$, where $\|\bullet\|$ is the norm of a vector, $\hat{\beta}$'s are estimated parameter vectors, and $\hat{\sigma}_{regr}$ is the estimated error variance in a conjoint model. Here, one assumes that the errors in both models have the same variance.

How much gain can be expected from these choice designs customized for each respondent? We showed in the previous chapter how to measure the gain from utility balance and that this gain depends on the magnitude of the parameter vector, measured by its scale (or norm, the square root of scale). Since larger logit coefficients lead to probabilities closer to zero or one, they increase the expected efficiency gains from utility balance (by making choice probabilities closer to one another). Using our method, we found that the theoretical efficiency of the customized choice designs increases by about 60-70% compared with designs assuming no prior information. This efficiency gain means that, theoretically, 30-40 choices provide as much accuracy, in terms of the size of the errors around the estimated parameters, as 100 choices from an uncustomized design.

It is worth noting that these expected gains from utility balance are considerably higher than the 10-50% gains documented in Chapter 4. The efficiency gains are greater here because the individual-level norms are much greater than aggregate-level ones. When the respondents were aggregated in the pretest, their norms dropped from 5.0 to about 1.5. Stated otherwise, utility balance is far more effective at the individual than at the group level because pooling choices across heterogeneous respondents already "balances" the (aggregate) choice probabilities.

Determining the Number of Required Choice Sets. Given this gain in efficiency, the next task is to estimate the number of choice sets needed so that the accuracy of the individual choice model approximates that of a conjoint model with 18 judgments (ratings). While there is no general way to answer this question, we performed an approximate test by assuming that the errors in both conjoint regression and the logistic choice model have the same variance. That is, the model underlying conjoint regression has an individual error term that was assumed to be i.i.d. normal; in parallel, the logistic model has an error term that was assumed to be i.i.d. Gumbel. To the extent that the underlying evaluation processes are similar, the variances of their errors may be similar as well. Scaling both models to equal variances of $\pi^2/6$ (a value which is implicit in logit models), and assuming a within-respondent norm of 5.0, we simulated 2500 decision processes (for choice and ratings) based upon different parameter vectors which were randomly drawn from a uniform distribution. Then, we measured how well the models recover the true parameter vectors. This measure of reliability was calculated as the average correlation through the origin between the estimated and true parameter vectors. We repeated this process for different choice designs with the number of choice sets ranging from 15 to 35.

Figure 5.1
NUMBER OF CHOICE SETS NEEDED TO EQUAL 18 CONJOINT JUDGMENTS

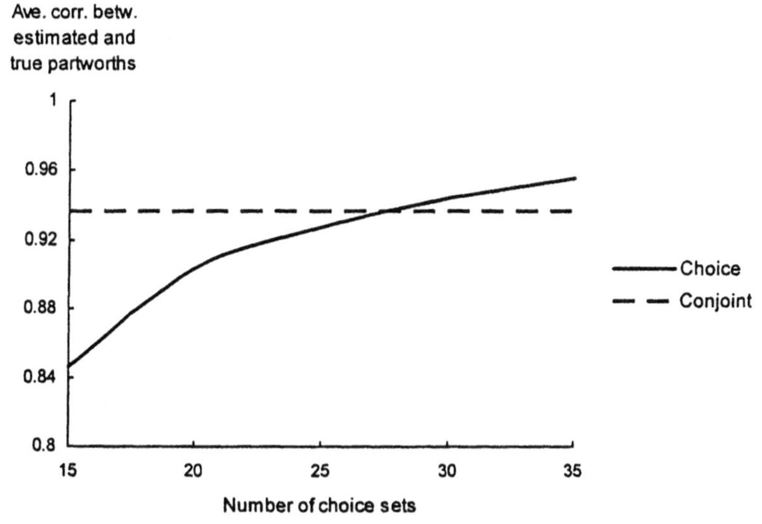

Figure 5.1 shows that roughly 30 (utility-balanced) choice sets, each composed of three alternatives, should be sufficient for the individual choice model to approximate the reliability of a 18 profile, ratings-based conjoint model. This number seems surprisingly small compared with previous approaches to individual-level choice models. However, it remained an empirical question whether this result would hold with real respondents.

5.1.3 Model Estimation Stage

We follow the assumption that the actual choice process among multiattribute alternatives can be approximated by a multinomial logit model (Ben-Akiva and Lerman 1985, Maddala 1983, McFadden 1974). For each respondent, a multinomial logit model, based upon 30 customized choices, is estimated by maximum likelihood. One difficulty we have with individual-level data is nonconvergence. McFadden (1974) documents a necessary and sufficient condition for the likelihood function to converge. Nonconvergence is not a design problem rather than a data problem that occurs when, for example, a respondent would only buy one brand, or never choose the highest-priced alternative. In those cases, the appropriate logit coefficient would be positive infinity for the brand, or negative infinity for the high price.

We found that in over 50% of the cases, the individual choice models failed to converge without utility balancing. Utility balancing reduced the probability of nonconvergence to 17%. To eliminate the technical problem of nonconvergence completely, we "fuzzed" or added a small amount of noise to the dependent variable. For example, if a respondent chose the first alternative among a set of three alternatives, then we used the triple (.999,.0005,.0005) instead of (1,0,0). This slight change of the dependent variable had virtually no effect on estimated probabilities but was sufficient to assure convergence for all our respondents.

5.2 Empirical Test of the Individual Choice Model

The aim of the empirical test is to examine whether the proposed individual choice model also works with real respondents as opposed to simulated ones mentioned earlier. We perform this test by comparing the predictive validity of the proposed approach with two traditional models of individual preference measurement, that is, a conjoint model and a self-explicated model. Note, that our primary concern here is *not* to compare the relative performance of different models (as has been done in numerous conjoint studies), but to assess the *functioning* of this new method using well-known approaches as benchmarks.

We measure predictive validity in two ways: first, the ability to correctly predict holdout choices, and second, the ability to precisely predict aggregate choice shares. If the individual choice model can produce reliable estimates, we expect it to outperform the traditional models in terms of predictive validity, simply because *models based upon choices* should be more appropriate in *predicting choices* than models based upon ratings or rankings of profiles. The critical empirical question is: will the reliability of the individual choice model be sufficient to produce stable and managerially useful parameter estimates?

5.2.1 Study Design

Context. Respondents were told that the study was conducted for a computer company that in the past only sold PC's and planned to enter the laptop market. The respondents were then asked to imagine that their laptop computer broke down and they had to purchase a new one, described using the attributes shown in Table 5.1.

Subjects. 50 MBA students at an Eastern business school participated in the experiment. We offered five cash prizes of $100 as an incentive. We told the students that their chances to win one of the prizes would be greater if they completed the questionnaire more accurately. The winners were those with the five highest test-retest reliabilities in a holdout choice task.

Data Collection. The study employed a self-administered, computer-based questionnaire. This method has the advantage of avoiding variable interviewer influence or putting time pressure on respondents. The data collection entailed two stages and was administered over a period of two weeks.

In the first stage, each respondent received a disk containing three tasks: a holdout choice task, a self-explicated task, and a conjoint task. After respondents became familiar with the different laptop attributes, they completed the holdout task by choosing their most preferred laptop from six choice sets each comprised of three alternatives. These choice sets were Pareto-optimal and the same across all respondents (see appendix E). Then, respondents completed the self-explicated and the conjoint tasks. The self-explicated task was conducted according to section 5.1.1 (see appendix B for an example screen). The conjoint task required respondents to evaluate 18 profiles composed from an orthogonal main effects plan (Addelman 1962). They rated each profile on a 0 to 100 point likelihood-of-purchase scale (see appendix C for an example screen). In addition to the 18 profiles for estimation, two profiles, one very unattractive and the other very attractive, were shown at the beginning of the conjoint section as warm-up tasks (the conjoint design is shown in appendix F). In this way, the respondents became familiar with the anchors of the rating scale (Louviere 1988). Respondents had to complete the holdout choices, the self-explicated task and the conjoint task in one session and return the disk within a week.

In the second stage, a week later, each respondent received a disk containing 36 choice questions (see appendix D for an example screen). The first six choice sets were replicas of the holdout sets, asked a week before, and served to estimate the test-retest reliability of choices. The other 30 choices were customized ("utility-balanced") for each respondent and used to estimate the individual choice models (the individual choice designs are given in appendix G).

5.2.2 Results

Individual conjoint partworths were obtained from the conjoint task by using OLS estimation. Calibration fits were generally good, with an average R^2, the percentage of explained variance, of 90%. Individual choice partworths were obtained from the choice task by using a maximum-likelihood procedure to estimate the individual choice models. The average ρ^2, the percentage gain in the log-likelihood function, was 91%. This ρ^2 is considerably higher than typically found with (aggregate) logit models, a manifestation of the greater consistency in the individual choice models; in this study, the pooled ρ^2 was about 20%. The probability that a respondent would choose the same alternative from an identical choice set was 77.3%, about the same test-retest reliability as found by Huber et al. (1993). The median decision time to make a choice was 11 seconds, and to rate a profile 7 seconds, implying that an entire rating task took about 2 and a choice task took about 6 minutes.

5.2.3 Predictive Validity

Next, we compare the predictive validity obtained by the proposed individual choice model with the conjoint and the self-explicated model. The first test is with respect to hit rates, measuring the extent to which each of the models predict holdout choices. Often in conjoint studies, tests of predictive validity are based upon only a small number of holdout sets (one to three) per respondent, which may not provide very reliable conclusions. To avoid this problem, we used a total of $6 \times 2 = 12$ holdout sets per respondent. Table 5.2 reports the predictive validity in terms of correctly predicted first choices. The highest hit rate came from the proposed individual choice model; it correctly predicted 73.3% of the holdout choices. It performed significantly better (p<.01, using the McNemar-test for correlated samples) than the conjoint and the self-explicated model, with hit rates of 64.7% and 65.3%, respectively. The difference in hit rates of the latter two models was not significant.[4]

---

[4] In a recent study by Srinivasan and Park (1995), this self-explicated model performed significantly better than traditional conjoint in predicting actual job choices of MBA students.

Table 5.2
COMPARISON OF PREDICTIVE VALIDITY

Model	Correctly predicted first choices		Actual vs. predicted choice shares	
	Absolute values (%)	Relative to test-retest (%)	Absolute values (MAE)	Relative to test-retest (%)
Self-explicated model	65.3	84.5	.127	18.9
Conjoint model	64.7	83.7	.122	19.7
Individual choice model	73.3	94.8	.032	75.0
Test-retest reliability	77.3	100.0	.024[a]	100.0

[a] Calculated as deviations from the average of actual choice shares.

Next, we compare the predictive validity of the three different approaches in terms of accuracy in predicting aggregate choice shares. For each of the six different market scenarios (holdout sets), we calculated choice shares by summing actual choices across respondents. These actual choice shares were then compared with the predicted choice shares obtained from the three different approaches. Predicted choice shares followed the maximum-utility rule, typically used in conjoint simulators (e.g., Green and Krieger 1988). Table 5.2 displays the mean absolute errors (MAE) between actual and predicted choice shares as a measure of predictive accuracy.

Again, the individual choice model outperformed the two alternative models. Its relative performance was even greater in predicting choice shares as opposed to individual choices, with the individual choice model (MAE=.032) predicting almost four times more precisely than the conjoint model (MAE=.122) or the self-explicated model (MAE=.127), respectively. Since the aggregate choice shares average over individual errors, this result suggests that the individual choice model produced less biased estimates of the true (choice-based) preference structures compared with the alternative models.

In the predictive tests described above, we merged the two holdout tasks into one. This may distort results since the conjoint and the self-explicated task were performed at the time of the first holdouts, while the choice task was a week later, at the time of the second holdouts. We tested whether the holdouts favored those models that occurred at the same time. We found that the models were indeed more accurate in predicting the more proximal holdout task. However, the direction of the combined results described above held regardless whether the first or the second holdout task was used. In particular, the individual choice model remained superior to either the conjoint or the self-explicated model even when "predicting" the earlier holdout task (although the significance level of the difference in hit rates dropped to $p<.10$).

In summary, two important results emerged. First, the use of customized choice designs enabled us to obtain reliable estimates from the individual choice models based upon a relatively small number of choices. Second, the proposed approach significantly outperformed traditional approaches to consumer preference structure measurement in correctly predicting both first choices and aggregate choice shares. The results suggest that the individual choice model produced less biased estimates of the true (choice-based) preference structures.

5.2.4 Heterogeneity Problem in Logit

According to McFadden (1974) the deterministic part of the utility function in the logit model reflects the "representative tastes" or average utilities of the population and all idiosyncrasies in individual utilities are assumed to be random which are captured by the stochastic component in that utility function (see section 2.2.1). Stated otherwise, the logit model assumes homogeneity of preference structures. It is well known that in the presence of heterogeneity, a nonlinear model, such as the logit model, produces biased estimates. Note that this heterogeneity problem generally does not occur in conjoint that underlies a linear model; here, the pooled or aggregate partworth estimate is the same as the average of the individual partworth estimates (Moore 1980).

Since we are now able to estimate individual-level partworths from choices, we can contrast the results obtained from a traditional logit model, which obtains estimates by pooling choices across all respondents, with the average of the individual choice estimates. We know that the pooled logit model will result in biased estimates of the average partworths (or preference structure), however, usually there is no way to tell to what extent these results will be biased. A comparison of the two different estimation procedures enables us to gauge the aggregation bias in the logit model. Figure 5.2 displays the resultant partworth estimates.

Figure 5.2
COMPARISON BETWEEN POOLED CHOICE ESTIMATE AND AVERAGE OF INDIVIDUAL CHOICE ESTIMATES

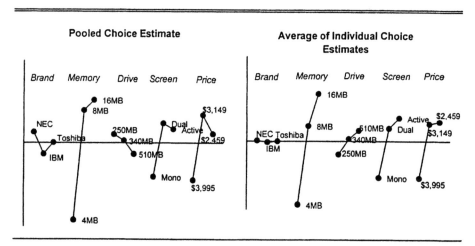

The four attributes memory, drive, screen, and price have expected partworth functions that are monotonically increasing in their levels. The average of the individual choice estimates shows greater face validity than the pooled estimate reflected in utility functions that follow the expected pattern. The pooled logit model surprisingly produced quite severe biases in the estimates (all partworth estimates except for 340 MB were statistically significant at $p<.01$). Three out of four attributes revealed perverse partworth patterns; the attribute Drive showed even a complete reversal of partworths.

Summarizing, in the presence of heterogeneity, the (pooled) logit model suffers from two important problems. First, as in any pooled analysis, there is the problem of "majority fallacy" (Kuehn and Day 1962), which means that the alternative chosen by the "average" customer is not the one chosen most often. For example, if half of the people in a population like large cars and the other half like small cars, then the "average" person likes medium-sized cars best, even though no real person may want one. Typically, heterogeneity reduces the predictive ability of the aggregate model. In this study, the pooled logit model predicted only 57% of the holdout choices (compared with 73.3% with the individual choice model).

While less good than the individual choice model, the pooled logit model usually does a reasonable job in predicting market shares compared to conjoint (see Elrod, Louviere, and Davey 1992, Huber et al. 1993). We found that the pooled logit model predicted actual choice shares almost as precisely as conjoint (MAE=.131 and MAE=.122, respectively).

Second, and perhaps more important, not only do we lose valuable information by aggregating respondents, but also the estimate of the average preference structure will be biased, aggravating the heterogeneity problem. In general, the magnitude of bias depends on the degree of heterogeneity in the data. What is surprising is the fact that the aggregation bias was even quite strong in our relatively small sample size of 50 respondents.[5]

An interesting study would involve a comparison of choice models that explicitly account for heterogeneity (e.g., random effects or latent class models) relative to these two anchors, that is, the pooled logit model and the average of individual choice estimates. One would expect such "heterogeneity" models to produce estimates that lie somewhere within that range defined by the two anchor models. A better "heterogeneity" model would produce results closer to the average of the individual choice estimates. Investigating this issue further, however, is beyond the scope of this thesis.

---

[5] It should be noted that the resultant biases in the aggregate estimates might have been smaller if each respondent had faced the same choice design (cf. discussions by Allenby and Rossi 1991, Foekens, Leefang and Wittink 1994).

5.2.5 Direct Use of Prior Information

In the individual choice model, self-explicated partworths were used to generate customized choice designs, but not used in the model estimation stage. Previous studies have shown that the predictive validity of conjoint models can be improved by incorporating such prior information in partworth estimates (e.g., Allenby et al. 1995, van der Lans and Heiser 1992, Srinivasan, Jain, and Malhotra 1983). In the remainder of this section, we investigate the extent to which order constraints on partworths improve the predictive validity of either the individual choice or the conjoint model.

We derived order constraints on partworths within attributes from the self-explicated tasks. A relatively simple quasi-Newton algorithm incorporated these priors into the partworth estimations, requiring, for example, that a more preferred brand would receive at least as high a partworth as a less preferred one. The algorithm maximizes an objective function (likelihood for choices and least squares for conjoint) within the subspace defined by order constraints (Hartmann, Kim, and So 1995). (Individual partworth estimates for all models considered are provided in appendix G.)

Consistent with previous studies, Table 5.3 shows that the predictive validity of the conjoint model improved by incorporating priors. The percentage of correctly predicted first choices increased significantly from 64.7% to 70.2% ($p<.01$), and the precision in predicted choice shares increased by 34% (from MAE=.122 to MAE=.080). Similarly, the constrained individual choice model increased in the percentage of correctly predicted first choices from 73.3% to 76.3% ($p<.01$). Surprisingly, a reversed effect occurred for the individual choice model; adding self-explicated constraints to the choice model "weakened" its ability to predict aggregate choice shares by 22% (MAE=.032 versus MAE=.041).

Table 5.3
PREDICTIVE VALIDITY OF CONSTRAINED MODEL ESTIMATION

Model	Correctly predicted first choices		Actual vs. predicted choice shares	
	Absolute values (%)	Relative to test-retest (%)	Absolute values (MAE)	Relative to test-retest (%)
Constrained conjoint model	70.2	90.8	.080	30.0
Constrained individual choice model	76.3	98.7	.041	58.5

This differential impact of constraints is an important result. The fact that constraints helped all models at predicting hit rates implies that they reduced noise in the individual-level estimates. However, the fact that adding self-explicated information deteriorated choice share predictions in the individual choice model suggests that here the bias they added was greater than the increase in reliability. Generally speaking, as constraints are incorporated into the model estimation, the quality of the predictive validity obtained depends on the trade-off between a reduction in error variance and an increase in bias. This result is similar to Hagerty's (1985, 1986) finding that more complex models perform better for aggregate data and worse than simpler, but more biased models for individual data. For the individual choice model, it appears that, in order to make aggregate-level predictions, it is more important to use unbiased, if perhaps more noisy estimates.

5.2.6 Differences between Partworths in Different Models

Is there any direct evidence of greater noise, but lower bias for the individual choice model? This question is difficult to answer with aggregate data because the heterogeneity in preference structures across respondents clouds consistent characterization of the partworths. With individual data, we provide evidence of a smaller reliability for the individual choice model as opposed to the alternative models and examine ways in which self-explication and judgment reflect consistently different evaluation processes than choice.

5.2.6.1 Reliability

As a measure of reliability, we examined the ordering of the levels within attributes to see the extent to which these orderings agree with their logical orderings (inferred from the self-explicated task). We focus our attention on the two most important attributes for each respondent, as these have the greatest stability, making interpretations less ambiguous. In the conjoint model, 10% of the most important attribute and 16% of the second most important attribute showed such order violations. In the choice model, 24% of the most important attribute and 32% of the second most important attribute showed order violations. The difference in percentages was only statistically significant ($p<.05$, using the McNemar-test for correlated samples) for the most important attribute. Consequently, in terms of attribute levels following expected patterns, the individual choice model yielded less reliable partworth estimates than the conjoint model.

5.2.6.2 Systematic Differences (Biases)

To the extent that choice differs systematically from judgment or self-explication, the only unbiased way to predict choice will be from choices themselves. We examine two ways in which choice may reflect a cognitively different task evaluation compared with judgment or self-explication. First, choice may put greater weight on a few attributes, particularly compared with the self-explicated task, which focuses attention on each attribute individually (Montgomery et al. 1994, Payne 1976). Second, choice may exhibit greater local loss aversion, the tendency to give proportionally greater weight to the lowest of the three attribute levels. This same pattern of concave partworth functions also occurs if there is a greater tendency to use conjunctive cutoffs in choice as opposed to ratings (Einhorn 1970). Thus, two quite different processes lead to the expectation of greater curvature in choice over judgment.

Importance Weights. We measured attribute importance as the range of partworths for an attribute divided by the sum of the ranges of the other attributes. Then, we averaged weights of the individually most and second most important attributes across respondents. Table 5.4 shows that in the self-explicated task, respondents put less weight on more important attributes, reflected in significantly smaller weights (.301) on the most important attribute compared with the conjoint (.426) and the choice task (.448) ($p<.05$).

The difference between conjoint and choice in their weighting of the most important attribute described above was not significant. When we combined the effects of the most and second most important attribute, however, we found a nearly significant difference ($p<.10$) between conjoint (($.426+.252)/2 =.339$) and choice (($.448+.265)/2 =.357$). In sum, there was strong evidence that self-explication underweighted the most important attribute and marginal evidence that conjoint underweighted the first two, relative to choice.

Table 5.4
COMPARISON OF PARTWORTHS FOR INDIVIDUALLY MOST AND SECOND MOST IMPORTANT ATTRIBUTES

Model	Most important attribute Weight (std.dev.)	Most important attribute Curvature (std.dev.)	Second most important attribute Weight (std.dev.)	Second most important attribute Curvature (std.dev.)
Self-explicated model	.301 (.033)	.458 (.268)	.248 (.026)	.479 (.250)
Conjoint model	.426 (.124)	.472 (.297)	.252 (.067)	.424 (.332)
Individual choice model	**.448** (.179)	**.630** (.384)	.265 (.107)	.499 (.283)

NOTE: Numbers in bold are significantly different (p<.05) from others in the same column.

Curvature. The second hypothesis is that choice would exhibit greater curvature than the other two tasks. We calculated measures of curvature for the attributes by setting the highest and lowest level of each attribute at +1 and -1, respectively. Curvature was then expressed as the position of the intermediate attribute level relative to these two anchors. Thus, positive values indicate concavity and negative values indicate convexity of the within-attribute partworth functions. As is evident from Table 5.4, choice exhibited greater positive curvature (p<.05) with respect to the most important attribute (.630) compared to the other two tasks (.458 and .472, respectively). There was no significant difference in curvature for the second most important attribute.

To summarize, the within-respondent analysis revealed that the conjoint model was more reliable in capturing expected attribute-level orderings than the individual choice model. However, the conjoint model and the self-explicated model were less successful at capturing the differences in attribute weights and local loss aversion found in choice.

5.3 Summary and Discussion

In this chapter, we presented the first *practical* approach, to our knowledge, for estimating individual choice models. In the past, researchers have assumed that the estimation of individual choice models would not be possible without overloading respondents with impractical numbers of choices. We showed that by using extremely efficient choice designs, reliable individual-level estimations are possible with relatively small numbers of choices. These customized choice designs were built by a computer program utilizing individual priors from a simple self-explicated task. Convergence was further assured by adding a small amount of noise to the choices.

We conducted an empirical study to test the new approach, comparing its predictive validity with two traditional approaches to preference structure measurement, a self-explicated and a ratings-based conjoint model. The proposed individual choice model significantly outperformed the alternative models both in predicting first choices and aggregate choice shares. Additionally, constraining the individual choice model improved its ability to predict individual choices, but, surprisingly deteriorated its ability to predict aggregate choices (market shares). These results and a direct comparison of the within-respondent partworths indicated that the self-explicated and the conjoint model were more reliable, but also more biased, than the choice model in predicting choices.

The importance of the comparison of individual choice with conjoint and self-explicated models is that it illustrates not only that individual preference structures can come from a logit analysis of choices, but also that other surrogate measures (such as direct elicitation or ratings) can be fundamentally different from choices. We found consistent differences between individual ratings-based and choice-based preference structures; i.e., choice revealed greater simplification and greater loss aversion compared to judgment. The implication is clear; if one wants to build a general model of choice, then choices are the most appropriate input. Further, we demonstrated that individual choice models offer a way to avoid the heterogeneity problem in (aggregate) choice models.

The ability to produce individual choice models is important in the commercial use of preference models. Individual choice estimates can simplify and augment the traditional aggregate analysis from choice experiments. Segmentation is easier when executed at the individual level, rather than at the level of *a priori* or latent segments. Storing information at the individual level also facilitates a direct relation of consumer choice to demographics or buyer behavior. In short, most of the benefits of an individual-level analysis enjoyed by standard conjoint analysis can now be applied to choice experiments.

The main contribution of the research in this chapter lies in demonstrating that something that was considered infeasible, individual-level choice models, can be done. Significant effort still remains to make the method a practical reality, but the ability to model and analyze choices at the individual level will allow us to better understand both the content and the processes of those critical decisions.

6. Conclusion

This thesis developed criteria for choice design efficiency when one has prior estimates about the model parameters, specified procedures for generating efficient choice designs, and finally, used this knowledge to develop and test individual-level choice models. In this final chapter, we summarize the findings of the thesis, discuss limitations, and provide directions for future research.

6.1 Summary

The thesis began with a review of basic concepts of linear design theory and probabilistic choice models. The section on design theory captured the principles of confounding and resolution in fractional factorial designs, linear models, and efficiency in linear designs. From this section followed two important lessons. First, the type of coding of a design does affect the interpretability of the estimated parameters, but not the overall fit or explained variance of the model. Thus, the choice of a particular coding is basically a matter of which contrasts are focused on. Second, efficiency is an important concept in design selection. A design is efficient if it produces precise parameter estimates. Two principles affect efficiency in linear designs, level balance and orthogonality. Generating an efficient design generally requires optimally trading off these two principles. Computer searches are the only general way to generate efficient designs (Kuhfeld et al. 1994).

The section on probabilistic choice models derived the formulation of the well-known multinomial logit model, discussed its properties, and provided a brief overview of other important choice models. Probabilistic choice models can be derived from a common framework, the random utility theory. Different choice models are defined by making different assumptions regarding the error component. For example, the probit model assumes that the errors are multivariate normally distributed, and the logit model assumes that the errors are identically and independently Gumbel distributed. The logit model is by far the most widely used discrete choice model because its important computational advantages. A major criticism of the logit model is that it is subject to the independence from irrelevant alternatives (IIA) property, implying that a newly introduced alternative draws proportionally choice probabilities from existing alternatives regardless of substitutability among alternatives. The IIA property generally does not hold at the aggregate level, even if each individual is consistent with IIA. This circumstance has important practical implications, suggesting that the IIA problem in logit can be alleviated by properly segmenting respondents in homogeneous groups (see McAlister et al. 1991, Swait et al. 1993). Alternatively, the generalization of the logit model, the universal logit model, can be used to account for substitutability effects among alternatives. The UL model accounts for IIA violations by modeling an alternative's utility as a function of its own attributes and the attributes (or availability) of other alternatives in the choice set. Consequently, the logit model remains an important and useful tool in investigating consumer choice and played an important role in this thesis.

Chapter 3 began with a review of previous approaches to building choice designs. Most of these methods rely on extensions of the general linear design theory. We pointed out that carefully selected linear designs provide reasonable, general-purpose choice designs, but they are generally nonoptimal in a statistical sense. Experimental designs for linear (e.g., conjoint) models are substantially different from designs for (nonlinear) choice models. First, choice design efficiency depends both on the creation of appropriate profiles and properly placing them into several choice sets. Second, probabilistic choice models are nonlinear in the parameters, implying that the statistical efficiency of a choice design depends on an (unknown) parameter vector. This property suggests to incorporate prior estimates on model parameters in choice designs.

We then identified four principles of choice design efficiency: orthogonality, level balance, minimal overlap, and utility balance. The first two principles come from the linear design theory, whereas the latter two are new and specific to choice designs. Minimal overlap means that the alternatives in a choice set are as different as possible in terms of their attribute levels. This is an important property because the contrasts necessary to estimate the effects are only meaningful as differences in attribute levels within a choice set. Utility balance means that the alternatives in a choice set are as similar as possible in terms of their utilities. Utility balance requires prior information on the model parameters. A choice design is optimal (i.e., it has maximum efficiency or minimum variances of the estimates) if it satisfies all four principles simultaneously. However, there are only a few special cases where those principles can be satisfies at once; in general, constructing an efficient choice designs requires optimally trading off all four principles.

In order to simplify the choice design problem, choice designs have traditionally been built under the assumption that all model parameters are zero. While this assumption is justified when one has very little information on model parameters, the analyst typically has some idea about the magnitude or directions of certain attributes, such as price or quality. We showed in Chapter 4 that if one has reasonable prior estimates on model parameters, then these can be used to generate considerably more efficient choice designs. These designs are more efficient because the alternatives within choice sets are balanced in terms of utilities. We provided two procedures, relabeling and swapping, to generate such utility-balanced choice designs. Relabeling is less flexible than swapping in that it increases utility balance without affecting the other three principles. Swapping is more effective than relabeling because its greater flexibility, trading off orthogonality against utility balance in order to improve design efficiency. The procedures for generating utility-balanced designs were applied to several different choice designs and was shown to reduce by 10-50% the number of respondents needed to achieve a certain error level around the model parameters. A sensitivity analysis revealed that the efficiency gains from utility balance are diminished, but still substantial, despite quite strong misspecifications of prior parameter estimates. The bottom line is that one can use even quite rough prior estimates and is still better off than assuming the parameters to be zero. Furthermore, the idea that the experiment should mimic marketplace choices (Carson et al. 1994) makes utility balance strategies additionally appealing; to the extent that marketplace dynamics tend to force out competitors with very low shares, market choice sets tend to be utility-balanced. Thus, utility balance may serve a dual role of increasing both the efficiency and the realism of a choice experiment.

Current wisdom holds that individual-level choice models require too many responses to be feasible, particularly for commercial projects. In Chapter 5, we presented the first practical approach to an individual-level choice model. We showed that it is possible to reliably estimate 10 individual parameters of a choice model with only 30 choices among three alternatives. An empirical test showed that the proposed model predicted individual choices and aggregate choice shares better than a ratings-based conjoint and self-explicated analysis. Reliability in the estimates came from the use of each individual's self-explicated data to generate extremely statistically efficient, customized choice designs. This reliability of individual choice estimates means that segmentation and simulation of choices can proceed at the individual level rather than at the aggregate or latent segment level.

We demonstrated the heterogeneity problem in (aggregate) choice models and showed how individual choice models overcome this problem. Finally, we illustrated how the proposed approach permits the exploration of behavioral differences between judgment (ratings) and choice without having to aggregate across heterogeneous respondents. The results indicated greater simplification and greater loss aversion in choice as opposed to judgment. In short, we demonstrated the usefulness and validity of individual choice models in both behavioral and marketing research areas.

6.2 Limitations and Future Research

Following, we discuss limitations of this dissertation and suggest directions for future research in both behavioral and methodological areas.

6.2.1 Behavioral Areas

In developing choice designs, our focus was on statistical efficiency. We showed that if we make a choice harder, i.e. more utility-balanced, then efficiency can be improved, producing more precise estimates. When respondents face harder choices, however, they may resort in simplifying tactics which potentially introduces biases in the estimates. In addition, we implicitly assumed that the error levels are constant across different choice sets; if they do increase, then the gain from theoretical efficiency could be lessened or even reversed. As an empirical test of utility balance, Huber, Zwerina, and Pinnell (1996) re-analyzed data from a large commercial study that used randomly generated choice tasks (Sawtooth Software 1993). After fitting a logit model to the data, the choice sets were evaluated and equally divided into hard (or utility-balanced) and easy (or utility-imbalanced) ones. Running separate logit analyses in the two groups, the authors found identical parameter estimates, but with the estimates from the group with utility-balanced choices having 30% smaller error variances compared to the group with utility-imbalanced choices. This test indicates that utility-balance is able to produce also in practice better estimation results, however, more empirical research is needed to explore under what circumstances utility balance produces a positive trade-off between (statistical) estimation error and (behavioral) respondents' error.

While Chapter 5 showed that respondents were able to accomplish 30 choices in about six minutes (which indicates that the time cost for respondents making numerous choices is not great) there is a need for more research on the impact of the number of choices per respondent on both the validity and the reliability of the ultimate choice model (see Johnson and Orme 1996 for a pioneering effort in this direction). It may be possible for each respondent to make a large number of choices by performing them in separate sittings. Splitting the task over several sittings is more feasible for choices than for ratings; in conjoint, it is important that a person uses a rating of, say, "6" the same way throughout the tasks performed in different sittings. In contrast, choice has its own context, making it possible for a person to make, say, 8 choices each day for 15 days, rather than, say, 120 choices in one sitting. Little in known about the effect on reliability and validity of the results stemming from these changes.

There are many difficult theoretical problems that can be better resolved with the use of individual choice models. Such models allow one to study differences between different decision processes (e.g., ratings vs. choice) or various task effects on choice without having to aggregate across heterogeneous respondents. As an example, the phenomenon of information overload on respondents and its effect on decision strategies can be investigated in a more direct way than was done in previous studies (e.g., Keller and Staelin 1987, Meyer and Johnson 1989, Payne 1976). Finally, future studies utilizing individual choice models may be able to optimize choice experiments by trading-off the efficiency advantage of complex choice tasks against an increase in within-respondent error.

6.2.2 Methodological Areas

While we are confident that utility balance applies to models similar to those that were explored in this thesis, i.e. multinomial logit models, more theoretical and empirical work is needed to construct designs that are appropriate for, say, nested logit or probit models with explicit heterogeneity terms. Also, we did not consider a constant alternative, such as "I would not buy any of these brands", in our designs (see Zwerina and Huber 1996 for a discussion of efficiency issues with respect to constant alternatives). The methods to generate utility-balanced designs described in Chapter 4 are attractive because they make intuitive sense and are useful in describing what makes a choice design efficient. However, these methods are difficult to operationalize for more complex choice designs (e.g., availability or attribute cross effects designs) and may be nonoptimal because they do not trade off all four efficiency principles simultaneously. For example, the swapping procedure only trades off orthogonality against utility balance—minimal overlap and level balance remain unchanged. Future research would be useful to develop more flexible and reliable algorithms, generating efficient and more complex choice design in a reasonable amount of time (see Zwerina, Huber, and Kuhfeld 1996 for a general method for constructing efficient choice designs).

The availability of individual choice models has important implications not only for behavioral research, but also for commercial applications. Before individual choice models are appropriate for commercial studies, however, additional research is needed. First, it would be useful to provide general guidelines on how many choices are required depending on the number of parameters and the number of alternatives per choice set. Second, many commercial studies involve large numbers of parameters. Hybrid models may play the same role for choice as they have for conjoint (e.g., Green 1984, Green and Krieger 1996, Srinivasan and Park 1995). One promising approach would be to limit each respondent's choices to, say, the five attributes they consider most important. Less important attributes can be given weights proportional to their self-explicated partworths.

There are a number of alternative design approaches that deserve attention. One approach is to use sequential or batch-sequential designs as opposed to static designs in which all design points are preselected. In a sequential design, each design point is selected using a well-defined rule that is based on the previously observed design points and responses. So far, very little is known about their statistical properties. A second approach is the use of Bayesian-motivated designs. Both approaches usually involve important statistical difficulty and computational cost, having limited their use to a few special cases (see Ford, Titterington, and Kitsos 1989 for an overview of nonlinear design issues). Such designs have typically been developed for problems in biology and physics, where the numbers of parameters usually do not exceed three or four, an impractical number for most marketing problems, involving large multifactor experiments.

Until recently, the application of Bayesian methods has been limited to special cases in which the posterior distribution has a (mathematically tractable) closed form. Recent progress in estimation techniques, such as Gibbs sampler (Gelfand and Smith 1990), overcome many of these limitations. Some successfully implemented Bayesian methods have been published in marketing (e.g., Allenby et al. 1995, Allenby and Ginter 1995, Lenk et al. 1996, Rossi and Allenby 1993). The use of Bayesian methods to building choice designs for marketing applications, however, have yet to be explored. With new estimation techniques, the problem in Bayesian methods lies no longer in mathematical tractability rather than in considerable computational cost. As computing power increases, these methods may become more attractive, replacing simpler and less reliable design approaches.

Appendix A: Derivation of Probability-Centered Estimation Error

EFFECTS-CODED DESIGN MATRIX OF ORIGINAL $3^3/3/9$ CHOICE DESIGN: X

X1.1	X1.2	X2.1	X2.2	X3.1	X3.2	Probabilities (from Eq 3.1)
1	0	1	0	1	0	0.002
0	1	0	1	0	1	0.047
-1	-1	-1	-1	-1	-1	0.951
1	0	0	1	0	1	0.045
0	1	-1	-1	-1	-1	0.910
-1	-1	1	0	1	0	0.045
1	0	-1	-1	-1	-1	0.488
0	1	1	0	1	0	0.024
-1	-1	0	1	0	1	0.488
0	1	1	0	-1	-1	0.333
-1	-1	0	1	1	0	0.333
1	0	-1	-1	0	1	0.333
0	1	0	1	1	0	0.045
-1	-1	-1	-1	0	1	0.910
1	0	1	0	-1	-1	0.045
0	1	-1	-1	0	1	0.488
-1	-1	1	0	-1	-1	0.488
1	0	0	1	1	0	0.024
-1	-1	1	0	0	1	0.333
1	0	0	1	-1	-1	0.333
0	1	-1	-1	1	0	0.333
-1	-1	0	1	-1	-1	0.910
1	0	-1	-1	1	0	0.045
0	1	1	0	0	1	0.045
-1	-1	-1	-1	1	0	0.488
1	0	1	0	0	1	0.024
0	1	0	1	-1	-1	0.488

$\beta' =$

-1	0	-1	0	-1	0

PROBABILITY-CENTERED DESIGN MATRIX: Z (from Eq 3.3)

Z1.1	Z1.2	Z2.1	Z2.2	Z3.1	Z3.2
1.95	0.90	1.95	0.90	1.95	0.90
0.95	1.90	0.95	1.90	0.95	1.90
-0.05	-0.10	-0.05	-0.10	-0.05	-0.10
1.00	-0.86	0.86	1.86	0.86	1.86
0.00	0.14	-0.14	-0.14	-0.14	-0.14
-1.00	-1.86	1.86	0.86	1.86	0.86
1.00	0.46	-0.54	-1.00	-0.54	-1.00
0.00	1.46	1.46	0.00	1.46	0.00
-1.00	-0.54	0.46	1.00	0.46	1.00
0.00	1.00	1.00	0.00	-1.00	-1.00
-1.00	-1.00	0.00	1.00	1.00	0.00
1.00	0.00	-1.00	-1.00	0.00	1.00
0.86	1.86	0.86	1.86	1.00	-0.86
-0.14	-0.14	-0.14	-0.14	0.00	0.14
1.86	0.86	1.86	0.86	-1.00	-1.86
0.46	1.00	-1.00	-0.54	0.46	1.00
-0.54	-1.00	1.00	0.46	-0.54	-1.00
1.46	0.00	0.00	1.46	1.46	0.00
-1.00	-1.00	1.00	0.00	0.00	1.00
1.00	0.00	0.00	1.00	-1.00	-1.00
0.00	1.00	-1.00	-1.00	1.00	0.00
-0.14	-0.14	0.00	0.14	-0.14	-0.14
1.86	0.86	-1.00	-1.86	1.86	0.86
0.86	1.86	1.00	-0.86	0.86	1.86
-0.54	-1.00	-0.54	-1.00	1.00	0.46
1.46	0.00	1.46	0.00	0.00	1.46
0.46	1.00	0.46	1.00	-1.00	-0.54

PROBABILITY-CENTERED COVARIANCE MATRIX

$$\Sigma_p = (Z'PZ)^{-1}$$

(from Eq 3.3)

	Z1.1	Z1.2	Z2.1	Z2.2	Z3.1	Z3.2
Z1.1	0.67	-0.30	0.20	0.02	0.20	0.02
Z1.2	-0.30	0.41	0.02	-0.02	0.02	-0.02
Z2.1	0.20	0.02	0.67	-0.30	0.20	0.02
Z2.2	0.02	-0.02	-0.30	0.41	0.02	-0.02
Z3.1	0.20	0.02	0.20	0.02	0.67	-0.30
Z3.2	0.02	-0.02	0.02	-0.02	-0.30	0.41

$$D_P - Error = (\det \Sigma_p)^{1/6} = .381$$

Appendix B: Example Screens of Self-Explicated Task

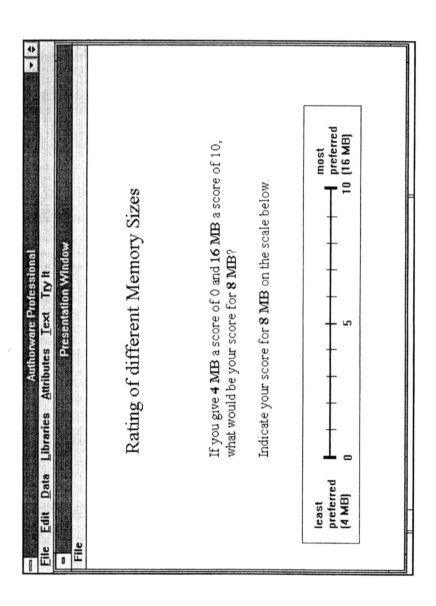

Appendices

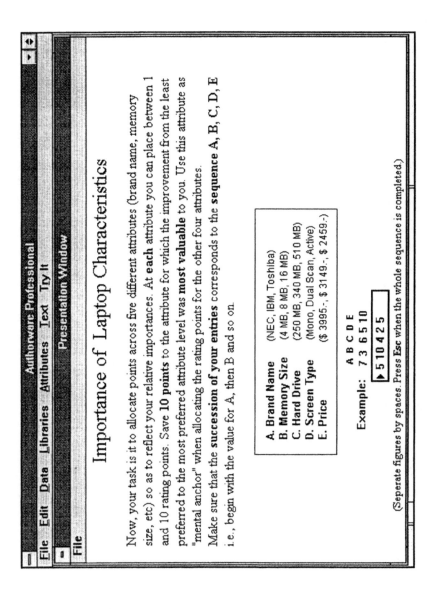

Appendix C: Example Screen of Conjoint Task

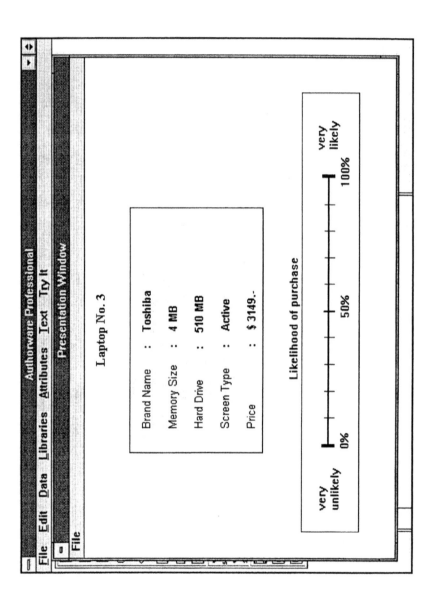

Appendices

Appendix D: Example Screen of Choice Task

```
Authorware Professional
File  Edit  Data  Libraries  Attributes  Text  Try It
          Presentation Window

                    Choice No. 2

    Laptop A              Laptop B              Laptop C

Brand Name : Toshiba   Brand Name : IBM      Brand Name : NEC
Memory Size : 8 MB     Memory Size : 8 MB    Memory Size : 16 MB
Hard Drive  : 250 MB   Hard Drive  : 510 MB  Hard Drive  : 340 MB
Screen Type : Dual Scan Screen Type : Active Screen Type : Mono
Price       : $ 3149.- Price       : $ 3995.- Price     : $ 2459.-

          Which one would you choose?
    (Indicate your choice by clicking on the object)
```

Appendix E: Holdout Choice Sets

The following table includes the six Pareto-optimal holdout sets which were used to evaluate predictive validity of the different models.

		Profile Descriptions				
Set	Altern.	Brand Name	Memory Size	Hard Drive	Screen Type	Price Level
1	I	IBM	8MB	340MB	Mono	$3149
	II	NEC	16MB	510MB	Mono	$3995
	III	Toshiba	16MB	250MB	DualScan	$2459
2	I	Toshiba	8MB	250MB	DualScan	$3149
	II	IBM	8MB	510MB	Active	$3995
	III	NEC	16MB	340MB	Mono	$2459
3	I	NEC	8MB	340MB	Active	$3995
	II	IBM	16MB	510MB	Mono	$3149
	III	Toshiba	4MB	510MB	Active	$2459
4	I	Toshiba	8MB	340MB	Mono	$2459
	II	IBM	16MB	340MB	DualScan	$3149
	III	NEC	4MB	510MB	Active	$2459
5	I	IBM	8MB	510MB	Mono	$2459
	II	NEC	16MB	340MB	DualScan	$3149
	III	Toshiba	8MB	250MB	Active	$2459
6	I	NEC	16MB	340MB	Mono	$3995
	II	IBM	8MB	340MB	Active	$3149
	III	Toshiba	4MB	250MB	DualScan	$2459

Appendix F: Experimental Conjoint Design

The following table includes the experimental design for the conjoint task. The first two profiles (one very attractive and one very unattractive) were used as warm-ups. The subsequent 18 profiles constitute an orthogonal main-effects plan and was used to estimate the conjoint partworths.

No.	Brand Name	Memory Size	Hard Drive	Screen Type	Price Level
1	NEC	4MB	250MB	Mono	$3995
2	Toshiba	16MB	510MB	Active	$2459
3	Toshiba	4MB	510MB	Active	$3149
4	NEC	4MB	250MB	Mono	$3995
5	IBM	4MB	340MB	DualScan	$3149
6	NEC	8MB	340MB	Active	$3149
7	IBM	8MB	510MB	Mono	$2459
8	NEC	16MB	510MB	DualScan	$2459
9	Toshiba	8MB	250MB	DualScan	$2459
10	IBM	16MB	250MB	Active	$3995
11	NEC	4MB	510MB	DualScan	$3995
12	Toshiba	16MB	340MB	Mono	$3995
13	NEC	8MB	250MB	Mono	$3149
14	IBM	4MB	250MB	Active	$2459
15	NEC	16MB	340MB	Active	$2459
16	Toshiba	4MB	340MB	Mono	$2459
17	Toshiba	8MB	510MB	Active	$3995
18	IBM	8MB	340MB	DualScan	$3995
19	Toshiba	16MB	250MB	DualScan	$3149
20	IBM	16MB	510MB	Mono	$3149

Appendix G: Experimental Choice Designs and Partworth Values

The following pages show the choice designs and partworth values for each of the 50 respondents used in the individual choice study. The upper panel on each page displays an utility-balanced choice design which was customized for a particular respondent (using his/her self-explicated data). There are 30 choice sets each consisting three laptop alternatives. A laptop alternative is characterized by five attributes with three different levels each.

The lower panel displays the respondent-specific partworth values, estimated from five different models. For readability purposes, these partworths are normalized as follows: first, attribute weights, defined as the maximum range of partworths within an attribute, sum to one; second, the smallest partworth within an attribute is set to zero. Due to rounding errors, the attribute weights do not always sum to one exactly.

Respondent No. 1

Experimental Choice Design

Set		Laptop A					Laptop B					Laptop C			
1	NEC	8MB	510MB	Mono	$3995	IBM	16MB	250MB	DualScan	$2459	Toshiba	4MB	340MB	Active	$3149
2	NEC	8MB	510MB	DualScan	$3995	IBM	16MB	250MB	Active	$3149	Toshiba	4MB	340MB	Mono	$2459
3	NEC	4MB	340MB	Active	$2459	IBM	16MB	510MB	Mono	$3995	Toshiba	8MB	250MB	DualScan	$3149
4	NEC	4MB	510MB	Mono	$2459	Toshiba	8MB	250MB	Active	$3995	IBM	16MB	340MB	DualScan	$3149
5	IBM	16MB	340MB	DualScan	$3995	Toshiba	4MB	510MB	Active	$3149	NEC	8MB	250MB	Mono	$2459
6	NEC	16MB	340MB	Mono	$3149	IBM	4MB	510MB	DualScan	$2459	Toshiba	8MB	250MB	Active	$3995
7	NEC	16MB	250MB	Active	$3995	IBM	8MB	340MB	Mono	$2459	Toshiba	4MB	510MB	DualScan	$3149
8	NEC	8MB	340MB	Mono	$3149	IBM	4MB	510MB	Active	$2459	Toshiba	16MB	250MB	DualScan	$3995
9	NEC	16MB	250MB	Active	$3995	IBM	8MB	340MB	DualScan	$3149	Toshiba	4MB	510MB	Mono	$2459
10	NEC	4MB	250MB	DualScan	$3149	IBM	8MB	340MB	Active	$2459	Toshiba	16MB	510MB	Mono	$3995
11	IBM	8MB	510MB	DualScan	$3995	Toshiba	16MB	250MB	Mono	$2459	NEC	4MB	340MB	Active	$3149
12	IBM	16MB	250MB	Active	$3149	Toshiba	4MB	340MB	DualScan	$2459	NEC	8MB	510MB	Mono	$3995
13	IBM	8MB	250MB	Active	$3149	NEC	4MB	340MB	Mono	$2459	Toshiba	16MB	510MB	DualScan	$3995
14	IBM	8MB	250MB	Active	$3149	Toshiba	16MB	340MB	DualScan	$3995	NEC	4MB	510MB	Mono	$2459
15	IBM	16MB	510MB	Mono	$3995	NEC	8MB	250MB	DualScan	$3149	Toshiba	4MB	340MB	Active	$2459
16	IBM	16MB	340MB	DualScan	$3149	NEC	4MB	250MB	Active	$3995	Toshiba	8MB	510MB	Mono	$2459
17	IBM	16MB	510MB	Mono	$3149	Toshiba	8MB	250MB	DualScan	$3995	NEC	4MB	340MB	Active	$2459
18	IBM	16MB	250MB	Mono	$3995	Toshiba	8MB	340MB	DualScan	$3149	NEC	4MB	510MB	Active	$2459
19	IBM	16MB	510MB	Mono	$2459	Toshiba	4MB	250MB	DualScan	$3995	NEC	8MB	340MB	Active	$3149
20	IBM	16MB	250MB	DualScan	$2459	NEC	4MB	510MB	Active	$3995	Toshiba	8MB	340MB	Mono	$3149
21	Toshiba	16MB	250MB	Active	$3995	NEC	8MB	340MB	Mono	$3149	IBM	4MB	510MB	DualScan	$2459
22	NEC	16MB	250MB	DualScan	$3149	Toshiba	4MB	510MB	Mono	$2459	IBM	8MB	340MB	Active	$3995
23	Toshiba	4MB	510MB	DualScan	$3995	NEC	16MB	250MB	Active	$3995	IBM	8MB	340MB	Mono	$2459
24	Toshiba	4MB	510MB	Mono	$3149	NEC	8MB	250MB	DualScan	$2459	IBM	16MB	340MB	Active	$3995
25	Toshiba	4MB	340MB	DualScan	$2459	NEC	8MB	510MB	Active	$3995	IBM	16MB	250MB	Mono	$3149
26	Toshiba	8MB	250MB	Mono	$3149	NEC	16MB	510MB	DualScan	$3995	IBM	4MB	340MB	Active	$3149
27	Toshiba	8MB	250MB	Mono	$2459	NEC	16MB	340MB	DualScan	$3995	IBM	4MB	510MB	Active	$3149
28	Toshiba	4MB	340MB	Active	$2459	NEC	16MB	250MB	Mono	$3149	IBM	8MB	510MB	DualScan	$3995
29	Toshiba	8MB	340MB	DualScan	$3149	NEC	4MB	510MB	Active	$3149	IBM	16MB	250MB	Mono	$3995
30	Toshiba	16MB	250MB	DualScan	$3995	IBM	8MB	510MB	Mono	$3149	NEC	4MB	340MB	Active	$2459

Partworth Values

Model	Brand Name			Memory Size				Hard Drive			Screen Type			Price Level		
	NEC	IBM	Toshiba	4MB	8MB	16MB	250MB	340MB	510MB	Mono	DualScan	Active	$3995	$3149	$2459
Self-Explicated	.083	.000	.125	.000	.243	.312	.000	.097	.219	.000	.069	.156	.000	.104	.187
Conjoint	.067	.000	.000	.000	.358	.692	.000	.010	.048	.024	.029	.000	.000	.120	.164
Choice	.034	.000	.030	.000	.263	.492	.000	.035	.133	.042	.000	.039	.000	.299	.226
Constr. Conjoint	.000	.000	.000	.000	.396	.766	.000	.011	.053	.000	.000	.000	.000	.133	.181
Constr. Choice	.047	.000	.069	.000	.313	.463	.000	.066	.184	.000	.015	.077	.000	.208	.208

Appendices

Respondent No. 2

Experimental Choice Design

Set	Laptop A					Laptop B					Laptop C				
1	NEC	8MB	510MB	Mono	$2459	IBM	16MB	250MB	DualScan	$3995	Toshiba	4MB	340MB	Active	$3149
2	NEC	8MB	510MB	DualScan	$3995	IBM	4MB	250MB	Active	$2459	Toshiba	16MB	340MB	Mono	$3149
3	NEC	4MB	340MB	Active	$3149	Toshiba	16MB	510MB	Mono	$3995	IBM	8MB	250MB	DualScan	$2459
4	NEC	4MB	510MB	Active	$3995	Toshiba	8MB	340MB	Mono	$2459	IBM	16MB	250MB	DualScan	$3149
5	NEC	16MB	340MB	Mono	$2459	IBM	4MB	510MB	DualScan	$3149	Toshiba	8MB	250MB	Active	$3995
6	NEC	16MB	340MB	Mono	$3995	IBM	4MB	510MB	DualScan	$2459	Toshiba	8MB	250MB	Active	$3149
7	IBM	8MB	250MB	Active	$3149	NEC	16MB	340MB	Mono	$2459	Toshiba	4MB	510MB	DualScan	$3995
8	IBM	4MB	340MB	Active	$3995	NEC	8MB	510MB	Mono	$2459	Toshiba	16MB	250MB	DualScan	$3149
9	IBM	4MB	510MB	Mono	$3149	NEC	8MB	340MB	DualScan	$3995	Toshiba	16MB	250MB	Mono	$2459
10	IBM	8MB	340MB	Mono	$2459	NEC	16MB	250MB	Active	$3995	Toshiba	4MB	510MB	DualScan	$3149
11	Toshiba	16MB	510MB	Mono	$3995	IBM	8MB	250MB	DualScan	$3149	NEC	4MB	340MB	Active	$2459
12	Toshiba	4MB	250MB	Active	$2459	IBM	8MB	340MB	DualScan	$3995	NEC	16MB	510MB	Mono	$3149
13	IBM	4MB	340MB	Active	$3149	NEC	8MB	510MB	Mono	$2459	Toshiba	16MB	250MB	DualScan	$3995
14	IBM	8MB	250MB	Active	$3149	NEC	16MB	340MB	Mono	$3995	Toshiba	4MB	510MB	DualScan	$2459
15	Toshiba	8MB	340MB	DualScan	$3995	NEC	16MB	510MB	Active	$3149	IBM	4MB	250MB	Active	$2459
16	IBM	16MB	340MB	Mono	$3149	Toshiba	4MB	510MB	DualScan	$2459	NEC	8MB	250MB	DualScan	$3995
17	IBM	8MB	510MB	Mono	$2459	NEC	16MB	250MB	Active	$3995	Toshiba	4MB	340MB	Active	$3149
18	IBM	16MB	340MB	Mono	$2459	Toshiba	8MB	250MB	DualScan	$3149	NEC	4MB	510MB	Active	$3995
19	Toshiba	8MB	340MB	Mono	$2459	IBM	4MB	510MB	Active	$3995	NEC	16MB	250MB	DualScan	$3149
20	NEC	16MB	250MB	DualScan	$3149	IBM	8MB	340MB	DualScan	$3995	Toshiba	8MB	510MB	Mono	$2459
21	Toshiba	16MB	510MB	Active	$3995	NEC	4MB	340MB	Active	$3149	IBM	4MB	250MB	Mono	$2459
22	NEC	16MB	510MB	Mono	$2459	IBM	8MB	250MB	Active	$3149	Toshiba	8MB	340MB	DualScan	$3995
23	NEC	16MB	510MB	Active	$3149	Toshiba	4MB	250MB	Mono	$3995	IBM	16MB	340MB	DualScan	$2459
24	Toshiba	4MB	510MB	Mono	$3995	NEC	8MB	250MB	Active	$2459	IBM	16MB	340MB	DualScan	$3149
25	Toshiba	4MB	340MB	DualScan	$2459	NEC	8MB	250MB	Active	$3995	IBM	16MB	510MB	Mono	$3149
26	Toshiba	16MB	250MB	Mono	$3149	NEC	4MB	510MB	DualScan	$3995	IBM	8MB	340MB	Active	$2459
27	Toshiba	8MB	510MB	Mono	$3995	IBM	16MB	340MB	DualScan	$3149	NEC	4MB	250MB	Active	$2459
28	NEC	8MB	250MB	DualScan	$2459	IBM	16MB	510MB	Mono	$3149	Toshiba	4MB	340MB	Active	$3995
29	Toshiba	8MB	340MB	Active	$3149	IBM	16MB	510MB	DualScan	$2459	NEC	4MB	250MB	Mono	$3995
30	Toshiba	16MB	340MB	Mono	$3149	NEC	4MB	510MB	DualScan	$2459	IBM	8MB	250MB	Active	$3995

Partworth Values

Model	Brand Name			Memory Size			Hard Drive			Screen Type			Price Level		
	NEC	IBM	Toshiba	4MB	8MB	16MB	250MB	340MB	510MB	Mono	DualScan	Active	$3995	$3149	$2459
Self-Explicated	.000	.036	.065	.000	.172	.258	.000	.129	.194	.000	.215	.323	.000	.090	.161
Conjoint	.069	.000	.055	.000	.269	.551	.077	.031	.000	.000	.168	.136	.041	.000	.135
Choice	.000	.023	.024	.000	.291	.443	.011	.000	.086	.000	.285	.258	.000	.041	.161
Constr. Conjoint	.000	.000	.024	.000	.322	.658	.000	.000	.000	.000	.182	.182	.000	.000	.136
Constr. Choice	.000	.014	.024	.000	.283	.426	.000	.000	.085	.000	.284	.284	.000	.046	.180

Appendices

Respondent No. 3

Experimental Choice Design

Set	Laptop A					Laptop B					Laptop C				
1	NEC	8MB	510MB	Mono	$2459	IBM	16MB	250MB	DualScan	$3995	Toshiba	4MB	340MB	Active	$3149
2	NEC	8MB	340MB	Active	$3995	Toshiba	4MB	250MB	DualScan	$2459	IBM	16MB	510MB	Mono	$3149
3	NEC	4MB	340MB	DualScan	$2459	IBM	8MB	510MB	Mono	$3149	Toshiba	16MB	250MB	Active	$3995
4	IBM	4MB	510MB	DualScan	$3995	NEC	16MB	340MB	Mono	$2459	Toshiba	8MB	250MB	Active	$3149
5	Toshiba	8MB	340MB	Mono	$2459	NEC	4MB	510MB	Active	$3149	IBM	16MB	250MB	DualScan	$3995
6	IBM	8MB	510MB	Mono	$3149	NEC	4MB	340MB	DualScan	$2459	Toshiba	16MB	250MB	Active	$3995
7	Toshiba	4MB	250MB	DualScan	$2459	IBM	16MB	510MB	Mono	$3149	NEC	8MB	340MB	Active	$3995
8	NEC	16MB	340MB	Active	$3149	IBM	4MB	510MB	DualScan	$2459	Toshiba	8MB	250MB	Mono	$3995
9	NEC	16MB	250MB	DualScan	$3149	IBM	4MB	340MB	Active	$3995	Toshiba	8MB	510MB	Mono	$2459
10	NEC	16MB	250MB	DualScan	$3995	IBM	8MB	340MB	Mono	$2459	Toshiba	4MB	510MB	Active	$3149
11	NEC	8MB	510MB	DualScan	$3995	IBM	4MB	250MB	Active	$2459	Toshiba	16MB	340MB	Mono	$3149
12	Toshiba	4MB	510MB	DualScan	$3149	IBM	8MB	250MB	Active	$3995	NEC	16MB	340MB	Mono	$2459
13	IBM	4MB	340MB	Active	$3149	Toshiba	8MB	510MB	Mono	$2459	NEC	16MB	250MB	DualScan	$3995
14	NEC	8MB	250MB	Active	$3149	Toshiba	16MB	340MB	Mono	$2459	IBM	4MB	510MB	DualScan	$3995
15	IBM	4MB	340MB	Mono	$3149	Toshiba	4MB	510MB	DualScan	$3995	NEC	8MB	250MB	Active	$2459
16	IBM	8MB	340MB	Active	$2459	Toshiba	16MB	510MB	DualScan	$3995	NEC	8MB	250MB	Mono	$3149
17	IBM	4MB	510MB	Active	$3995	Toshiba	4MB	250MB	DualScan	$3149	NEC	16MB	340MB	Mono	$2459
18	Toshiba	16MB	510MB	Mono	$2459	IBM	8MB	250MB	DualScan	$3149	NEC	4MB	340MB	Active	$3995
19	NEC	16MB	510MB	Mono	$2459	IBM	4MB	340MB	Active	$3995	Toshiba	8MB	250MB	DualScan	$3149
20	IBM	16MB	250MB	DualScan	$2459	NEC	4MB	510MB	Mono	$3995	Toshiba	8MB	340MB	Active	$3149
21	Toshiba	8MB	250MB	Active	$3995	NEC	4MB	340MB	DualScan	$2459	IBM	16MB	510MB	Mono	$3149
22	NEC	8MB	510MB	DualScan	$3995	Toshiba	4MB	250MB	Mono	$2459	IBM	16MB	340MB	Active	$3149
23	Toshiba	16MB	510MB	Active	$3149	NEC	4MB	340MB	Mono	$3149	IBM	8MB	250MB	DualScan	$2459
24	IBM	4MB	250MB	Mono	$3149	NEC	8MB	340MB	Active	$2459	Toshiba	16MB	510MB	DualScan	$3995
25	NEC	4MB	250MB	DualScan	$2459	Toshiba	8MB	510MB	Active	$3995	IBM	16MB	340MB	Mono	$3149
26	Toshiba	16MB	250MB	Mono	$2459	NEC	8MB	340MB	DualScan	$3995	IBM	4MB	510MB	Active	$3149
27	Toshiba	8MB	510MB	Mono	$2459	NEC	16MB	340MB	DualScan	$3149	IBM	4MB	250MB	Active	$3995
28	IBM	8MB	340MB	DualScan	$3995	Toshiba	16MB	250MB	Mono	$2459	NEC	4MB	510MB	Active	$3149
29	Toshiba	8MB	340MB	DualScan	$3149	NEC	16MB	250MB	Active	$2459	IBM	4MB	510MB	Mono	$3995
30	IBM	16MB	340MB	Mono	$3149	NEC	8MB	510MB	DualScan	$3995	Toshiba	4MB	250MB	Active	$2459

Partworth Values

Model	Brand Name			Memory Size				Hard Drive			Screen Type			Price Level		
	NEC	IBM	Toshiba	4MB	8MB	16MB	250MB	340MB	510MB	Mono	DualScan	Active	$3995	$3149	$2459
Self-Explicated	.000	.094	.052	.000	.170	.219	.000	.122	.156	.000	.278	.312	.000	.097	.219
Conjoint	.107	.000	.030	.000	.161	.239	.000	.069	.025	.000	.229	.306	.000	.155	.278
Choice	.000	.024	.001	.000	.088	.132	.000	.096	.120	.000	.411	.407	.000	.157	.314
Constr. Conjoint	.000	.000	.000	.000	.196	.290	.000	.000	.000	.000	.278	.372	.000	.189	.338
Constr. Choice	.000	.026	.003	.000	.089	.133	.000	.096	.121	.000	.409	.409	.000	.153	.311

Respondent No. 4

Experimental Choice Design

Set	Laptop A					Laptop B					Laptop C				
1	Toshiba	8MB	510MB	Mono	$2459	IBM	16MB	250MB	DualScan	$3995	NEC	4MB	340MB	Active	$3149
2	Toshiba	8MB	510MB	DualScan	$3995	IBM	4MB	340MB	Active	$3149	NEC	16MB	250MB	Mono	$2459
3	NEC	4MB	340MB	DualScan	$2459	IBM	16MB	510MB	Mono	$3995	Toshiba	8MB	250MB	Active	$3149
4	NEC	4MB	510MB	Active	$2459	Toshiba	8MB	250MB	DualScan	$3995	IBM	16MB	340MB	DualScan	$3995
5	NEC	16MB	250MB	Mono	$3995	IBM	4MB	510MB	DualScan	$3149	Toshiba	8MB	340MB	Active	$3149
6	NEC	16MB	510MB	Mono	$3995	IBM	8MB	340MB	DualScan	$2459	Toshiba	8MB	250MB	Active	$3149
7	IBM	16MB	250MB	Active	$3149	NEC	8MB	510MB	Mono	$3149	Toshiba	4MB	340MB	DualScan	$2459
8	NEC	8MB	340MB	Active	$2459	Toshiba	4MB	510MB	DualScan	$2459	IBM	16MB	250MB	Mono	$3995
9	Toshiba	4MB	510MB	DualScan	$3149	NEC	8MB	340MB	Active	$3995	IBM	16MB	250MB	Mono	$2459
10	NEC	4MB	250MB	Active	$2459	IBM	8MB	340MB	DualScan	$3149	Toshiba	16MB	510MB	Mono	$3149
11	IBM	8MB	510MB	DualScan	$3995	Toshiba	16MB	250MB	DualScan	$3995	NEC	4MB	340MB	Mono	$2459
12	IBM	8MB	250MB	Active	$3149	Toshiba	4MB	340MB	DualScan	$2459	NEC	16MB	510MB	Mono	$3149
13	IBM	4MB	340MB	Active	$3995	Toshiba	8MB	510MB	Mono	$2459	NEC	16MB	250MB	DualScan	$3995
14	IBM	8MB	250MB	Active	$3149	Toshiba	16MB	340MB	Mono	$2459	NEC	4MB	510MB	DualScan	$3995
15	IBM	16MB	340MB	DualScan	$3995	Toshiba	8MB	510MB	Mono	$3149	NEC	4MB	250MB	Active	$2459
16	NEC	16MB	340MB	Active	$2459	Toshiba	4MB	510MB	DualScan	$3995	IBM	8MB	250MB	Mono	$3149
17	IBM	4MB	510MB	Active	$3995	Toshiba	16MB	250MB	DualScan	$3149	NEC	8MB	340MB	Mono	$2459
18	IBM	16MB	250MB	Mono	$2459	Toshiba	8MB	510MB	DualScan	$3995	NEC	4MB	340MB	Active	$3149
19	IBM	16MB	250MB	Mono	$2459	NEC	4MB	510MB	Active	$2459	Toshiba	8MB	340MB	DualScan	$3149
20	IBM	4MB	340MB	DualScan	$2459	Toshiba	8MB	510MB	Active	$3995	NEC	16MB	250MB	Mono	$3995
21	Toshiba	16MB	340MB	Active	$3995	NEC	4MB	250MB	Mono	$2459	IBM	8MB	510MB	DualScan	$3149
22	IBM	8MB	510MB	Mono	$3149	NEC	4MB	250MB	Active	$2459	Toshiba	16MB	340MB	DualScan	$3995
23	IBM	16MB	510MB	Active	$3995	NEC	4MB	250MB	Mono	$3149	Toshiba	8MB	340MB	DualScan	$2459
24	IBM	4MB	510MB	Mono	$2459	NEC	8MB	250MB	DualScan	$3995	Toshiba	16MB	340MB	Active	$3149
25	Toshiba	4MB	250MB	Active	$2459	NEC	8MB	510MB	DualScan	$3149	IBM	16MB	340MB	Mono	$3995
26	Toshiba	8MB	340MB	Mono	$2459	NEC	16MB	250MB	DualScan	$3995	IBM	4MB	510MB	Active	$3149
27	IBM	8MB	340MB	Mono	$2459	NEC	16MB	250MB	Active	$3995	Toshiba	4MB	510MB	DualScan	$3149
28	NEC	4MB	510MB	DualScan	$3149	IBM	8MB	340MB	Active	$2459	Toshiba	16MB	250MB	DualScan	$3995
29	IBM	8MB	340MB	Active	$2459	NEC	16MB	510MB	DualScan	$3149	Toshiba	4MB	250MB	Mono	$3995
30	Toshiba	4MB	340MB	Mono	$3995	IBM	8MB	510MB	Active	$3149	NEC	16MB	250MB	DualScan	$2459

Partworth Values

Model	Brand Name			Memory Size			Hard Drive			Screen Type			Price Level		
	NEC	IBM	Toshiba	4MB	8MB	16MB	250MB	340MB	510MB	Mono	DualScan	Active	$3995	$3149	$2459
Self-Explicated	.027	.061	.000	.000	.162	.242	.000	.081	.182	.000	.212	.273	.000	.108	.242
Conjoint	.098	.000	.011	.000	.223	.351	.000	.100	.072	.000	.134	.242	.000	.030	.209
Choice	.020	.000	.063	.000	.335	.350	.132	.180	.000	.000	.341	.349	.058	.000	.054
Constr. Conjoint	.000	.000	.000	.000	.251	.395	.000	.097	.097	.000	.151	.272	.000	.034	.236
Constr. Choice	.000	.000	.000	.000	.310	.365	.000	.047	.047	.000	.348	.394	.000	.046	.194

Respondent No. 5

Experimental Choice Design

Set	Laptop A					Laptop B					Laptop C				
1	NEC	8MB	510MB	Mono	$2459	IBM	16MB	250MB	DualScan	$3995	Toshiba	4MB	340MB	Active	$3149
2	Toshiba	4MB	510MB	DualScan	$3995	IBM	8MB	250MB	Active	$2459	NEC	16MB	340MB	Mono	$3149
3	NEC	8MB	340MB	DualScan	$2459	Toshiba	16MB	510MB	Mono	$3995	IBM	4MB	250MB	Active	$3149
4	NEC	8MB	510MB	Active	$2459	IBM	4MB	250MB	Mono	$3149	IBM	16MB	340MB	DualScan	$3995
5	Toshiba	16MB	340MB	Mono	$3149	IBM	4MB	510MB	DualScan	$3995	NEC	8MB	250MB	Active	$3149
6	NEC	16MB	340MB	Mono	$3149	Toshiba	4MB	510MB	DualScan	$2459	IBM	8MB	250MB	Active	$3995
7	NEC	16MB	250MB	Active	$3995	IBM	4MB	340MB	Mono	$3149	IBM	8MB	510MB	DualScan	$2459
8	NEC	4MB	250MB	Active	$3149	NEC	16MB	340MB	Mono	$2459	Toshiba	8MB	510MB	DualScan	$3995
9	Toshiba	16MB	250MB	DualScan	$2459	NEC	8MB	340MB	DualScan	$3995	IBM	8MB	510MB	Mono	$3149
10	IBM	4MB	250MB	Active	$2459	IBM	4MB	340MB	Active	$3149	Toshiba	16MB	510MB	Mono	$3995
11	IBM	8MB	510MB	DualScan	$3995	Toshiba	8MB	340MB	DualScan	$2459	NEC	16MB	250MB	Mono	$2459
12	IBM	16MB	250MB	DualScan	$3149	Toshiba	4MB	340MB	Active	$3995	NEC	4MB	510MB	Mono	$2459
13	IBM	4MB	340MB	DualScan	$3995	NEC	8MB	510MB	Mono	$3149	NEC	16MB	250MB	DualScan	$3149
14	IBM	8MB	250MB	Active	$3149	Toshiba	16MB	340MB	Mono	$2459	NEC	4MB	510MB	DualScan	$3995
15	IBM	4MB	340MB	DualScan	$3149	NEC	16MB	510MB	Mono	$3995	Toshiba	8MB	250MB	Active	$2459
16	Toshiba	4MB	340MB	DualScan	$2459	IBM	8MB	250MB	Active	$3149	NEC	16MB	510MB	Mono	$3995
17	Toshiba	16MB	510MB	Mono	$3995	IBM	8MB	250MB	Active	$3995	NEC	4MB	340MB	DualScan	$2459
18	Toshiba	8MB	250MB	Mono	$2459	IBM	16MB	340MB	DualScan	$3149	NEC	4MB	510MB	Active	$3149
19	IBM	8MB	510MB	Active	$3149	Toshiba	4MB	250MB	Mono	$3995	NEC	16MB	340MB	DualScan	$2459
20	IBM	16MB	250MB	DualScan	$2459	Toshiba	4MB	340MB	Active	$3995	NEC	8MB	510MB	Mono	$3149
21	Toshiba	16MB	250MB	Active	$3995	NEC	4MB	510MB	Mono	$3149	IBM	8MB	340MB	DualScan	$2459
22	IBM	16MB	340MB	Mono	$3149	NEC	8MB	250MB	Active	$2459	Toshiba	4MB	510MB	DualScan	$3995
23	Toshiba	16MB	250MB	Active	$3995	NEC	4MB	510MB	Mono	$2459	IBM	8MB	340MB	DualScan	$3149
24	Toshiba	8MB	510MB	Mono	$2459	NEC	16MB	250MB	DualScan	$3149	IBM	4MB	340MB	Active	$3995
25	NEC	4MB	510MB	DualScan	$2459	Toshiba	8MB	340MB	Active	$3995	IBM	16MB	250MB	Active	$3149
26	Toshiba	8MB	250MB	Mono	$2459	NEC	16MB	340MB	DualScan	$3149	IBM	4MB	510MB	Active	$3149
27	Toshiba	8MB	340MB	Mono	$3149	NEC	16MB	340MB	DualScan	$3995	IBM	4MB	510MB	Active	$2459
28	IBM	8MB	510MB	Mono	$2459	Toshiba	16MB	250MB	DualScan	$3149	NEC	4MB	340MB	Active	$3995
29	Toshiba	16MB	340MB	DualScan	$3149	NEC	8MB	510MB	Active	$2459	IBM	4MB	250MB	Mono	$3995
30	NEC	4MB	340MB	Mono	$2459	Toshiba	8MB	510MB	DualScan	$3149	IBM	16MB	250MB	Active	$3995

Partworth Values

Model	Brand Name			Memory Size			Hard Drive			Screen Type			Price Level		
	NEC	IBM	Toshiba	4MB	8MB	16MB	250MB	340MB	510MB	Mono	DualScan	Active	$3995	$3149	$2459
Self-Explicated	.019	.033	.000	.000	.059	.267	.000	.200	.300	.000	.222	.333	.000	.059	.067
Conjoint	.098	.000	.076	.000	.223	.322	.000	.004	.006	.000	.261	.408	.167	.000	.093
Choice	.031	.000	.028	.000	.106	.304	.000	.087	.193	.000	.327	.424	.000	.049	.004
Constr. Conjoint	.000	.000	.000	.000	.299	.432	.000	.006	.008	.000	.351	.547	.000	.000	.013
Constr. Choice	.000	.000	.000	.000	.123	.316	.000	.055	.188	.000	.424	.496	.000	.000	.000

Respondent No. 6

Experimental Choice Design

Set	Laptop A					Laptop B					Laptop C				
1	Toshiba	340MB	8MB	Mono	$2459	IBM	250MB	16MB	DualScan	$3995	NEC	510MB	4MB	Active	$3149
2	NEC	510MB	8MB	Mono	$3149	IBM	250MB	16MB	Active	$3995	Toshiba	340MB	4MB	DualScan	$2459
3	NEC	250MB	8MB	Active	$2459	IBM	340MB	16MB	Mono	$3995	Toshiba	510MB	4MB	DualScan	$3149
4	NEC	510MB	4MB	Active	$3149	IBM	250MB	16MB	Mono	$2459	Toshiba	340MB	8MB	DualScan	$3995
5	NEC	510MB	16MB	Mono	$3995	IBM	340MB	4MB	DualScan	$2459	Toshiba	250MB	8MB	Active	$3149
6	NEC	340MB	16MB	Mono	$3149	IBM	510MB	4MB	DualScan	$2459	Toshiba	250MB	8MB	Active	$3995
7	NEC	250MB	16MB	Active	$3995	IBM	340MB	8MB	Mono	$2459	Toshiba	510MB	4MB	DualScan	$3149
8	NEC	340MB	8MB	Active	$3149	IBM	510MB	4MB	Mono	$2459	Toshiba	250MB	16MB	DualScan	$3995
9	NEC	250MB	4MB	DualScan	$3149	IBM	340MB	16MB	Active	$3995	Toshiba	510MB	8MB	Mono	$2459
10	Toshiba	250MB	16MB	DualScan	$3149	NEC	340MB	4MB	Active	$2459	IBM	510MB	8MB	Mono	$3995
11	IBM	510MB	8MB	DualScan	$3995	Toshiba	250MB	16MB	Active	$3149	NEC	340MB	4MB	Mono	$2459
12	IBM	250MB	8MB	DualScan	$3149	Toshiba	340MB	4MB	Active	$2459	NEC	510MB	16MB	Mono	$3995
13	NEC	340MB	4MB	Active	$2459	Toshiba	510MB	8MB	Mono	$3149	IBM	250MB	16MB	DualScan	$3995
14	NEC	250MB	8MB	Active	$3149	Toshiba	340MB	4MB	Mono	$3995	IBM	510MB	16MB	DualScan	$2459
15	IBM	340MB	8MB	Active	$3995	NEC	250MB	16MB	DualScan	$3149	Toshiba	510MB	4MB	Mono	$2459
16	NEC	340MB	16MB	DualScan	$2459	Toshiba	510MB	8MB	Active	$3995	IBM	250MB	4MB	Mono	$3149
17	Toshiba	510MB	4MB	DualScan	$3995	NEC	250MB	8MB	DualScan	$2459	IBM	340MB	16MB	Mono	$3149
18	Toshiba	250MB	16MB	Mono	$2459	IBM	340MB	8MB	DualScan	$3995	NEC	510MB	4MB	Active	$3149
19	NEC	510MB	4MB	DualScan	$2459	Toshiba	340MB	16MB	Mono	$3995	IBM	250MB	8MB	Active	$3149
20	IBM	250MB	16MB	DualScan	$3995	Toshiba	340MB	4MB	Active	$2459	NEC	510MB	8MB	Mono	$3149
21	Toshiba	250MB	8MB	Active	$3995	NEC	510MB	16MB	Mono	$3149	IBM	340MB	4MB	DualScan	$2459
22	NEC	250MB	16MB	DualScan	$3149	Toshiba	340MB	4MB	Active	$2459	IBM	510MB	8MB	Mono	$3995
23	Toshiba	510MB	16MB	DualScan	$3995	NEC	250MB	4MB	Mono	$2459	IBM	340MB	8MB	Active	$3149
24	Toshiba	510MB	4MB	Active	$2459	NEC	250MB	8MB	DualScan	$2459	IBM	340MB	16MB	Mono	$3149
25	Toshiba	340MB	4MB	Active	$3995	NEC	510MB	8MB	DualScan	$3995	IBM	250MB	16MB	Mono	$3149
26	Toshiba	250MB	8MB	Mono	$2459	NEC	340MB	16MB	DualScan	$3995	IBM	510MB	4MB	Active	$3149
27	Toshiba	250MB	8MB	Mono	$2459	NEC	340MB	16MB	DualScan	$3995	IBM	510MB	4MB	Active	$3149
28	NEC	510MB	4MB	Active	$3149	IBM	250MB	16MB	Mono	$2459	Toshiba	340MB	8MB	DualScan	$3995
29	Toshiba	340MB	8MB	DualScan	$3149	NEC	510MB	4MB	Active	$2459	IBM	250MB	16MB	Mono	$3995
30	Toshiba	340MB	4MB	Mono	$3995	IBM	510MB	8MB	DualScan	$3149	NEC	250MB	16MB	Active	$2459

Partworth Values

Model	Brand Name			Memory Size			Hard Drive			Screen Type			Price Level		
	NEC	IBM	Toshiba	4MB	8MB	16MB	250MB	340MB	510MB	Mono	DualScan	Active	$3995	$3149	$2459
Self-Explicated	.000	.044	.067	.000	.222	.333	.000	.104	.233	.000	.133	.200	.000	.074	.167
Conjoint	.084	.000	.053	.000	.426	.752	.000	.012	.012	.000	.068	.114	.030	.000	.038
Choice	.000	.000	.000	.000	.000	.999	.000	.000	.000	.000	.000	.000	.000	.000	.000
Constr. Conjoint	.000	.012	.012	.000	.468	.825	.000	.013	.013	.000	.074	.125	.000	.000	.025
Constr. Choice	.000	.000	.000	.000	.000	1.000	.000	.000	.000	.000	.000	.000	.000	.000	.000

Appendices

Respondent No. 7

Experimental Choice Design

Set	Laptop A					Laptop B					Laptop C				
1	NEC	8MB	510MB	Mono	$3149	Toshiba	16MB	340MB	Active	$3995	IBM	4MB	250MB	DualScan	$2459
2	IBM	8MB	510MB	DualScan	$3995	Toshiba	16MB	340MB	Mono	$3149	NEC	4MB	250MB	Active	$2459
3	Toshiba	4MB	510MB	Mono	$2459	IBM	8MB	340MB	Active	$3995	NEC	16MB	250MB	DualScan	$3149
4	NEC	4MB	250MB	Active	$2459	IBM	8MB	510MB	DualScan	$3995	Toshiba	16MB	340MB	Mono	$3149
5	NEC	16MB	340MB	Active	$3995	IBM	4MB	510MB	DualScan	$2459	Toshiba	8MB	250MB	Mono	$2459
6	NEC	16MB	340MB	Mono	$3149	Toshiba	4MB	510MB	DualScan	$3149	IBM	8MB	250MB	Active	$3995
7	Toshiba	4MB	250MB	Active	$2459	NEC	16MB	340MB	Mono	$2459	IBM	8MB	510MB	DualScan	$3995
8	IBM	8MB	340MB	Active	$3995	IBM	4MB	510MB	Active	$3149	IBM	16MB	250MB	DualScan	$3149
9	NEC	4MB	510MB	Mono	$2459	IBM	8MB	340MB	DualScan	$3995	Toshiba	16MB	250MB	DualScan	$3149
10	NEC	8MB	250MB	Active	$3149	Toshiba	4MB	340MB	DualScan	$2459	IBM	16MB	510MB	Mono	$3995
11	Toshiba	8MB	510MB	DualScan	$3995	IBM	16MB	250MB	Mono	$3149	NEC	4MB	340MB	Active	$2459
12	IBM	8MB	250MB	Active	$3149	Toshiba	4MB	340MB	Mono	$2459	NEC	16MB	510MB	DualScan	$3995
13	Toshiba	4MB	510MB	DualScan	$3149	IBM	8MB	250MB	Mono	$2459	NEC	16MB	340MB	Active	$3995
14	IBM	8MB	250MB	Active	$3149	Toshiba	4MB	340MB	Mono	$2459	NEC	16MB	510MB	DualScan	$3995
15	IBM	16MB	340MB	Mono	$3149	Toshiba	8MB	510MB	DualScan	$3995	NEC	4MB	250MB	Active	$2459
16	IBM	16MB	340MB	DualScan	$3149	Toshiba	4MB	510MB	Active	$3149	NEC	8MB	250MB	Mono	$2459
17	NEC	4MB	510MB	Mono	$2459	IBM	8MB	250MB	Active	$3149	Toshiba	16MB	340MB	DualScan	$3995
18	IBM	16MB	250MB	Mono	$2459	NEC	4MB	510MB	DualScan	$3995	Toshiba	8MB	340MB	Active	$3149
19	IBM	16MB	510MB	Mono	$3995	Toshiba	4MB	250MB	Active	$2459	NEC	8MB	340MB	DualScan	$3149
20	IBM	4MB	340MB	DualScan	$2459	Toshiba	16MB	510MB	Active	$3149	IBM	4MB	340MB	Mono	$2459
21	NEC	16MB	250MB	Active	$3995	Toshiba	8MB	510MB	Mono	$2459	IBM	8MB	340MB	DualScan	$3149
22	IBM	16MB	510MB	Mono	$3995	NEC	4MB	250MB	Active	$2459	Toshiba	8MB	340MB	DualScan	$3149
23	Toshiba	16MB	510MB	Active	$3149	NEC	8MB	250MB	Mono	$2459	IBM	16MB	340MB	DualScan	$3995
24	IBM	4MB	510MB	Active	$3149	NEC	8MB	250MB	DualScan	$2459	Toshiba	16MB	250MB	Mono	$3149
25	IBM	4MB	340MB	Mono	$2459	NEC	8MB	510MB	Active	$3995	Toshiba	16MB	510MB	DualScan	$3149
26	Toshiba	8MB	250MB	Mono	$2459	NEC	16MB	340MB	DualScan	$3995	IBM	4MB	510MB	Active	$3149
27	Toshiba	8MB	250MB	Mono	$2459	NEC	16MB	340MB	DualScan	$3995	IBM	4MB	510MB	Active	$3149
28	Toshiba	8MB	510MB	Active	$3995	NEC	16MB	250MB	DualScan	$3149	IBM	4MB	340MB	Mono	$2459
29	NEC	8MB	340MB	Active	$2459	Toshiba	16MB	510MB	DualScan	$3149	IBM	4MB	250MB	Mono	$3995
30	IBM	4MB	340MB	DualScan	$2459	NEC	8MB	510MB	Mono	$3149	Toshiba	16MB	250MB	Active	$3995

Partworth Values

Model	Brand Name			Memory Size			Hard Drive			Screen Type			Price Level		
	NEC	IBM	Toshiba	4MB	8MB	16MB	250MB	340MB	510MB	Mono	DualScan	Active	$3995	$3149	$2459
Self-Explicated	.000	.032	.022	.000	.194	.290	.000	.086	.194	.000	.072	.161	.000	.143	.323
Conjoint	.015	.000	.004	.000	.109	.308	.000	.221	.134	.000	.120	.147	.013	.000	.309
Choice	.014	.000	.001	.000	.358	.500	.000	.116	.179	.000	.124	.081	.000	.128	.183
Constr. Conjoint	.000	.000	.000	.000	.116	.329	.000	.190	.190	.000	.128	.157	.000	.000	.324
Constr. Choice	.000	.000	.000	.000	.548	.681	.000	.154	.166	.000	.000	.000	.000	.143	.153

Respondent No. 8

Experimental Choice Design

Set	Laptop A					Laptop B					Laptop C				
1	NEC	8MB	340MB	Mono	$2459	IBM	16MB	250MB	Active	$3995	Toshiba	4MB	510MB	DualScan	$3149
2	NEC	8MB	510MB	DualScan	$3995	IBM	16MB	250MB	Active	$3149	Toshiba	4MB	340MB	Mono	$2459
3	Toshiba	8MB	340MB	Active	$3995	NEC	16MB	250MB	Mono	$2459	IBM	4MB	510MB	DualScan	$3149
4	IBM	4MB	510MB	Active	$2459	NEC	8MB	250MB	DualScan	$3995	Toshiba	16MB	340MB	DualScan	$3149
5	NEC	16MB	340MB	Mono	$3995	IBM	4MB	510MB	DualScan	$3149	Toshiba	8MB	250MB	Active	$2459
6	NEC	16MB	340MB	Mono	$3995	Toshiba	4MB	510MB	DualScan	$3149	IBM	8MB	250MB	Active	$3149
7	NEC	16MB	250MB	DualScan	$3995	IBM	8MB	340MB	Mono	$2459	Toshiba	4MB	510MB	DualScan	$3995
8	NEC	16MB	250MB	Mono	$2459	Toshiba	4MB	510MB	Active	$3149	IBM	8MB	340MB	DualScan	$3149
9	NEC	4MB	510MB	DualScan	$3995	Toshiba	8MB	340MB	Active	$3149	IBM	16MB	250MB	Mono	$2459
10	IBM	4MB	340MB	DualScan	$2459	NEC	8MB	250MB	Active	$3149	IBM	16MB	510MB	Mono	$3995
11	IBM	8MB	340MB	DualScan	$3995	Toshiba	16MB	250MB	Active	$3149	NEC	4MB	510MB	Mono	$2459
12	IBM	4MB	510MB	DualScan	$3995	Toshiba	8MB	340MB	Mono	$2459	NEC	16MB	250MB	Mono	$3149
13	IBM	4MB	340MB	Active	$3149	Toshiba	8MB	510MB	Mono	$2459	NEC	16MB	250MB	DualScan	$3995
14	IBM	8MB	250MB	Active	$3995	Toshiba	16MB	340MB	Mono	$2459	NEC	4MB	510MB	DualScan	$3995
15	IBM	16MB	340MB	Mono	$3995	IBM	4MB	510MB	DualScan	$2459	NEC	8MB	250MB	Active	$3149
16	Toshiba	16MB	250MB	DualScan	$2459	IBM	4MB	510MB	Mono	$3995	NEC	8MB	340MB	Active	$3149
17	IBM	8MB	510MB	Mono	$3149	Toshiba	16MB	250MB	Active	$3149	NEC	4MB	340MB	DualScan	$2459
18	IBM	16MB	250MB	Mono	$2459	NEC	4MB	340MB	DualScan	$3149	Toshiba	8MB	510MB	Active	$3995
19	Toshiba	8MB	510MB	Active	$3149	NEC	4MB	340MB	DualScan	$3995	IBM	16MB	340MB	DualScan	$3995
20	Toshiba	16MB	250MB	DualScan	$2459	NEC	4MB	340MB	Active	$3149	IBM	8MB	510MB	Mono	$3149
21	IBM	16MB	250MB	DualScan	$2459	NEC	4MB	340MB	Active	$3149	Toshiba	8MB	510MB	Mono	$2459
22	Toshiba	16MB	510MB	Mono	$3995	IBM	8MB	250MB	DualScan	$2459	NEC	4MB	340MB	Active	$3995
23	Toshiba	16MB	510MB	Active	$3995	NEC	4MB	340MB	Mono	$3149	IBM	8MB	340MB	DualScan	$2459
24	Toshiba	4MB	510MB	DualScan	$2459	NEC	8MB	250MB	Active	$3149	IBM	16MB	340MB	Mono	$3995
25	Toshiba	8MB	510MB	Mono	$2459	NEC	4MB	340MB	Active	$3995	IBM	16MB	250MB	DualScan	$3149
26	NEC	16MB	250MB	Mono	$2459	IBM	8MB	340MB	Active	$3995	Toshiba	4MB	510MB	DualScan	$3149
27	NEC	4MB	250MB	Active	$2459	Toshiba	16MB	340MB	DualScan	$3995	IBM	8MB	510MB	Mono	$3149
28	Toshiba	8MB	340MB	DualScan	$3149	IBM	8MB	250MB	Mono	$2459	NEC	4MB	510MB	Active	$3995
29	Toshiba	16MB	340MB	DualScan	$3149	NEC	8MB	510MB	Active	$3995	IBM	4MB	250MB	Mono	$2459
30	Toshiba	4MB	340MB	Mono	$3995	NEC	8MB	510MB	DualScan	$3149	IBM	16MB	250MB	Active	$2459

Partworth Values

Model	Brand Name			Memory Size			Hard Drive			Screen Type			Price Level		
	NEC	IBM	Toshiba	4MB	8MB	16MB	250MB	340MB	510MB	Mono	DualScan	Active	$3995	$3149	$2459
Self-Explicated	.139	.108	.000	.000	.123	.278	.000	.167	.250	.000	.151	.194	.000	.077	.139
Conjoint	.000	.027	.078	.000	.148	.371	.000	.124	.305	.000	.101	.136	.109	.000	.004
Choice	.000	.092	.130	.000	.367	.373	.000	.277	.348	.081	.004	.000	.000	.068	.043
Constr. Conjoint	.000	.000	.000	.000	.182	.456	.000	.152	.376	.000	.124	.168	.000	.000	.000
Constr. Choice	.000	.000	.000	.000	.339	.435	.000	.332	.431	.000	.013	.025	.000	.108	.108

Respondent No. 9

Experimental Choice Design

Set	Laptop A					Laptop B					Laptop C				
1	NEC	8MB	510MB	Mono	$2459	IBM	16MB	250MB	DualScan	$3995	Toshiba	4MB	340MB	Active	$3149
2	Toshiba	8MB	340MB	DualScan	$3995	NEC	16MB	250MB	Active	$3149	IBM	4MB	510MB	Mono	$2459
3	NEC	8MB	250MB	Active	$2459	IBM	16MB	510MB	Mono	$3995	Toshiba	4MB	340MB	DualScan	$3149
4	NEC	4MB	510MB	Active	$2459	Toshiba	16MB	250MB	Mono	$3149	IBM	8MB	340MB	DualScan	$3995
5	NEC	16MB	340MB	Mono	$2459	IBM	4MB	510MB	DualScan	$3149	Toshiba	8MB	250MB	Active	$3995
6	NEC	8MB	510MB	Mono	$3995	IBM	4MB	340MB	DualScan	$3149	Toshiba	16MB	250MB	Active	$2459
7	Toshiba	16MB	250MB	DualScan	$3149	IBM	8MB	340MB	Mono	$3149	NEC	4MB	510MB	Active	$2459
8	NEC	16MB	250MB	Active	$3149	IBM	4MB	510MB	Mono	$2459	Toshiba	8MB	340MB	DualScan	$3995
9	NEC	4MB	250MB	DualScan	$3995	IBM	8MB	340MB	Active	$3149	Toshiba	16MB	510MB	Mono	$2459
10	NEC	8MB	510MB	DualScan	$3149	IBM	4MB	340MB	Mono	$2459	Toshiba	16MB	250MB	Active	$3995
11	IBM	8MB	510MB	DualScan	$3995	16MB	340MB	Active	$3149	NEC	4MB	250MB	Mono	$2459
12	IBM	16MB	250MB	DualScan	$3149	Toshiba	8MB	340MB	Mono	$2459	NEC	4MB	510MB	Active	$3995
13	IBM	4MB	340MB	Active	$3149	Toshiba	8MB	250MB	Mono	$3995	NEC	16MB	510MB	DualScan	$2459
14	IBM	8MB	250MB	DualScan	$3149	NEC	16MB	340MB	Mono	$2459	Toshiba	4MB	510MB	Active	$3995
15	IBM	8MB	340MB	Mono	$3149	Toshiba	4MB	510MB	Active	$3995	NEC	16MB	250MB	DualScan	$2459
16	IBM	8MB	340MB	DualScan	$3995	Toshiba	4MB	510MB	Active	$3149	NEC	16MB	250MB	Mono	$2459
17	IBM	4MB	510MB	Mono	$2459	Toshiba	8MB	250MB	Active	$3995	NEC	16MB	340MB	DualScan	$3149
18	IBM	16MB	250MB	Mono	$2459	Toshiba	4MB	510MB	DualScan	$3995	NEC	8MB	340MB	Active	$3149
19	IBM	4MB	250MB	Active	$2459	Toshiba	16MB	510MB	Mono	$3995	NEC	8MB	340MB	DualScan	$3149
20	NEC	16MB	250MB	DualScan	$2459	Toshiba	4MB	510MB	Active	$3995	IBM	8MB	340MB	Mono	$3149
21	IBM	16MB	250MB	Active	$3995	NEC	8MB	340MB	DualScan	$3149	Toshiba	4MB	510MB	Mono	$2459
22	Toshiba	4MB	340MB	DualScan	$3149	NEC	8MB	250MB	Active	$2459	IBM	16MB	510MB	Mono	$3995
23	Toshiba	16MB	340MB	Active	$3995	NEC	4MB	510MB	Mono	$3149	IBM	8MB	250MB	DualScan	$2459
24	NEC	4MB	510MB	Mono	$3149	Toshiba	8MB	250MB	DualScan	$2459	IBM	16MB	340MB	Active	$3995
25	Toshiba	4MB	340MB	DualScan	$2459	NEC	8MB	510MB	Active	$3995	IBM	16MB	250MB	Mono	$3149
26	Toshiba	16MB	250MB	Mono	$3995	NEC	8MB	510MB	Active	$3149	IBM	4MB	340MB	DualScan	$2459
27	Toshiba	8MB	250MB	Mono	$2459	NEC	16MB	340MB	DualScan	$3995	IBM	8MB	510MB	Active	$3149
28	Toshiba	4MB	510MB	DualScan	$3149	NEC	16MB	340MB	Mono	$2459	IBM	8MB	250MB	Active	$3995
29	Toshiba	8MB	340MB	DualScan	$3149	NEC	16MB	510MB	Active	$3149	IBM	4MB	250MB	Mono	$3995
30	Toshiba	4MB	340MB	Mono	$3995	NEC	16MB	510MB	DualScan	$3149	IBM	8MB	250MB	Active	$2459

Partworth Values

	Brand Name			Memory Size			Hard Drive			Screen Type			Price Level		
Model	NEC	IBM	Toshiba	4MB	8MB	16MB	250MB	340MB	510MB	Mono	DualScan	Active	$3995	$3149	$2459
Self-Explicated	.000	.160	.179	.000	.199	.256	.000	.120	.179	.000	.140	.179	.000	.137	.205
Conjoint	.000	.084	.012	.000	.174	.320	.000	.044	.173	.000	.064	.072	.000	.139	.351
Choice	.000	.129	.141	.000	.204	.138	.188	.004	.000	.000	.232	.230	.224	.236	.000
Constr. Conjoint	.000	.000	.000	.000	.190	.349	.000	.048	.189	.000	.070	.079	.000	.152	.383
Constr. Choice	.000	.274	.274	.000	.345	.363	.000	.000	.000	.000	.342	.363	.000	.000	.000

Respondent No. 10

Experimental Choice Design

Set	Laptop A					Laptop B					Laptop C				
1	Toshiba	8MB	510MB	Mono	$3995	IBM	16MB	250MB	DualScan	$3149	NEC	4MB	340MB	Active	$2459
2	NEC	8MB	510MB	DualScan	$3995	IBM	16MB	250MB	Mono	$2459	Toshiba	4MB	340MB	Active	$3149
3	NEC	8MB	340MB	Active	$3995	IBM	16MB	250MB	Mono	$3149	Toshiba	4MB	510MB	DualScan	$2459
4	Toshiba	4MB	510MB	Mono	$2459	IBM	8MB	250MB	Active	$3149	NEC	16MB	340MB	DualScan	$3995
5	Toshiba	16MB	340MB	Mono	$3149	IBM	4MB	510MB	Active	$3995	NEC	8MB	250MB	DualScan	$2459
6	IBM	8MB	340MB	Mono	$3995	NEC	4MB	510MB	DualScan	$2459	Toshiba	16MB	340MB	Active	$3995
7	Toshiba	16MB	250MB	Active	$3995	IBM	8MB	340MB	Mono	$3149	NEC	4MB	510MB	DualScan	$2459
8	NEC	16MB	250MB	Active	$3149	IBM	4MB	510MB	Mono	$2459	Toshiba	8MB	340MB	DualScan	$3995
9	Toshiba	4MB	250MB	DualScan	$3995	IBM	8MB	340MB	Active	$3149	NEC	16MB	510MB	Mono	$2459
10	Toshiba	8MB	250MB	DualScan	$2459	IBM	4MB	340MB	Active	$3149	NEC	16MB	510MB	Mono	$3995
11	IBM	16MB	340MB	DualScan	$3995	NEC	8MB	250MB	Active	$2459	Toshiba	4MB	510MB	Mono	$3149
12	Toshiba	8MB	340MB	DualScan	$3995	IBM	4MB	250MB	Active	$2459	NEC	16MB	510MB	Mono	$3149
13	IBM	4MB	340MB	Active	$3149	Toshiba	8MB	510MB	Mono	$3995	NEC	16MB	250MB	DualScan	$3995
14	Toshiba	8MB	250MB	Active	$3149	NEC	16MB	340MB	Mono	$2459	IBM	4MB	510MB	DualScan	$3995
15	Toshiba	8MB	510MB	Mono	$3995	IBM	4MB	250MB	DualScan	$3149	NEC	4MB	340MB	Active	$2459
16	IBM	16MB	340MB	Mono	$3995	Toshiba	4MB	510MB	DualScan	$3149	NEC	8MB	250MB	Active	$2459
17	IBM	4MB	510MB	DualScan	$3995	Toshiba	8MB	250MB	Active	$3149	NEC	16MB	340MB	Mono	$3149
18	Toshiba	16MB	250MB	Mono	$2459	IBM	8MB	340MB	DualScan	$3995	NEC	4MB	510MB	Active	$3149
19	IBM	4MB	510MB	Mono	$2459	Toshiba	16MB	250MB	Active	$3995	NEC	8MB	340MB	DualScan	$3149
20	IBM	16MB	250MB	DualScan	$3995	Toshiba	4MB	340MB	Active	$2459	NEC	8MB	510MB	Mono	$3149
21	IBM	16MB	250MB	Active	$3995	NEC	8MB	510MB	Mono	$3149	Toshiba	4MB	340MB	DualScan	$2459
22	Toshiba	16MB	250MB	DualScan	$3995	NEC	4MB	340MB	Active	$2459	IBM	8MB	510MB	Mono	$3995
23	NEC	16MB	510MB	Active	$3995	Toshiba	4MB	250MB	Mono	$3149	IBM	8MB	340MB	DualScan	$2459
24	Toshiba	4MB	510MB	DualScan	$3149	IBM	8MB	250MB	Mono	$2459	NEC	16MB	340MB	Active	$3995
25	NEC	8MB	250MB	DualScan	$2459	Toshiba	4MB	510MB	Active	$3995	IBM	4MB	340MB	Mono	$3149
26	IBM	8MB	250MB	Mono	$2459	NEC	16MB	340MB	DualScan	$3995	Toshiba	4MB	510MB	Active	$3149
27	Toshiba	16MB	250MB	Mono	$2459	NEC	8MB	340MB	Active	$3995	IBM	4MB	510MB	DualScan	$3149
28	IBM	8MB	510MB	Mono	$3995	NEC	16MB	250MB	DualScan	$2459	Toshiba	4MB	340MB	Active	$3149
29	Toshiba	8MB	340MB	DualScan	$3995	IBM	4MB	510MB	Active	$3149	NEC	16MB	250MB	Mono	$2459
30	IBM	4MB	340MB	Mono	$3995	NEC	16MB	510MB	DualScan	$3149	Toshiba	8MB	250MB	Active	$2459

Partworth Values

Model	Brand Name			Memory Size			Hard Drive			Screen Type			Price Level		
	NEC	IBM	Toshiba	4MB	8MB	16MB	250MB	340MB	510MB	Mono	DualScan	Active	$3995	$3149	$2459
Self-Explicated	.000	.108	.084	.000	.210	.270	.000	.135	.243	.000	.105	.189	.000	.084	.189
Conjoint	.060	.057	.000	.000	.464	.445	.000	.136	.084	.000	.224	.276	.000	.002	.064
Choice	.013	.000	.010	.000	.484	.530	.000	.074	.143	.000	.141	.156	.000	.158	.100
Constr. Conjoint	.000	.029	.000	.000	.488	.488	.000	.119	.119	.000	.241	.296	.000	.002	.002
Constr. Choice	.000	.000	.000	.000	.760	.779	.000	.038	.088	.000	.125	.132	.000	.000	.000

Respondent No. 11

Experimental Choice Design

Set		Laptop A					Laptop B					Laptop C			
1	NEC	16MB	510MB	Mono	$2459	IBM	8MB	250MB	Active	$3149	Toshiba	4MB	340MB	DualScan	$3995
2	NEC	8MB	510MB	DualScan	$3995	IBM	16MB	250MB	Active	$3149	Toshiba	4MB	340MB	Mono	$2459
3	NEC	8MB	510MB	Active	$3995	IBM	16MB	340MB	Mono	$3149	Toshiba	4MB	250MB	DualScan	$2459
4	NEC	16MB	510MB	Mono	$2459	IBM	4MB	340MB	Active	$3149	Toshiba	8MB	250MB	DualScan	$3149
5	NEC	8MB	510MB	Active	$3995	IBM	4MB	340MB	DualScan	$3149	Toshiba	16MB	250MB	Mono	$2459
6	Toshiba	8MB	340MB	Mono	$2459	NEC	8MB	510MB	DualScan	$3149	IBM	16MB	250MB	Active	$3995
7	IBM	4MB	250MB	Active	$2459	NEC	16MB	340MB	DualScan	$3149	Toshiba	16MB	510MB	Mono	$3995
8	NEC	4MB	340MB	Active	$2459	IBM	16MB	510MB	Mono	$3149	Toshiba	16MB	250MB	DualScan	$3995
9	NEC	4MB	510MB	DualScan	$3149	IBM	16MB	250MB	Active	$3995	Toshiba	8MB	340MB	Mono	$2459
10	NEC	4MB	250MB	Mono	$2459	IBM	8MB	340MB	Active	$3149	Toshiba	8MB	510MB	DualScan	$3995
11	NEC	8MB	340MB	DualScan	$3995	Toshiba	4MB	250MB	Active	$3149	IBM	16MB	510MB	Mono	$2459
12	Toshiba	4MB	250MB	Active	$3149	IBM	8MB	510MB	Mono	$2459	NEC	16MB	340MB	DualScan	$3995
13	IBM	4MB	510MB	DualScan	$3995	Toshiba	8MB	340MB	Mono	$3149	NEC	16MB	250MB	Active	$2459
14	IBM	8MB	250MB	Active	$3149	Toshiba	4MB	340MB	Mono	$2459	NEC	16MB	510MB	DualScan	$3995
15	Toshiba	8MB	250MB	Active	$3995	Toshiba	4MB	510MB	Mono	$3149	NEC	16MB	340MB	DualScan	$2459
16	NEC	8MB	340MB	Active	$3149	IBM	16MB	510MB	DualScan	$3995	NEC	16MB	250MB	Mono	$2459
17	Toshiba	4MB	510MB	Mono	$2459	IBM	4MB	510MB	DualScan	$3149	NEC	4MB	340MB	Active	$3995
18	Toshiba	8MB	510MB	Mono	$3149	IBM	16MB	250MB	DualScan	$3995	NEC	8MB	340MB	Active	$2459
19	IBM	16MB	340MB	Mono	$2459	IBM	4MB	340MB	Active	$3995	NEC	4MB	510MB	DualScan	$3149
20	NEC	16MB	250MB	DualScan	$2459	IBM	4MB	250MB	Active	$3149	Toshiba	8MB	510MB	Mono	$2459
21	Toshiba	16MB	250MB	DualScan	$3995	NEC	4MB	340MB	Active	$3149	IBM	8MB	510MB	Mono	$2459
22	Toshiba	16MB	340MB	Mono	$2459	NEC	8MB	250MB	Active	$2459	IBM	4MB	510MB	DualScan	$3995
23	Toshiba	16MB	510MB	Active	$3995	NEC	4MB	250MB	Mono	$3149	IBM	8MB	340MB	DualScan	$3995
24	Toshiba	4MB	510MB	Mono	$3149	IBM	8MB	250MB	DualScan	$2459	NEC	16MB	340MB	Active	$3995
25	Toshiba	4MB	250MB	DualScan	$2459	NEC	8MB	340MB	Active	$3995	IBM	16MB	510MB	Mono	$3149
26	Toshiba	16MB	250MB	Mono	$2459	IBM	8MB	340MB	DualScan	$3995	NEC	4MB	510MB	Active	$3149
27	Toshiba	16MB	250MB	Mono	$2459	NEC	8MB	340MB	DualScan	$3149	IBM	4MB	510MB	Active	$3995
28	Toshiba	8MB	250MB	Mono	$3149	NEC	16MB	250MB	DualScan	$2459	IBM	4MB	340MB	Active	$3995
29	IBM	16MB	340MB	DualScan	$3149	NEC	8MB	510MB	Active	$2459	Toshiba	4MB	250MB	Mono	$3995
30	Toshiba	16MB	340MB	Mono	$3149	NEC	8MB	510MB	DualScan	$3995	IBM	4MB	250MB	Active	$2459

Partworth Values

Model	Brand Name			Memory Size			Hard Drive			Screen Type			Price Level		
	NEC	IBM	Toshiba	4MB	8MB	16MB	250MB	340MB	510MB	Mono	DualScan	Active	$3995	$3149	$2459
Self-Explicated	.000	.108	.194	.000	.086	.129	.000	.176	.226	.000	.258	.290	.000	.090	.161
Conjoint	.133	.000	.196	.000	.059	.138	.000	.039	.048	.000	.351	.337	.000	.267	.168
Choice	.000	.105	.080	.000	.079	.149	.000	.066	.156	.000	.398	.408	.000	.118	.182
Constr. Conjoint	.000	.000	.148	.000	.067	.157	.000	.044	.055	.000	.392	.392	.000	.248	.248
Constr. Choice	.000	.108	.108	.000	.079	.143	.000	.097	.167	.000	.380	.397	.000	.110	.186

Appendices   123

Respondent No. 12

Experimental Choice Design

Set	Laptop A					Laptop B					Laptop C				
1	IBM	8MB	510MB	Mono	$3149	NEC	16MB	250MB	DualScan	$3995	Toshiba	4MB	340MB	Active	$2459
2	IBM	8MB	510MB	DualScan	$3995	Toshiba	16MB	250MB	Active	$3149	NEC	4MB	340MB	Mono	$2459
3	NEC	8MB	250MB	Mono	$2459	Toshiba	16MB	510MB	DualScan	$3995	IBM	4MB	340MB	Active	$3149
4	NEC	4MB	510MB	Mono	$3995	IBM	8MB	340MB	DualScan	$3995	Toshiba	16MB	250MB	Active	$3149
5	NEC	16MB	340MB	Mono	$2459	IBM	4MB	510MB	Active	$3149	Toshiba	8MB	250MB	Active	$2459
6	NEC	8MB	340MB	Mono	$3149	IBM	4MB	250MB	Active	$2459	Toshiba	16MB	510MB	DualScan	$3995
7	NEC	8MB	250MB	Active	$3995	IBM	16MB	340MB	Mono	$2459	Toshiba	4MB	510MB	DualScan	$3149
8	IBM	16MB	340MB	Mono	$3149	NEC	4MB	510MB	Active	$3995	Toshiba	8MB	250MB	DualScan	$2459
9	NEC	4MB	250MB	DualScan	$2459	IBM	8MB	340MB	Active	$3995	Toshiba	16MB	510MB	Mono	$3149
10	NEC	4MB	340MB	DualScan	$3149	IBM	16MB	250MB	Mono	$2459	Toshiba	8MB	510MB	Active	$3995
11	IBM	8MB	510MB	DualScan	$3995	NEC	16MB	250MB	Active	$3149	Toshiba	4MB	340MB	Mono	$2459
12	IBM	8MB	250MB	Active	$3149	Toshiba	4MB	340MB	DualScan	$2459	NEC	16MB	510MB	Mono	$3995
13	IBM	4MB	340MB	Active	$3149	Toshiba	8MB	510MB	Mono	$2459	NEC	16MB	250MB	DualScan	$3995
14	IBM	8MB	250MB	DualScan	$3149	Toshiba	16MB	340MB	Mono	$2459	NEC	4MB	510MB	Active	$3995
15	NEC	16MB	340MB	Mono	$3995	Toshiba	8MB	510MB	DualScan	$3149	IBM	4MB	250MB	Active	$2459
16	NEC	16MB	250MB	Active	$3995	Toshiba	4MB	340MB	DualScan	$2459	IBM	8MB	510MB	Mono	$3149
17	IBM	4MB	510MB	Mono	$2459	NEC	8MB	250MB	Active	$3149	Toshiba	16MB	340MB	DualScan	$3995
18	Toshiba	16MB	250MB	Mono	$2459	IBM	8MB	340MB	Active	$3995	NEC	4MB	510MB	DualScan	$3149
19	IBM	16MB	510MB	Active	$3995	Toshiba	4MB	250MB	Mono	$2459	NEC	8MB	340MB	DualScan	$3149
20	IBM	4MB	250MB	Active	$2459	Toshiba	16MB	340MB	DualScan	$3995	NEC	8MB	510MB	Mono	$3149
21	Toshiba	16MB	340MB	Active	$3995	NEC	4MB	510MB	DualScan	$3149	IBM	8MB	250MB	Mono	$2459
22	Toshiba	16MB	510MB	Mono	$3149	NEC	4MB	250MB	Active	$2459	IBM	8MB	340MB	DualScan	$3995
23	NEC	4MB	510MB	Active	$3995	IBM	16MB	250MB	DualScan	$3149	Toshiba	8MB	340MB	Mono	$2459
24	NEC	4MB	510MB	Active	$3995	Toshiba	8MB	250MB	DualScan	$2459	IBM	16MB	340MB	Mono	$3149
25	Toshiba	4MB	340MB	DualScan	$2459	IBM	8MB	510MB	Active	$3995	NEC	16MB	250MB	Mono	$3149
26	Toshiba	16MB	250MB	Mono	$2459	NEC	8MB	340MB	DualScan	$3995	IBM	4MB	510MB	Active	$3149
27	Toshiba	16MB	250MB	Mono	$2459	NEC	8MB	340MB	DualScan	$3995	IBM	4MB	510MB	Active	$3149
28	Toshiba	8MB	510MB	Active	$3995	NEC	16MB	250MB	Mono	$2459	IBM	4MB	340MB	DualScan	$3149
29	IBM	8MB	340MB	DualScan	$2459	NEC	16MB	510MB	Active	$3149	Toshiba	4MB	250MB	Mono	$3995
30	Toshiba	4MB	510MB	Mono	$3995	NEC	8MB	340MB	Active	$3149	IBM	16MB	250MB	DualScan	$2459

Partworth Values

Model	Brand Name			Memory Size			Hard Drive			Screen Type			Price Level		
	NEC	IBM	Toshiba	4MB	8MB	16MB	250MB	340MB	510MB	Mono	DualScan	Active	$3995	$3149	$2459
Self-Explicated	.143	.095	.000	.000	.152	.229	.000	.133	.171	.000	.156	.200	.000	.114	.257
Conjoint	.180	.000	.147	.000	.128	.202	.000	.000	.011	.000	.244	.244	.000	.223	.363
Choice	.073	.065	.000	.000	.282	.351	.000	.057	.078	.000	.132	.094	.000	.226	.366
Constr. Conjoint	.114	.000	.000	.000	.138	.218	.000	.000	.012	.000	.264	.264	.000	.241	.392
Constr. Choice	.000	.000	.000	.000	.422	.502	.000	.000	.000	.000	.000	.000	.000	.369	.498

Appendices 125

Respondent No. 13

Experimental Choice Design

Set	Laptop A					Laptop B					Laptop C				
1	NEC	8MB	510MB	Mono	$2459	Toshiba	16MB	250MB	DualScan	$3995	IBM	4MB	340MB	Active	$3149
2	NEC	8MB	340MB	Active	$3995	IBM	16MB	250MB	Mono	$3149	Toshiba	4MB	510MB	DualScan	$2459
3	Toshiba	4MB	340MB	Active	$2459	IBM	16MB	510MB	Mono	$3995	NEC	8MB	250MB	DualScan	$3149
4	IBM	4MB	250MB	Active	$2459	NEC	16MB	510MB	Mono	$3149	Toshiba	8MB	340MB	Mono	$3149
5	Toshiba	16MB	250MB	Active	$3995	IBM	4MB	510MB	DualScan	$3149	IBM	8MB	340MB	Mono	$2459
6	NEC	16MB	340MB	Mono	$3149	IBM	4MB	510MB	DualScan	$2459	Toshiba	8MB	250MB	Active	$3995
7	Toshiba	16MB	250MB	DualScan	$3995	IBM	8MB	510MB	Mono	$3149	NEC	4MB	340MB	Active	$2459
8	NEC	16MB	250MB	Mono	$3149	IBM	4MB	340MB	Active	$2459	IBM	8MB	510MB	DualScan	$3995
9	Toshiba	4MB	250MB	DualScan	$3149	IBM	8MB	340MB	Active	$3149	NEC	16MB	510MB	Mono	$2459
10	Toshiba	8MB	510MB	Mono	$3149	NEC	4MB	340MB	DualScan	$2459	IBM	16MB	250MB	Active	$3995
11	IBM	16MB	510MB	DualScan	$3995	Toshiba	8MB	250MB	Active	$3149	NEC	4MB	340MB	Mono	$2459
12	IBM	16MB	340MB	DualScan	$3149	NEC	8MB	510MB	Active	$2459	Toshiba	4MB	510MB	Mono	$3995
13	IBM	4MB	340MB	Active	$3149	Toshiba	8MB	510MB	Mono	$2459	NEC	16MB	250MB	DualScan	$3995
14	IBM	8MB	250MB	DualScan	$3149	Toshiba	16MB	340MB	Mono	$3995	NEC	4MB	510MB	Active	$2459
15	IBM	8MB	510MB	DualScan	$3995	Toshiba	16MB	340MB	Mono	$3149	NEC	4MB	250MB	Active	$2459
16	IBM	16MB	510MB	Mono	$3995	NEC	4MB	340MB	Active	$2459	Toshiba	8MB	250MB	DualScan	$3149
17	IBM	16MB	510MB	Mono	$3995	Toshiba	8MB	250MB	DualScan	$3149	NEC	4MB	340MB	Active	$2459
18	Toshiba	16MB	250MB	Mono	$2459	IBM	8MB	340MB	DualScan	$3995	NEC	4MB	510MB	Active	$3149
19	Toshiba	16MB	250MB	Active	$3995	NEC	4MB	510MB	DualScan	$3149	IBM	8MB	340MB	Mono	$2459
20	Toshiba	16MB	340MB	DualScan	$3995	IBM	4MB	250MB	Active	$2459	NEC	8MB	510MB	Mono	$3149
21	NEC	16MB	250MB	DualScan	$3995	IBM	8MB	340MB	Mono	$2459	Toshiba	4MB	510MB	Active	$3149
22	Toshiba	16MB	250MB	Mono	$3149	NEC	4MB	510MB	DualScan	$2459	IBM	8MB	340MB	Active	$3995
23	Toshiba	16MB	340MB	Active	$3995	NEC	4MB	250MB	DualScan	$3149	IBM	8MB	510MB	Mono	$2459
24	IBM	4MB	510MB	Active	$3149	NEC	8MB	250MB	Mono	$2459	Toshiba	16MB	340MB	DualScan	$3995
25	Toshiba	4MB	340MB	DualScan	$2459	NEC	8MB	510MB	Active	$3995	IBM	16MB	250MB	Mono	$3149
26	Toshiba	8MB	250MB	Mono	$2459	NEC	16MB	340MB	DualScan	$3995	IBM	4MB	510MB	Active	$3149
27	Toshiba	8MB	250MB	Mono	$2459	NEC	16MB	340MB	DualScan	$3995	IBM	4MB	510MB	Active	$3149
28	Toshiba	8MB	510MB	Active	$3995	NEC	16MB	340MB	Mono	$3149	IBM	4MB	250MB	DualScan	$2459
29	NEC	16MB	250MB	Mono	$3149	Toshiba	4MB	510MB	DualScan	$2459	IBM	8MB	340MB	Active	$3995
30	Toshiba	4MB	340MB	Mono	$3995	NEC	8MB	510MB	Active	$3149	IBM	16MB	250MB	DualScan	$2459

Partworth Values

Model	Brand Name			Memory Size				Hard Drive			Screen Type			Price Level		
	NEC	IBM	Toshiba	4MB	8MB	16MB	250MB	340MB	510MB	Mono	DualScan	Active	$3995	$3149	$2459
Self-Explicated	.023	.034	.000	.000	.230	.345	.000	.034	.103	.000	.188	.241	.000	.184	.276
Conjoint	.092	.013	.000	.000	.220	.412	.000	.008	.066	.000	.157	.096	.000	.204	.272
Choice	.033	.038	.000	.000	.356	.466	.014	.000	.029	.000	.102	.190	.000	.067	.276
Constr. Conjoint	.000	.000	.000	.000	.251	.470	.000	.009	.076	.000	.145	.145	.000	.233	.310
Constr. Choice	.021	.024	.000	.000	.343	.459	.000	.000	.043	.000	.108	.192	.000	.077	.283

Respondent No. 14

Experimental Choice Design

Set			Laptop A					Laptop B					Laptop C		
1	NEC	8MB	340MB	DualScan	$2459	IBM	16MB	250MB	Mono	$3995	Toshiba	4MB	510MB	Active	$3149
2	IBM	8MB	510MB	Mono	$3995	NEC	16MB	250MB	DualScan	$3149	Toshiba	4MB	340MB	Active	$2459
3	NEC	8MB	250MB	Active	$2459	IBM	16MB	340MB	DualScan	$3995	Toshiba	4MB	510MB	Mono	$3149
4	NEC	4MB	510MB	DualScan	$2459	IBM	16MB	250MB	Active	$3995	Toshiba	8MB	340MB	Mono	$3149
5	NEC	16MB	340MB	Active	$3995	Toshiba	4MB	510MB	DualScan	$2459	IBM	8MB	250MB	Mono	$3149
6	NEC	16MB	340MB	Mono	$3995	Toshiba	8MB	510MB	DualScan	$2459	IBM	8MB	250MB	Active	$3995
7	Toshiba	16MB	250MB	Active	$3149	IBM	8MB	340MB	Mono	$3149	NEC	4MB	510MB	DualScan	$2459
8	NEC	16MB	340MB	Active	$3995	IBM	4MB	510MB	Mono	$2459	Toshiba	8MB	250MB	DualScan	$3149
9	Toshiba	4MB	250MB	DualScan	$3995	IBM	8MB	340MB	Active	$3149	NEC	16MB	510MB	Mono	$2459
10	NEC	4MB	250MB	DualScan	$3995	Toshiba	8MB	340MB	Mono	$2459	IBM	16MB	510MB	Active	$3149
11	IBM	8MB	510MB	DualScan	$3995	NEC	16MB	250MB	Mono	$3149	Toshiba	4MB	340MB	Active	$2459
12	IBM	8MB	250MB	Mono	$2459	Toshiba	4MB	340MB	Active	$3149	NEC	16MB	510MB	DualScan	$3995
13	Toshiba	4MB	340MB	Active	$3149	IBM	8MB	510MB	DualScan	$3995	NEC	16MB	250MB	Mono	$2459
14	Toshiba	8MB	340MB	Active	$3995	NEC	16MB	250MB	Mono	$2459	IBM	4MB	510MB	DualScan	$3149
15	Toshiba	8MB	340MB	Mono	$3149	IBM	16MB	250MB	Active	$3995	NEC	4MB	510MB	DualScan	$2459
16	Toshiba	16MB	340MB	DualScan	$3995	IBM	8MB	250MB	Active	$2459	NEC	4MB	510MB	Mono	$3149
17	Toshiba	4MB	510MB	Mono	$2459	IBM	8MB	250MB	DualScan	$3149	NEC	16MB	340MB	Active	$3995
18	Toshiba	16MB	340MB	Mono	$2459	IBM	4MB	250MB	DualScan	$3995	NEC	8MB	510MB	Active	$3149
19	IBM	4MB	340MB	Active	$2459	Toshiba	16MB	250MB	DualScan	$3995	NEC	8MB	510MB	Mono	$3149
20	Toshiba	16MB	340MB	DualScan	$3995	IBM	4MB	250MB	Active	$3149	NEC	8MB	510MB	Mono	$3149
21	Toshiba	16MB	250MB	Active	$3995	NEC	8MB	340MB	Mono	$2459	IBM	4MB	510MB	DualScan	$3149
22	Toshiba	8MB	250MB	DualScan	$3149	NEC	4MB	510MB	Mono	$2459	IBM	16MB	340MB	Mono	$3995
23	Toshiba	16MB	510MB	Active	$3995	NEC	4MB	250MB	Mono	$3149	IBM	8MB	340MB	DualScan	$2459
24	Toshiba	4MB	510MB	Mono	$2459	NEC	16MB	250MB	DualScan	$3149	IBM	8MB	340MB	Active	$3995
25	Toshiba	4MB	340MB	DualScan	$2459	NEC	8MB	510MB	Active	$3995	IBM	16MB	250MB	Mono	$3149
26	NEC	8MB	250MB	DualScan	$2459	Toshiba	16MB	510MB	Active	$3995	IBM	4MB	340MB	Mono	$3149
27	Toshiba	8MB	250MB	Mono	$2459	NEC	16MB	340MB	DualScan	$3149	IBM	4MB	510MB	Active	$3995
28	IBM	4MB	340MB	Active	$3149	NEC	16MB	250MB	Mono	$2459	Toshiba	8MB	510MB	DualScan	$3995
29	Toshiba	8MB	250MB	DualScan	$3149	IBM	4MB	510MB	Active	$2459	NEC	16MB	340MB	Mono	$3995
30	IBM	4MB	340MB	DualScan	$2459	NEC	16MB	510MB	Mono	$3995	Toshiba	8MB	250MB	Active	$3149

Partworth Values

Model	Brand Name			Memory Size			Hard Drive			Screen Type			Price Level		
	NEC	IBM	Toshiba	4MB	8MB	16MB	250MB	340MB	510MB	Mono	DualScan	Active	$3995	$3149	$2459
Self-Explicated	.000	.121	.094	.000	.202	.303	.000	.081	.182	.000	.067	.152	.000	.162	.242
Conjoint	.089	.024	.000	.000	.336	.403	.000	.050	.142	.000	.130	.066	.000	.078	.237
Choice	.000	.001	.000	.000	.285	.480	.000	.007	.010	.022	.030	.000	.000	.478	.477
Constr. Conjoint	.000	.000	.000	.000	.382	.459	.000	.057	.161	.000	.111	.111	.000	.089	.269
Constr. Choice	.000	.011	.007	.000	.283	.486	.000	.012	.022	.000	.000	.000	.000	.478	.481

Respondent No. 15

Experimental Choice Design

Set	Laptop A				Laptop B				Laptop C			
1	NEC	8MB	510MB	Mono	$2459	IBM	16MB	250MB	DualScan	$3995	Toshiba	4MB	340MB	Active	$3149
2	NEC	8MB	510MB	DualScan	$3995	IBM	16MB	250MB	Mono	$2459	Toshiba	4MB	340MB	Active	$3149
3	NEC	8MB	340MB	DualScan	$3149	Toshiba	16MB	250MB	Mono	$2459	IBM	4MB	510MB	Active	$3995
4	Toshiba	4MB	510MB	DualScan	$2459	IBM	16MB	250MB	Active	$3149	NEC	8MB	340MB	DualScan	$3995
5	NEC	16MB	340MB	Mono	$3995	IBM	4MB	510MB	Active	$3149	Toshiba	8MB	250MB	DualScan	$2459
6	NEC	16MB	510MB	Mono	$3995	IBM	4MB	340MB	DualScan	$2459	Toshiba	8MB	250MB	Active	$3149
7	NEC	16MB	250MB	Active	$2459	IBM	8MB	340MB	Mono	$3149	Toshiba	4MB	510MB	DualScan	$3995
8	NEC	4MB	340MB	Active	$2459	IBM	8MB	510MB	Mono	$3995	Toshiba	16MB	250MB	DualScan	$3149
9	Toshiba	8MB	250MB	DualScan	$2459	IBM	4MB	510MB	Active	$3149	NEC	16MB	340MB	Mono	$3995
10	IBM	4MB	340MB	DualScan	$3149	NEC	8MB	250MB	Active	$2459	Toshiba	16MB	510MB	Mono	$3995
11	IBM	8MB	510MB	DualScan	$3995	NEC	16MB	250MB	Mono	$2459	Toshiba	4MB	340MB	Active	$3149
12	IBM	4MB	340MB	DualScan	$2459	Toshiba	8MB	250MB	Active	$3149	NEC	16MB	510MB	Mono	$3995
13	IBM	4MB	340MB	Active	$3149	Toshiba	8MB	510MB	Mono	$3995	NEC	16MB	250MB	DualScan	$2459
14	IBM	8MB	250MB	Active	$3149	Toshiba	16MB	340MB	Mono	$2459	NEC	4MB	510MB	DualScan	$3995
15	Toshiba	8MB	510MB	DualScan	$3995	IBM	16MB	250MB	Mono	$2459	NEC	4MB	340MB	Active	$3149
16	Toshiba	16MB	250MB	DualScan	$3995	NEC	4MB	510MB	Active	$2459	IBM	8MB	340MB	Mono	$3149
17	IBM	16MB	340MB	Mono	$2459	NEC	8MB	250MB	Active	$3149	Toshiba	4MB	510MB	DualScan	$3995
18	Toshiba	16MB	250MB	Mono	$2459	IBM	4MB	510MB	Active	$3995	NEC	8MB	340MB	DualScan	$3149
19	IBM	8MB	340MB	Active	$2459	NEC	4MB	250MB	Mono	$3995	Toshiba	16MB	510MB	DualScan	$3149
20	IBM	8MB	250MB	DualScan	$3995	NEC	4MB	510MB	Active	$3149	Toshiba	16MB	340MB	Mono	$2459
21	NEC	16MB	250MB	Active	$2459	Toshiba	4MB	510MB	DualScan	$3149	IBM	8MB	340MB	Mono	$3995
22	NEC	16MB	250MB	DualScan	$3149	Toshiba	8MB	340MB	Mono	$2459	IBM	4MB	510MB	Active	$3995
23	Toshiba	16MB	340MB	Active	$3995	NEC	4MB	250MB	Mono	$3149	IBM	8MB	510MB	DualScan	$2459
24	Toshiba	4MB	510MB	DualScan	$3149	NEC	8MB	250MB	Active	$2459	IBM	16MB	340MB	Mono	$3995
25	Toshiba	4MB	340MB	DualScan	$2459	NEC	8MB	510MB	Active	$3995	IBM	16MB	250MB	Mono	$3149
26	IBM	8MB	340MB	Mono	$2459	NEC	16MB	250MB	DualScan	$3995	Toshiba	4MB	510MB	Active	$3149
27	Toshiba	8MB	510MB	Mono	$2459	NEC	16MB	250MB	DualScan	$3149	IBM	4MB	340MB	Active	$3995
28	NEC	4MB	510MB	Active	$3149	Toshiba	16MB	250MB	Mono	$2459	IBM	8MB	340MB	DualScan	$3995
29	Toshiba	8MB	340MB	Active	$3995	NEC	4MB	510MB	DualScan	$2459	IBM	16MB	250MB	Mono	$3149
30	Toshiba	16MB	340MB	Mono	$3995	NEC	8MB	510MB	DualScan	$3149	IBM	4MB	250MB	Active	$2459

Partworth Values

Model	Brand Name			Memory Size			Hard Drive			Screen Type			Price Level		
	NEC	IBM	Toshiba	4MB	8MB	16MB	250MB	340MB	510MB	Mono	DualScan	Active	$3995	$3149	$2459
Self-Explicated	.000	.097	.065	.000	.143	.323	.000	.151	.194	.000	.151	.226	.000	.090	.161
Conjoint	.105	.000	.013	.000	.252	.410	.000	.094	.035	.000	.204	.285	.000	.016	.107
Choice	.022	.000	.008	.000	.414	.367	.099	.000	.140	.000	.381	.317	.043	.043	.000
Constr. Conjoint	.000	.000	.000	.000	.314	.511	.000	.000	.000	.000	.255	.355	.000	.021	.133
Constr. Choice	.000	.028	.004	.000	.375	.431	.000	.000	.127	.000	.357	.357	.000	.056	.057

Respondent No. 16

Experimental Choice Design

Set	Laptop A				Laptop B					Laptop C				
1	NEC	8MB	510MB	Mono	$2459	IBM	16MB	250MB	DualScan	$3995	Toshiba	4MB	340MB	Active	$3149
2	NEC	8MB	510MB	DualScan	$3995	IBM	16MB	340MB	Mono	$3149	Toshiba	4MB	250MB	Active	$2459
3	Toshiba	8MB	340MB	Active	$3995	IBM	16MB	250MB	Mono	$2459	NEC	4MB	510MB	DualScan	$3149
4	IBM	4MB	340MB	Active	$2459	NEC	8MB	510MB	Mono	$3149	Toshiba	16MB	250MB	DualScan	$2459
5	NEC	16MB	340MB	Mono	$3149	IBM	4MB	510MB	DualScan	$3995	Toshiba	8MB	250MB	Active	$3995
6	Toshiba	16MB	250MB	Mono	$2459	NEC	8MB	510MB	DualScan	$3149	IBM	8MB	340MB	Active	$3995
7	NEC	16MB	250MB	Active	$3995	IBM	8MB	510MB	Mono	$2459	Toshiba	4MB	250MB	DualScan	$2459
8	NEC	8MB	340MB	DualScan	$3149	IBM	4MB	510MB	Mono	$2459	Toshiba	16MB	250MB	Active	$3995
9	IBM	4MB	250MB	Active	$3149	NEC	8MB	340MB	DualScan	$2459	Toshiba	16MB	510MB	Mono	$3995
10	NEC	8MB	250MB	Active	$3149	Toshiba	4MB	340MB	DualScan	$2459	IBM	16MB	510MB	Mono	$3995
11	IBM	4MB	510MB	Active	$3995	Toshiba	8MB	250MB	DualScan	$2459	NEC	16MB	340MB	Mono	$3149
12	IBM	8MB	340MB	DualScan	$2459	Toshiba	4MB	340MB	Active	$3149	NEC	16MB	510MB	Mono	$3995
13	IBM	4MB	340MB	Active	$3149	Toshiba	8MB	510MB	Mono	$2459	NEC	16MB	250MB	DualScan	$3995
14	NEC	8MB	250MB	Active	$3149	Toshiba	4MB	340MB	Mono	$2459	IBM	4MB	510MB	DualScan	$3995
15	Toshiba	8MB	340MB	Active	$3995	NEC	16MB	250MB	DualScan	$3149	IBM	4MB	510MB	Mono	$2459
16	IBM	16MB	340MB	Mono	$3149	Toshiba	4MB	510MB	DualScan	$3995	NEC	8MB	250MB	Active	$2459
17	NEC	16MB	510MB	Mono	$3995	IBM	8MB	250MB	DualScan	$2459	Toshiba	4MB	340MB	Active	$3149
18	Toshiba	16MB	340MB	Mono	$2459	IBM	8MB	250MB	Active	$3995	NEC	4MB	510MB	DualScan	$3149
19	Toshiba	8MB	340MB	Active	$3995	IBM	4MB	510MB	Mono	$2459	NEC	16MB	250MB	DualScan	$3149
20	IBM	16MB	250MB	DualScan	$3995	NEC	4MB	510MB	Active	$2459	Toshiba	8MB	510MB	Mono	$3149
21	NEC	16MB	250MB	Active	$3995	IBM	4MB	340MB	DualScan	$2459	Toshiba	8MB	510MB	Mono	$3149
22	Toshiba	16MB	250MB	Mono	$3149	NEC	4MB	510MB	DualScan	$2459	IBM	8MB	340MB	Active	$3995
23	Toshiba	4MB	510MB	Active	$3995	NEC	16MB	340MB	Mono	$3149	IBM	8MB	250MB	DualScan	$2459
24	IBM	8MB	510MB	Mono	$3149	Toshiba	4MB	340MB	DualScan	$2459	NEC	16MB	250MB	Active	$3995
25	Toshiba	4MB	340MB	Active	$2459	NEC	8MB	510MB	DualScan	$3995	IBM	16MB	250MB	Mono	$3149
26	IBM	8MB	250MB	Active	$3149	NEC	16MB	340MB	DualScan	$3995	Toshiba	4MB	510MB	Mono	$2459
27	IBM	8MB	250MB	Mono	$3149	Toshiba	16MB	340MB	DualScan	$3995	NEC	4MB	510MB	Active	$2459
28	Toshiba	8MB	250MB	Active	$2459	NEC	16MB	340MB	DualScan	$2459	IBM	4MB	510MB	DualScan	$3995
29	Toshiba	8MB	510MB	DualScan	$2459	IBM	16MB	340MB	Active	$3149	NEC	4MB	250MB	Mono	$3995
30	NEC	4MB	340MB	Mono	$3995	Toshiba	8MB	510MB	DualScan	$3149	IBM	16MB	250MB	Active	$2459

Partworth Values

Model	Brand Name			Memory Size			Hard Drive			Screen Type			Price Level		
	NEC	IBM	Toshiba	4MB	8MB	16MB	250MB	340MB	510MB	Mono	DualScan	Active	$3995	$3149	$2459
Self-Explicated	.000	.063	.049	.000	.125	.281	.000	.111	.250	.000	.194	.250	.000	.122	.156
Conjoint	.048	.000	.037	.000	.295	.376	.000	.096	.186	.000	.280	.379	.000	.011	.007
Choice	.000	.007	.016	.000	.115	.184	.000	.074	.105	.000	.515	.523	.000	.093	.171
Constr. Conjoint	.000	.000	.000	.000	.310	.396	.000	.101	.196	.000	.295	.399	.000	.009	.009
Constr. Choice	.000	.000	.000	.000	.113	.172	.000	.074	.088	.000	.562	.563	.000	.091	.176

Respondent No. 17

Experimental Choice Design

Set	Laptop A					Laptop B					Laptop C				
1	NEC	8MB	510MB	Mono	$3995	IBM	16MB	250MB	DualScan	$3149	Toshiba	4MB	340MB	Active	$2459
2	NEC	8MB	510MB	Mono	$3995	Toshiba	16MB	250MB	Active	$3149	IBM	4MB	340MB	DualScan	$2459
3	NEC	4MB	340MB	Active	$2459	Toshiba	8MB	510MB	Mono	$3995	IBM	16MB	250MB	DualScan	$3149
4	NEC	4MB	250MB	Active	$2459	IBM	8MB	510MB	DualScan	$3995	Toshiba	16MB	340MB	Mono	$3149
5	NEC	16MB	340MB	Mono	$3995	IBM	4MB	510MB	DualScan	$3149	Toshiba	8MB	250MB	Active	$2459
6	Toshiba	8MB	340MB	Mono	$3995	NEC	8MB	340MB	Active	$2459	NEC	16MB	250MB	Active	$3149
7	IBM	4MB	250MB	DualScan	$3995	NEC	8MB	340MB	Active	$3149	Toshiba	16MB	510MB	Mono	$2459
8	NEC	16MB	250MB	Active	$3149	Toshiba	4MB	510MB	DualScan	$2459	IBM	8MB	340MB	Mono	$3995
9	NEC	4MB	250MB	DualScan	$3995	IBM	8MB	340MB	Mono	$3149	Toshiba	16MB	510MB	Active	$2459
10	NEC	4MB	250MB	DualScan	$3149	IBM	8MB	340MB	Active	$2459	Toshiba	16MB	510MB	Mono	$3995
11	IBM	8MB	340MB	DualScan	$3995	Toshiba	16MB	250MB	Mono	$3149	NEC	4MB	510MB	Active	$2459
12	NEC	4MB	510MB	DualScan	$3149	IBM	8MB	250MB	Active	$2459	IBM	16MB	340MB	Mono	$3995
13	IBM	4MB	340MB	DualScan	$3149	Toshiba	8MB	510MB	Mono	$3995	NEC	16MB	250MB	DualScan	$2459
14	IBM	8MB	250MB	Active	$2459	Toshiba	16MB	340MB	DualScan	$3995	NEC	4MB	510MB	Mono	$3149
15	IBM	4MB	510MB	DualScan	$3149	Toshiba	16MB	340MB	Mono	$3995	NEC	8MB	250MB	Active	$2459
16	NEC	16MB	250MB	DualScan	$2459	IBM	4MB	510MB	Active	$3995	Toshiba	8MB	340MB	Mono	$3149
17	IBM	8MB	510MB	Mono	$3995	NEC	16MB	250MB	DualScan	$3149	Toshiba	4MB	340MB	Active	$2459
18	IBM	16MB	510MB	Mono	$2459	Toshiba	8MB	510MB	DualScan	$3995	NEC	4MB	340MB	Active	$3149
19	NEC	4MB	510MB	Mono	$2459	IBM	16MB	250MB	Active	$3995	Toshiba	8MB	340MB	DualScan	$3149
20	IBM	4MB	250MB	DualScan	$2459	Toshiba	16MB	340MB	Active	$3995	NEC	8MB	510MB	Mono	$3149
21	Toshiba	8MB	250MB	Active	$2459	IBM	16MB	340MB	Mono	$3995	NEC	4MB	510MB	DualScan	$3149
22	Toshiba	16MB	250MB	DualScan	$3995	IBM	4MB	250MB	Active	$2459	NEC	8MB	340MB	Mono	$3149
23	NEC	16MB	510MB	Active	$3995	IBM	4MB	250MB	Mono	$3149	Toshiba	8MB	340MB	DualScan	$2459
24	Toshiba	4MB	510MB	Active	$3149	NEC	8MB	250MB	DualScan	$2459	IBM	16MB	340MB	Mono	$3995
25	NEC	4MB	510MB	Active	$3149	Toshiba	8MB	340MB	DualScan	$3995	IBM	16MB	250MB	Mono	$2459
26	Toshiba	8MB	250MB	Mono	$2459	NEC	16MB	340MB	DualScan	$3995	IBM	4MB	510MB	Active	$3149
27	Toshiba	8MB	250MB	Mono	$2459	NEC	16MB	340MB	DualScan	$3995	IBM	4MB	510MB	Active	$3149
28	NEC	4MB	340MB	Active	$3995	IBM	16MB	250MB	DualScan	$2459	Toshiba	8MB	510MB	Active	$3149
29	Toshiba	8MB	340MB	Active	$3995	NEC	16MB	250MB	DualScan	$3149	IBM	4MB	510MB	Mono	$2459
30	NEC	4MB	510MB	DualScan	$2459	Toshiba	8MB	340MB	Mono	$3149	IBM	16MB	250MB	Active	$3995

Partworth Values

Model	Brand Name			Memory Size				Hard Drive			Screen Type			Price Level		
	NEC	IBM	Toshiba	4MB	8MB	16MB	250MB	340MB	510MB	Mono	DualScan	Active	$3995	$3149	$2459
Self-Explicated	.030	.067	.000	.000	.233	.300	.000	.233	.300	.000	.059	.133	.000	.133	.200
Conjoint	.123	.081	.000	.000	.264	.418	.000	.261	.340	.016	.000	.010	.037	.000	.103
Choice	.027	.000	.038	.000	.297	.267	.117	.000	.405	.016	.012	.000	.083	.000	.244
Constr. Conjoint	.107	.107	.000	.000	.279	.441	.000	.276	.359	.000	.000	.002	.000	.000	.089
Constr. Choice	.000	.000	.000	.000	.371	.371	.000	.000	.384	.000	.003	.020	.000	.000	.224

Respondent No. 18

Experimental Choice Design

Set	Laptop A					Laptop B					Laptop C			
1	NEC	8MB	510MB	Mono	$3995	IBM	16MB	250MB	DualScan	$3149	Toshiba	4MB	340MB	Active	$2459
2	NEC	8MB	340MB	DualScan	$3995	IBM	16MB	250MB	Active	$3149	Toshiba	4MB	510MB	Mono	$2459
3	NEC	8MB	340MB	Active	$3149	IBM	16MB	510MB	Mono	$3995	Toshiba	4MB	250MB	DualScan	$2459
4	NEC	4MB	510MB	Active	$2459	IBM	8MB	340MB	Mono	$3995	Toshiba	16MB	250MB	DualScan	$3149
5	NEC	16MB	340MB	Mono	$3995	IBM	4MB	510MB	DualScan	$3149	Toshiba	8MB	250MB	Active	$2459
6	NEC	16MB	340MB	Mono	$3149	IBM	4MB	510MB	DualScan	$2459	Toshiba	8MB	250MB	Active	$3995
7	IBM	16MB	250MB	Active	$3995	NEC	8MB	340MB	Mono	$2459	Toshiba	4MB	510MB	DualScan	$3149
8	IBM	16MB	250MB	Active	$3149	Toshiba	4MB	510MB	Mono	$2459	NEC	8MB	340MB	DualScan	$3995
9	IBM	4MB	250MB	DualScan	$3995	Toshiba	8MB	340MB	Active	$3149	NEC	16MB	510MB	Mono	$2459
10	NEC	4MB	340MB	DualScan	$3995	IBM	8MB	340MB	Active	$2459	Toshiba	16MB	510MB	Mono	$3149
11	NEC	16MB	250MB	DualScan	$3995	Toshiba	8MB	250MB	Active	$3149	IBM	4MB	510MB	Mono	$2459
12	IBM	4MB	250MB	Active	$3149	Toshiba	8MB	340MB	DualScan	$2459	NEC	16MB	510MB	Mono	$3995
13	NEC	4MB	510MB	Active	$3149	Toshiba	4MB	340MB	Mono	$3995	IBM	16MB	250MB	DualScan	$2459
14	NEC	8MB	250MB	Active	$2459	IBM	16MB	340MB	Mono	$3995	Toshiba	4MB	510MB	DualScan	$3149
15	NEC	8MB	510MB	Mono	$3995	Toshiba	16MB	340MB	DualScan	$3149	IBM	4MB	250MB	Active	$2459
16	IBM	16MB	250MB	DualScan	$2459	Toshiba	4MB	510MB	Active	$3995	NEC	8MB	340MB	Mono	$3149
17	IBM	4MB	510MB	Active	$3995	Toshiba	16MB	250MB	DualScan	$2459	NEC	8MB	340MB	Mono	$3149
18	NEC	16MB	250MB	DualScan	$2459	IBM	8MB	340MB	Mono	$3149	Toshiba	4MB	510MB	Active	$3995
19	NEC	16MB	340MB	Active	$3995	IBM	4MB	250MB	Mono	$2459	NEC	8MB	510MB	DualScan	$3149
20	IBM	16MB	250MB	DualScan	$3149	Toshiba	4MB	340MB	Active	$2459	NEC	8MB	510MB	Mono	$3995
21	Toshiba	8MB	250MB	Active	$3995	NEC	16MB	510MB	Mono	$3149	IBM	4MB	340MB	DualScan	$2459
22	Toshiba	8MB	250MB	Active	$3149	NEC	4MB	510MB	DualScan	$2459	IBM	16MB	340MB	Mono	$3995
23	Toshiba	8MB	510MB	DualScan	$3995	IBM	4MB	340MB	Mono	$3149	NEC	16MB	340MB	Active	$2459
24	Toshiba	4MB	510MB	Active	$3995	NEC	16MB	250MB	DualScan	$2459	IBM	8MB	340MB	Mono	$3149
25	Toshiba	4MB	510MB	Mono	$2459	NEC	8MB	340MB	DualScan	$3995	IBM	16MB	250MB	Active	$3149
26	Toshiba	8MB	250MB	Mono	$2459	NEC	16MB	340MB	DualScan	$3149	IBM	4MB	510MB	Active	$3995
27	Toshiba	8MB	250MB	Mono	$2459	NEC	16MB	340MB	DualScan	$3149	IBM	4MB	510MB	Active	$3995
28	Toshiba	4MB	510MB	DualScan	$3149	NEC	16MB	250MB	Active	$2459	IBM	8MB	340MB	Active	$3995
29	IBM	8MB	340MB	DualScan	$3995	NEC	4MB	510MB	Active	$3149	Toshiba	16MB	250MB	Mono	$2459
30	Toshiba	16MB	340MB	Mono	$3149	NEC	4MB	510MB	Active	$3995	IBM	8MB	250MB	DualScan	$2459

Partworth Values

Model	Brand Name			Memory Size			Hard Drive			Screen Type			Price Level		
	NEC	IBM	Toshiba	4MB	8MB	16MB	250MB	340MB	510MB	Mono	DualScan	Active	$3995	$3149	$2459
Self-Explicated	.000	.048	.071	.000	.286	.321	.000	.198	.357	.000	.063	.143	.000	.048	.107
Conjoint	.044	.083	.000	.000	.429	.465	.000	.180	.308	.054	.000	.062	.061	.000	.083
Choice	.100	.060	.000	.000	.258	.245	.000	.166	.227	.259	.175	.000	.156	.107	.000
Constr. Conjoint	.000	.000	.000	.000	.499	.541	.000	.210	.358	.000	.000	.041	.000	.000	.000
Constr. Choice	.000	.000	.000	.000	.498	.500	.000	.268	.500	.000	.000	.000	.000	.000	.061

Appendices

Respondent No. 19

Experimental Choice Design

Set		Laptop A					Laptop B					Laptop C			
1	NEC	8MB	510MB	Mono	$2459	IBM	16MB	250MB	DualScan	$3995	Toshiba	4MB	340MB	Active	$3149
2	IBM	8MB	510MB	DualScan	$3995	Toshiba	16MB	250MB	Mono	$2459	NEC	4MB	340MB	Active	$3149
3	NEC	8MB	340MB	Active	$2459	IBM	16MB	510MB	DualScan	$3995	Toshiba	4MB	250MB	Mono	$3149
4	NEC	4MB	510MB	Active	$2459	IBM	8MB	250MB	DualScan	$3995	Toshiba	16MB	340MB	Mono	$3149
5	NEC	16MB	340MB	Mono	$3995	IBM	4MB	510MB	DualScan	$3149	Toshiba	8MB	250MB	Active	$2459
6	NEC	16MB	340MB	Mono	$3995	IBM	4MB	510MB	DualScan	$3149	Toshiba	8MB	250MB	Active	$2459
7	NEC	4MB	340MB	Active	$2459	IBM	8MB	510MB	Mono	$3149	Toshiba	16MB	250MB	DualScan	$2459
8	IBM	16MB	250MB	Mono	$2459	Toshiba	4MB	340MB	Active	$3995	NEC	8MB	510MB	DualScan	$3149
9	NEC	4MB	250MB	DualScan	$3995	IBM	8MB	340MB	Active	$3149	Toshiba	16MB	510MB	Mono	$2459
10	NEC	4MB	250MB	DualScan	$3995	IBM	8MB	340MB	Active	$3149	Toshiba	16MB	510MB	Mono	$3149
11	IBM	8MB	510MB	Mono	$2459	NEC	16MB	250MB	DualScan	$2459	Toshiba	4MB	340MB	Active	$3995
12	NEC	4MB	250MB	DualScan	$3149	Toshiba	8MB	340MB	Active	$3149	IBM	16MB	510MB	Mono	$2459
13	IBM	4MB	340MB	Active	$3149	Toshiba	8MB	510MB	Mono	$2459	NEC	16MB	250MB	DualScan	$3995
14	IBM	8MB	250MB	Active	$3149	Toshiba	16MB	340MB	Mono	$3995	NEC	4MB	510MB	DualScan	$2459
15	IBM	16MB	340MB	Mono	$3995	Toshiba	8MB	510MB	DualScan	$3149	NEC	4MB	250MB	Active	$2459
16	IBM	8MB	340MB	DualScan	$2459	NEC	4MB	510MB	Active	$3995	Toshiba	16MB	250MB	Mono	$3149
17	IBM	8MB	510MB	DualScan	$3995	Toshiba	16MB	250MB	DualScan	$3149	NEC	4MB	340MB	Active	$2459
18	IBM	16MB	250MB	Mono	$2459	Toshiba	4MB	340MB	Active	$3995	NEC	8MB	510MB	DualScan	$3149
19	IBM	16MB	510MB	DualScan	$3149	Toshiba	4MB	250MB	Mono	$2459	IBM	8MB	340MB	Active	$3995
20	NEC	16MB	250MB	DualScan	$2459	Toshiba	4MB	340MB	Active	$3995	NEC	8MB	510MB	Mono	$3149
21	IBM	16MB	250MB	Active	$3995	IBM	4MB	510MB	Mono	$3149	IBM	8MB	340MB	DualScan	$2459
22	Toshiba	8MB	510MB	DualScan	$3995	NEC	4MB	340MB	Active	$3149	IBM	16MB	250MB	Mono	$2459
23	NEC	8MB	510MB	Active	$3995	IBM	4MB	250MB	Mono	$3149	IBM	16MB	340MB	DualScan	$2459
24	Toshiba	4MB	510MB	DualScan	$2459	IBM	8MB	250MB	Mono	$3149	NEC	16MB	340MB	Active	$3995
25	Toshiba	8MB	340MB	Mono	$2459	NEC	4MB	510MB	Active	$3995	IBM	16MB	250MB	DualScan	$3149
26	Toshiba	8MB	250MB	Mono	$2459	NEC	16MB	340MB	DualScan	$3995	IBM	4MB	510MB	Active	$3149
27	Toshiba	8MB	250MB	Mono	$2459	NEC	16MB	340MB	DualScan	$3995	IBM	4MB	510MB	Active	$3149
28	Toshiba	8MB	510MB	Mono	$3149	IBM	16MB	250MB	DualScan	$2459	IBM	4MB	340MB	Active	$3995
29	NEC	8MB	340MB	Active	$3149	IBM	16MB	510MB	DualScan	$3995	Toshiba	4MB	250MB	Mono	$2459
30	IBM	4MB	510MB	Mono	$3149	Toshiba	8MB	340MB	DualScan	$2459	NEC	16MB	250MB	Active	$3995

Partworth Values

Model	Brand Name			Memory Size			Hard Drive			Screen Type			Price Level		
	NEC	IBM	Toshiba	4MB	8MB	16MB	250MB	340MB	510MB	Mono	DualScan	Active	$3995	$3149	$2459
Self-Explicated	.000	.030	.033	.000	.148	.333	.000	.233	.300	.000	.059	.267	.000	.037	.067
Conjoint	.163	.000	.129	.000	.132	.121	.000	.184	.165	.000	.061	.445	.076	.049	.000
Choice	.057	.045	.000	.000	.150	.271	.000	.249	.287	.000	.280	.305	.000	.079	.040
Constr. Conjoint	.000	.000	.061	.000	.159	.159	.000	.220	.220	.000	.076	.561	.000	.000	.040
Constr. Choice	.000	.000	.000	.000	.150	.304	.000	.275	.275	.000	.320	.378	.000	.044	.044

Respondent No. 20

Experimental Choice Design

Set		Laptop A					Laptop B					Laptop C			
1	NEC	4MB	510MB	Mono	$2459	IBM	16MB	250MB	Active	$3995	Toshiba	8MB	340MB	DualScan	$3149
2	NEC	8MB	510MB	DualScan	$3995	IBM	16MB	250MB	Active	$3149	Toshiba	4MB	340MB	Mono	$2459
3	Toshiba	8MB	340MB	Mono	$2459	IBM	16MB	510MB	DualScan	$3995	NEC	4MB	250MB	Active	$3149
4	IBM	4MB	510MB	Active	$2459	NEC	8MB	250MB	Mono	$3995	Toshiba	16MB	340MB	DualScan	$3149
5	IBM	16MB	340MB	Mono	$2459	NEC	4MB	510MB	DualScan	$3149	Toshiba	8MB	250MB	Active	$3995
6	NEC	16MB	340MB	Mono	$3149	IBM	4MB	510MB	DualScan	$2459	Toshiba	8MB	250MB	Active	$3995
7	Toshiba	4MB	340MB	Active	$3995	IBM	8MB	510MB	Mono	$2459	NEC	16MB	250MB	DualScan	$3149
8	NEC	4MB	340MB	Active	$3149	IBM	8MB	510MB	Mono	$2459	Toshiba	16MB	250MB	DualScan	$3995
9	NEC	8MB	510MB	DualScan	$3995	IBM	4MB	340MB	Active	$3149	Toshiba	16MB	250MB	Mono	$2459
10	Toshiba	4MB	250MB	Active	$3149	IBM	8MB	340MB	DualScan	$2459	NEC	16MB	510MB	Mono	$3995
11	IBM	8MB	340MB	Active	$2459	NEC	16MB	250MB	DualScan	$3149	Toshiba	4MB	510MB	Mono	$3995
12	Toshiba	8MB	250MB	DualScan	$2459	IBM	4MB	340MB	Active	$3149	NEC	16MB	510MB	Mono	$3995
13	IBM	4MB	250MB	Active	$2459	Toshiba	8MB	510MB	Mono	$3149	NEC	16MB	340MB	DualScan	$3995
14	IBM	8MB	340MB	Active	$3149	NEC	16MB	250MB	Mono	$2459	Toshiba	4MB	510MB	DualScan	$3995
15	Toshiba	16MB	340MB	Mono	$3995	IBM	8MB	510MB	DualScan	$3149	NEC	4MB	250MB	Active	$2459
16	IBM	16MB	340MB	DualScan	$3149	NEC	4MB	250MB	Active	$3995	Toshiba	8MB	510MB	Mono	$2459
17	IBM	4MB	510MB	Active	$3995	Toshiba	8MB	250MB	DualScan	$2459	NEC	16MB	340MB	Mono	$3149
18	IBM	16MB	340MB	Mono	$2459	Toshiba	4MB	510MB	DualScan	$3995	NEC	8MB	250MB	Active	$3149
19	IBM	16MB	510MB	Mono	$3149	NEC	8MB	250MB	Active	$3149	Toshiba	4MB	340MB	DualScan	$2459
20	IBM	16MB	250MB	DualScan	$2459	Toshiba	4MB	340MB	Active	$3995	NEC	8MB	510MB	Mono	$3149
21	NEC	16MB	250MB	Active	$3995	Toshiba	4MB	510MB	Mono	$3149	IBM	8MB	340MB	DualScan	$2459
22	NEC	16MB	510MB	Mono	$3995	IBM	8MB	250MB	Active	$2459	Toshiba	4MB	340MB	DualScan	$3149
23	Toshiba	8MB	510MB	Mono	$3995	NEC	4MB	250MB	Active	$2459	IBM	16MB	340MB	DualScan	$3149
24	Toshiba	4MB	510MB	Mono	$3149	NEC	8MB	250MB	DualScan	$2459	IBM	16MB	340MB	Active	$3995
25	Toshiba	4MB	250MB	DualScan	$2459	NEC	8MB	340MB	Active	$3995	IBM	16MB	510MB	Mono	$3149
26	Toshiba	16MB	250MB	Mono	$2459	NEC	4MB	510MB	DualScan	$3149	IBM	8MB	340MB	Active	$3995
27	Toshiba	8MB	340MB	Mono	$2459	NEC	16MB	250MB	DualScan	$3149	IBM	4MB	510MB	Active	$3995
28	IBM	8MB	250MB	Active	$3149	NEC	16MB	340MB	Mono	$2459	Toshiba	4MB	510MB	DualScan	$3995
29	NEC	8MB	340MB	Active	$3149	IBM	16MB	510MB	DualScan	$2459	Toshiba	4MB	250MB	Mono	$3995
30	NEC	4MB	340MB	Active	$3995	IBM	8MB	510MB	DualScan	$3149	Toshiba	16MB	250MB	Mono	$2459

Partworth Values

	Brand Name			Memory Size			Hard Drive			Screen Type			Price Level		
Model	NEC	IBM	Toshiba	4MB	8MB	16MB	250MB	340MB	510MB	Mono	DualScan	Active	$3995	$3149	$2459
Self-Explicated	.090	.000	.162	.000	.084	.189	.000	.096	.216	.000	.120	.270	.000	.090	.162
Conjoint	.057	.000	.014	.000	.257	.438	.000	.016	.143	.000	.195	.224	.138	.000	.086
Choice	.077	.000	.086	.000	.108	.164	.000	.093	.182	.000	.202	.370	.000	.120	.198
Constr. Conjoint	.000	.000	.000	.000	.312	.532	.000	.020	.174	.000	.236	.273	.000	.000	.021
Constr. Choice	.077	.000	.086	.000	.108	.164	.000	.093	.182	.000	.202	.370	.000	.120	.198

Appendices

Respondent No. 21

Experimental Choice Design

Set	Laptop A				Laptop B				Laptop C			
1	NEC	8MB	250MB	Mono	$2459	IBM	16MB	510MB	DualScan	$3995	Toshiba	4MB	340MB	Active	$3149
2	NEC	8MB	510MB	DualScan	$3995	IBM	16MB	250MB	Active	$3149	Toshiba	4MB	340MB	Mono	$2459
3	Toshiba	8MB	340MB	Mono	$2459	NEC	4MB	510MB	Active	$3995	IBM	16MB	250MB	DualScan	$3149
4	Toshiba	4MB	510MB	DualScan	$2459	IBM	8MB	250MB	Mono	$3995	NEC	16MB	340MB	Active	$3149
5	NEC	16MB	340MB	Mono	$3995	IBM	4MB	510MB	DualScan	$3149	Toshiba	8MB	250MB	Active	$2459
6	Toshiba	16MB	340MB	DualScan	$3995	NEC	4MB	510MB	Mono	$3149	IBM	8MB	250MB	Active	$2459
7	NEC	4MB	250MB	Active	$2459	IBM	16MB	340MB	Mono	$3149	Toshiba	8MB	510MB	DualScan	$3995
8	NEC	8MB	340MB	Active	$3995	IBM	4MB	510MB	Mono	$2459	Toshiba	16MB	250MB	DualScan	$3149
9	NEC	4MB	250MB	DualScan	$2459	IBM	8MB	340MB	Active	$3149	Toshiba	16MB	510MB	Mono	$3995
10	Toshiba	4MB	250MB	Active	$2459	IBM	8MB	340MB	DualScan	$3149	NEC	16MB	510MB	Mono	$3995
11	IBM	8MB	510MB	DualScan	$3995	Toshiba	16MB	250MB	Mono	$3149	NEC	4MB	340MB	Active	$2459
12	NEC	4MB	340MB	Active	$3149	Toshiba	8MB	250MB	DualScan	$2459	IBM	16MB	510MB	Mono	$3995
13	IBM	4MB	340MB	DualScan	$2459	Toshiba	8MB	510MB	Mono	$3149	NEC	16MB	250MB	Active	$3995
14	Toshiba	8MB	340MB	DualScan	$3149	IBM	16MB	250MB	Mono	$2459	NEC	4MB	510MB	Active	$3995
15	IBM	8MB	510MB	Mono	$3149	Toshiba	16MB	340MB	Active	$3995	NEC	4MB	250MB	DualScan	$2459
16	IBM	16MB	250MB	Mono	$2459	Toshiba	4MB	340MB	Active	$3149	NEC	8MB	510MB	DualScan	$3995
17	IBM	4MB	510MB	Mono	$2459	Toshiba	16MB	250MB	DualScan	$3149	NEC	8MB	340MB	Active	$3995
18	IBM	16MB	250MB	Mono	$2459	Toshiba	4MB	510MB	DualScan	$3149	NEC	8MB	340MB	Active	$3995
19	IBM	16MB	510MB	Mono	$3995	NEC	8MB	250MB	Active	$2459	Toshiba	4MB	340MB	DualScan	$3149
20	Toshiba	8MB	510MB	DualScan	$2459	IBM	16MB	340MB	Active	$3995	NEC	4MB	250MB	Mono	$3149
21	NEC	16MB	250MB	Mono	$3149	IBM	4MB	340MB	DualScan	$2459	Toshiba	8MB	510MB	Active	$3995
22	Toshiba	8MB	510MB	DualScan	$3995	NEC	4MB	250MB	Active	$2459	IBM	16MB	340MB	Mono	$3149
23	IBM	16MB	510MB	DualScan	$3995	Toshiba	4MB	250MB	Active	$2459	NEC	8MB	340MB	Mono	$3149
24	Toshiba	4MB	510MB	Mono	$3149	NEC	8MB	250MB	DualScan	$2459	IBM	16MB	340MB	Active	$3995
25	Toshiba	4MB	340MB	Mono	$2459	IBM	8MB	510MB	Active	$3995	NEC	16MB	250MB	DualScan	$3149
26	NEC	8MB	250MB	Mono	$2459	Toshiba	16MB	340MB	DualScan	$3995	IBM	4MB	510MB	Active	$3149
27	Toshiba	8MB	250MB	Mono	$2459	NEC	16MB	340MB	DualScan	$3995	IBM	4MB	510MB	Active	$3149
28	Toshiba	8MB	510MB	DualScan	$3995	NEC	16MB	250MB	Mono	$3149	IBM	4MB	340MB	Active	$2459
29	IBM	8MB	340MB	DualScan	$3149	NEC	4MB	510MB	Active	$3995	Toshiba	16MB	250MB	Mono	$2459
30	IBM	8MB	340MB	Mono	$2459	NEC	4MB	510MB	Active	$3995	Toshiba	16MB	250MB	DualScan	$3149

Partworth Values

Model	Brand Name			Memory Size			Hard Drive			Screen Type			Price Level		
	NEC	IBM	Toshiba	4MB	8MB	16MB	250MB	340MB	510MB	Mono	DualScan	Active	$3995	$3149	$2459
Self-Explicated	.097	.000	.054	.000	.100	.226	.000	.143	.258	.000	.100	.129	.000	.161	.290
Conjoint	.090	.000	.132	.000	.132	.282	.067	.000	.208	.000	.196	.070	.000	.152	.183
Choice	.000	.000	.000	.000	.000	.000	.000	.000	.000	.000	.000	.000	.000	.999	.000
Constr. Conjoint	.148	.000	.148	.000	.176	.376	.000	.000	.232	.000	.000	.000	.000	.203	.244
Constr. Choice	.000	.000	.000	.000	.000	1.000	.000	.000	.000	.000	.000	.000	.000	.000	.000

Respondent No. 22

Experimental Choice Design

Set	Laptop A					Laptop B					Laptop C				
1	NEC	8MB	510MB	Mono	$2459	IBM	16MB	250MB	DualScan	$3995	Toshiba	4MB	340MB	Active	$3149
2	Toshiba	8MB	510MB	DualScan	$3995	IBM	4MB	250MB	Active	$3149	NEC	16MB	340MB	Mono	$2459
3	NEC	4MB	340MB	Active	$3149	IBM	8MB	510MB	Mono	$3995	Toshiba	16MB	250MB	DualScan	$2459
4	NEC	4MB	510MB	Active	$2459	IBM	8MB	250MB	DualScan	$3995	Toshiba	16MB	340MB	DualScan	$3149
5	Toshiba	16MB	340MB	Mono	$3995	IBM	4MB	510MB	DualScan	$3149	NEC	8MB	250MB	Active	$2459
6	NEC	16MB	510MB	Mono	$3149	IBM	4MB	340MB	DualScan	$2459	Toshiba	8MB	250MB	Active	$3995
7	NEC	16MB	250MB	Active	$3995	IBM	8MB	340MB	Mono	$2459	Toshiba	4MB	510MB	DualScan	$3149
8	NEC	8MB	250MB	Active	$3149	IBM	4MB	340MB	Mono	$3149	Toshiba	16MB	510MB	DualScan	$2459
9	NEC	16MB	250MB	Active	$3995	NEC	8MB	340MB	Mono	$2459	Toshiba	4MB	510MB	DualScan	$3149
10	IBM	8MB	250MB	DualScan	$2459	NEC	4MB	340MB	Active	$3149	Toshiba	16MB	510MB	Mono	$3995
11	IBM	8MB	510MB	DualScan	$3995	Toshiba	4MB	250MB	Active	$2459	NEC	16MB	340MB	Mono	$3149
12	IBM	8MB	250MB	DualScan	$2459	Toshiba	4MB	340MB	Active	$3995	NEC	16MB	510MB	Mono	$3149
13	IBM	4MB	340MB	Active	$3995	Toshiba	8MB	510MB	Mono	$3149	NEC	16MB	250MB	DualScan	$2459
14	NEC	8MB	250MB	Active	$3149	Toshiba	16MB	340MB	Mono	$2459	IBM	4MB	510MB	DualScan	$3995
15	IBM	8MB	340MB	DualScan	$3995	NEC	16MB	510MB	Mono	$3149	Toshiba	4MB	250MB	Active	$2459
16	IBM	16MB	250MB	DualScan	$3149	NEC	4MB	510MB	Active	$3995	Toshiba	8MB	340MB	Mono	$2459
17	IBM	16MB	510MB	Mono	$3995	Toshiba	8MB	250MB	Active	$2459	NEC	4MB	250MB	Active	$2459
18	Toshiba	16MB	340MB	Mono	$2459	IBM	4MB	250MB	Active	$3149	NEC	8MB	510MB	DualScan	$3995
19	IBM	16MB	510MB	Mono	$3995	IBM	4MB	340MB	Active	$2459	NEC	8MB	340MB	DualScan	$3149
20	IBM	16MB	250MB	DualScan	$2459	Toshiba	4MB	340MB	Active	$3995	NEC	8MB	510MB	Mono	$3149
21	IBM	16MB	250MB	Active	$3995	IBM	8MB	340MB	Mono	$3149	NEC	4MB	510MB	DualScan	$2459
22	Toshiba	8MB	510MB	DualScan	$3995	NEC	4MB	250MB	Active	$2459	IBM	16MB	340MB	Mono	$3149
23	Toshiba	8MB	510MB	Active	$3149	NEC	4MB	250MB	Mono	$3149	IBM	16MB	340MB	DualScan	$2459
24	IBM	8MB	510MB	Mono	$3149	NEC	4MB	250MB	Active	$2459	Toshiba	16MB	340MB	DualScan	$3995
25	IBM	8MB	340MB	Mono	$2459	NEC	4MB	510MB	Active	$3995	Toshiba	16MB	250MB	DualScan	$3149
26	Toshiba	8MB	510MB	Mono	$3149	NEC	16MB	340MB	DualScan	$3995	IBM	4MB	250MB	Active	$2459
27	Toshiba	8MB	510MB	Mono	$2459	NEC	16MB	340MB	DualScan	$3995	IBM	4MB	250MB	Active	$3149
28	IBM	8MB	250MB	Active	$3995	NEC	16MB	340MB	Mono	$2459	Toshiba	4MB	510MB	DualScan	$3149
29	Toshiba	8MB	340MB	Active	$3149	NEC	16MB	510MB	DualScan	$2459	IBM	4MB	250MB	Mono	$3995
30	IBM	4MB	510MB	Mono	$2459	NEC	8MB	340MB	DualScan	$3149	Toshiba	16MB	250MB	Active	$3995

Partworth Values

Model	Brand Name			Memory Size				Hard Drive			Screen Type			Price Level		
	NEC	IBM	Toshiba	4MB	8MB	16MB	250MB	340MB	510MB	Mono	DualScan	Active	$3995	$3149	$2459
Self-Explicated	.000	.091	.040	.000	.141	.212	.000	.162	.242	.000	.135	.303	.000	.101	.152
Conjoint	.184	.000	.012	.000	.139	.288	.016	.066	.000	.000	.207	.359	.103	.000	.053
Choice	.111	.068	.000	.000	.240	.279	.145	.000	.002	.000	.231	.282	.152	.183	.000
Constr. Conjoint	.000	.000	.000	.000	.215	.445	.000	.000	.000	.000	.319	.553	.000	.000	.000
Constr. Choice	.000	.080	.000	.000	.327	.410	.000	.000	.000	.000	.266	.510	.000	.000	.000

Respondent No. 23

Experimental Choice Design

Set		Laptop A					Laptop B					Laptop C			
1	NEC	8MB	340MB	Mono	$2459	IBM	16MB	250MB	Active	$3995	Toshiba	4MB	510MB	DualScan	$3149
2	NEC	8MB	510MB	DualScan	$3995	Toshiba	16MB	250MB	Active	$3149	IBM	4MB	340MB	Mono	$2459
3	Toshiba	8MB	340MB	Active	$2459	IBM	16MB	510MB	Mono	$3149	NEC	4MB	250MB	DualScan	$3995
4	Toshiba	4MB	510MB	Active	$3995	NEC	8MB	340MB	DualScan	$2459	IBM	16MB	250MB	DualScan	$3149
5	Toshiba	16MB	340MB	Active	$3995	IBM	4MB	510MB	DualScan	$2459	NEC	8MB	250MB	Mono	$2459
6	NEC	8MB	510MB	Mono	$3149	IBM	4MB	250MB	Mono	$2459	Toshiba	16MB	340MB	Active	$3995
7	IBM	16MB	250MB	Active	$3995	Toshiba	8MB	340MB	Mono	$2459	NEC	4MB	510MB	DualScan	$3149
8	NEC	16MB	250MB	Active	$3149	IBM	4MB	340MB	Mono	$3149	Toshiba	8MB	510MB	DualScan	$3995
9	Toshiba	4MB	340MB	DualScan	$2459	NEC	16MB	250MB	Active	$2459	IBM	8MB	510MB	Mono	$3995
10	NEC	4MB	250MB	DualScan	$2459	IBM	8MB	340MB	Mono	$3149	Toshiba	16MB	510MB	Mono	$3995
11	NEC	4MB	510MB	DualScan	$3995	IBM	16MB	250MB	Active	$3149	Toshiba	8MB	340MB	Mono	$2459
12	IBM	4MB	340MB	Active	$3149	Toshiba	8MB	250MB	DualScan	$2459	NEC	16MB	510MB	Mono	$3995
13	NEC	16MB	250MB	DualScan	$3995	Toshiba	4MB	510MB	Mono	$2459	IBM	8MB	340MB	Active	$3149
14	IBM	8MB	340MB	Active	$3149	Toshiba	16MB	250MB	Mono	$2459	NEC	4MB	510MB	DualScan	$3995
15	IBM	8MB	510MB	Mono	$3995	Toshiba	16MB	250MB	Active	$3149	NEC	4MB	340MB	DualScan	$2459
16	IBM	16MB	340MB	DualScan	$3149	NEC	4MB	510MB	Active	$2459	Toshiba	8MB	250MB	Mono	$2459
17	IBM	8MB	510MB	Mono	$3149	Toshiba	4MB	250MB	DualScan	$2459	NEC	16MB	340MB	Active	$3995
18	Toshiba	8MB	250MB	Mono	$2459	IBM	4MB	510MB	Active	$3995	NEC	16MB	340MB	DualScan	$3149
19	IBM	8MB	510MB	Active	$3149	NEC	4MB	340MB	Mono	$2459	Toshiba	16MB	250MB	DualScan	$2459
20	IBM	16MB	340MB	DualScan	$3995	NEC	4MB	250MB	Active	$2459	Toshiba	8MB	510MB	Mono	$3149
21	Toshiba	4MB	510MB	Active	$3995	NEC	16MB	340MB	Mono	$3149	IBM	8MB	250MB	Mono	$2459
22	NEC	8MB	510MB	DualScan	$3149	IBM	4MB	340MB	Mono	$2459	Toshiba	16MB	250MB	Active	$3995
23	Toshiba	8MB	510MB	Mono	$3149	NEC	16MB	250MB	Active	$3995	IBM	4MB	340MB	DualScan	$3995
24	Toshiba	16MB	510MB	Mono	$3149	NEC	8MB	250MB	DualScan	$2459	IBM	4MB	340MB	Active	$3149
25	Toshiba	4MB	340MB	Active	$2459	NEC	8MB	510MB	DualScan	$3995	IBM	16MB	250MB	Mono	$3995
26	NEC	8MB	250MB	Mono	$2459	IBM	16MB	340MB	DualScan	$3995	Toshiba	4MB	510MB	Active	$3149
27	IBM	8MB	250MB	Mono	$2459	NEC	16MB	340MB	DualScan	$3149	Toshiba	4MB	510MB	Active	$3995
28	Toshiba	8MB	510MB	Active	$3149	IBM	16MB	250MB	Mono	$2459	NEC	4MB	340MB	DualScan	$3995
29	NEC	16MB	340MB	Active	$3149	Toshiba	8MB	510MB	Mono	$3995	IBM	4MB	250MB	DualScan	$2459
30	IBM	16MB	250MB	Mono	$3149	Toshiba	8MB	510MB	DualScan	$3995	NEC	4MB	340MB	Active	$2459

Partworth Values

Model	Brand Name			Memory Size			Hard Drive			Screen Type			Price Level		
	NEC	IBM	Toshiba	4MB	8MB	16MB	250MB	340MB	510MB	Mono	DualScan	Active	$3995	$3149	$2459
Self-Explicated	.025	.057	.000	.000	.102	.229	.000	.029	.257	.000	.114	.171	.000	.032	.286
Conjoint	.248	.037	.000	.000	.048	.252	.000	.122	.156	.000	.085	.089	.000	.048	.256
Choice	.000	.013	.079	.000	.301	.082	.137	.283	.000	.085	.079	.000	.057	.252	.000
Constr. Conjoint	.000	.000	.000	.000	.064	.335	.000	.163	.207	.000	.113	.118	.000	.064	.340
Constr. Choice	.000	.013	.079	.000	.301	.082	.137	.283	.000	.085	.079	.000	.057	.252	.000

Appendices

Respondent No. 24

Experimental Choice Design

Set	Laptop A						Laptop B						Laptop C					
	Brand	Mem	HD	Screen	Price		Brand	Mem	HD	Screen	Price		Brand	Mem	HD	Screen	Price	
1	Toshiba	8MB	510MB	Mono	$2459		NEC	16MB	340MB	DualScan	$3995		IBM	4MB	250MB	Active	$3149
2	NEC	8MB	510MB	DualScan	$3149		Toshiba	16MB	250MB	Active	$2459		IBM	4MB	340MB	Mono	$3995
3	NEC	4MB	510MB	Active	$2459		IBM	16MB	340MB	Mono	$3149		Toshiba	8MB	250MB	DualScan	$3995
4	NEC	4MB	510MB	Active	$3995		IBM	8MB	340MB	Mono	$2459		Toshiba	16MB	250MB	DualScan	$3149
5	Toshiba	16MB	340MB	Mono	$3149		IBM	4MB	510MB	DualScan	$2459		NEC	8MB	250MB	Active	$3995
6	NEC	16MB	340MB	Mono	$3995		IBM	4MB	510MB	DualScan	$2459		Toshiba	8MB	250MB	Active	$3149
7	NEC	8MB	250MB	Active	$3149		IBM	16MB	340MB	Mono	$3149		Toshiba	4MB	510MB	DualScan	$2459
8	NEC	16MB	340MB	Active	$3995		Toshiba	4MB	510MB	Mono	$2459		IBM	8MB	250MB	DualScan	$3149
9	NEC	8MB	340MB	DualScan	$3149		IBM	4MB	250MB	Active	$2459		Toshiba	16MB	510MB	Mono	$3995
10	NEC	8MB	250MB	DualScan	$3149		IBM	4MB	340MB	Active	$3995		Toshiba	16MB	510MB	Mono	$2459
11	NEC	8MB	510MB	DualScan	$2459		Toshiba	16MB	250MB	Active	$3149		IBM	4MB	340MB	Mono	$3995
12	IBM	16MB	250MB	DualScan	$3995		NEC	8MB	340MB	Active	$3149		Toshiba	4MB	510MB	Mono	$2459
13	IBM	4MB	340MB	Active	$3149		Toshiba	8MB	510MB	Mono	$2459		NEC	16MB	250MB	DualScan	$3995
14	NEC	8MB	250MB	Active	$2459		Toshiba	16MB	340MB	Mono	$2459		IBM	4MB	510MB	DualScan	$3995
15	IBM	16MB	340MB	Mono	$3149		Toshiba	8MB	250MB	DualScan	$3995		NEC	4MB	510MB	Active	$2459
16	IBM	8MB	340MB	Mono	$2459		NEC	4MB	510MB	Active	$3995		NEC	16MB	250MB	DualScan	$3149
17	IBM	16MB	340MB	Mono	$3995		Toshiba	8MB	250MB	DualScan	$3149		NEC	4MB	510MB	Active	$2459
18	IBM	16MB	340MB	Mono	$3149		Toshiba	4MB	340MB	DualScan	$2459		NEC	8MB	510MB	Active	$3149
19	IBM	8MB	510MB	Mono	$3995		Toshiba	4MB	340MB	Active	$2459		NEC	16MB	250MB	DualScan	$3149
20	NEC	16MB	340MB	DualScan	$3995		Toshiba	4MB	250MB	Active	$2459		IBM	8MB	510MB	Mono	$3149
21	IBM	16MB	250MB	Active	$3149		NEC	4MB	510MB	Mono	$3995		Toshiba	8MB	340MB	DualScan	$2459
22	IBM	16MB	510MB	DualScan	$3995		NEC	4MB	340MB	Active	$2459		IBM	8MB	510MB	Mono	$3149
23	NEC	8MB	510MB	Active	$3995		NEC	4MB	340MB	Mono	$3149		IBM	16MB	250MB	DualScan	$2459
24	Toshiba	16MB	510MB	Mono	$3149		NEC	8MB	250MB	DualScan	$2459		IBM	4MB	340MB	Active	$3995
25	Toshiba	16MB	340MB	DualScan	$3149		NEC	8MB	510MB	Active	$2459		IBM	4MB	250MB	Mono	$3995
26	IBM	8MB	340MB	Mono	$2459		NEC	16MB	250MB	DualScan	$3995		Toshiba	4MB	510MB	Active	$3149
27	Toshiba	16MB	510MB	Mono	$3149		NEC	8MB	340MB	DualScan	$3995		IBM	4MB	250MB	Active	$2459
28	Toshiba	16MB	510MB	Mono	$2459		NEC	8MB	250MB	DualScan	$3149		IBM	4MB	340MB	Active	$3995
29	Toshiba	8MB	510MB	DualScan	$3149		NEC	16MB	250MB	Active	$2459		IBM	4MB	510MB	Mono	$3995
30	Toshiba	4MB	340MB	Mono	$3995		NEC	16MB	510MB	DualScan	$3149		IBM	8MB	250MB	Active	$2459

Partworth Values

Model	Brand Name			Memory Size			Hard Drive			Screen Type			Price Level		
	NEC	IBM	Toshiba	4MB	8MB	16MB	250MB	340MB	510MB	Mono	DualScan	Active	$3995	$3149	$2459
Self-Explicated	.000	.138	.077	.000	.245	.276	.000	.077	.172	.000	.268	.345	.000	.031	.069
Conjoint	.112	.000	.049	.000	.257	.287	.034	.078	.000	.000	.208	.434	.089	.000	.051
Choice	.121	.000	.060	.000	.369	.350	.161	.101	.000	.000	.076	.276	.073	.040	.000
Constr. Conjoint	.000	.000	.000	.000	.354	.394	.000	.000	.000	.000	.286	.596	.000	.000	.010
Constr. Choice	.000	.000	.000	.000	.497	.501	.000	.000	.000	.000	.267	.499	.000	.000	.000

Appendices

Respondent No. 25

Experimental Choice Design

Set	Laptop A					Laptop B					Laptop C				
1	NEC	8MB	510MB	Mono	$3149	Toshiba	16MB	250MB	DualScan	$2459	IBM	4MB	340MB	Active	$3995
2	Toshiba	4MB	510MB	DualScan	$3149	IBM	8MB	250MB	Active	$2459	NEC	16MB	340MB	Mono	$3995
3	IBM	8MB	340MB	DualScan	$2459	NEC	16MB	510MB	Mono	$3995	Toshiba	4MB	250MB	Active	$3149
4	NEC	4MB	250MB	Active	$2459	IBM	16MB	510MB	Mono	$3995	Toshiba	8MB	340MB	DualScan	$3149
5	NEC	16MB	340MB	Mono	$3149	Toshiba	4MB	510MB	DualScan	$2459	IBM	8MB	250MB	Active	$3995
6	IBM	16MB	340MB	Mono	$2459	Toshiba	4MB	510MB	DualScan	$3149	NEC	8MB	250MB	Active	$3995
7	NEC	4MB	250MB	Active	$3149	Toshiba	8MB	510MB	Mono	$3995	IBM	16MB	340MB	DualScan	$2459
8	Toshiba	4MB	250MB	Active	$3149	IBM	16MB	510MB	Mono	$3995	NEC	8MB	340MB	DualScan	$2459
9	NEC	4MB	510MB	DualScan	$2459	IBM	8MB	250MB	Active	$3149	NEC	16MB	340MB	Mono	$3995
10	Toshiba	4MB	250MB	Mono	$2459	NEC	8MB	340MB	Active	$3995	IBM	16MB	340MB	DualScan	$3149
11	IBM	8MB	510MB	DualScan	$3149	IBM	4MB	250MB	Active	$3995	Toshiba	16MB	340MB	Mono	$2459
12	NEC	4MB	250MB	Active	$3149	Toshiba	8MB	340MB	DualScan	$3995	NEC	16MB	510MB	Mono	$2459
13	IBM	4MB	340MB	Active	$3149	IBM	8MB	510MB	Mono	$3995	NEC	16MB	340MB	DualScan	$2459
14	IBM	8MB	250MB	Active	$3149	Toshiba	16MB	340MB	Mono	$2459	NEC	4MB	510MB	DualScan	$3995
15	Toshiba	16MB	340MB	Mono	$3149	IBM	8MB	510MB	DualScan	$3995	NEC	4MB	250MB	Active	$2459
16	NEC	16MB	340MB	DualScan	$3995	IBM	4MB	250MB	Active	$3149	Toshiba	8MB	510MB	Mono	$2459
17	NEC	8MB	510MB	Mono	$3149	Toshiba	16MB	250MB	DualScan	$2459	IBM	4MB	340MB	Active	$2459
18	IBM	16MB	510MB	Mono	$3995	Toshiba	8MB	340MB	DualScan	$2459	NEC	4MB	340MB	Active	$3995
19	IBM	16MB	510MB	Mono	$3149	Toshiba	4MB	340MB	DualScan	$3995	NEC	8MB	250MB	Active	$2459
20	NEC	16MB	250MB	DualScan	$2459	Toshiba	4MB	340MB	Active	$3995	IBM	8MB	340MB	DualScan	$2459
21	IBM	16MB	250MB	DualScan	$3149	NEC	4MB	340MB	Active	$3995	IBM	8MB	510MB	Mono	$2459
22	IBM	16MB	340MB	DualScan	$3149	NEC	4MB	250MB	Active	$2459	Toshiba	8MB	510MB	Mono	$3995
23	NEC	16MB	510MB	DualScan	$3149	IBM	4MB	250MB	Mono	$2459	IBM	8MB	340MB	Active	$3995
24	NEC	8MB	510MB	Mono	$2459	Toshiba	16MB	250MB	DualScan	$3149	IBM	4MB	340MB	Active	$3995
25	Toshiba	4MB	510MB	DualScan	$2459	IBM	8MB	250MB	Active	$3995	NEC	16MB	340MB	Mono	$3149
26	NEC	8MB	510MB	Mono	$3149	IBM	16MB	250MB	DualScan	$3995	IBM	4MB	340MB	Active	$2459
27	IBM	16MB	510MB	Mono	$2459	NEC	8MB	340MB	DualScan	$3995	Toshiba	4MB	250MB	Active	$3149
28	Toshiba	4MB	250MB	Active	$2459	NEC	8MB	340MB	DualScan	$3149	IBM	16MB	510MB	Mono	$3995
29	Toshiba	16MB	250MB	DualScan	$3995	IBM	8MB	510MB	Mono	$3149	NEC	4MB	340MB	Active	$3149
30	Toshiba	4MB	510MB	Mono	$3149	NEC	8MB	340MB	DualScan	$2459	IBM	16MB	250MB	Active	$3995

Partworth Values

Model	Brand Name			Memory Size				Hard Drive			Screen Type			Price Level		
	NEC	IBM	Toshiba	4MB	8MB	16MB	250MB	340MB	510MB	Mono	DualScan	Active	$3995	$3149	$2459
Self-Explicated	.071	.000	.107	.000	.167	.250	.000	.139	.250	.000	.119	.357	.000	.020	.036
Conjoint	.171	.000	.052	.000	.196	.244	.000	.086	.197	.000	.081	.045	.000	.091	.308
Choice	.165	.000	.149	.000	.250	.279	.000	.095	.062	.000	.076	.062	.000	.274	.386
Constr. Conjoint	.000	.000	.000	.000	.241	.301	.000	.106	.243	.000	.078	.078	.000	.112	.379
Constr. Choice	.157	.000	.157	.000	.242	.288	.000	.094	.094	.000	.069	.092	.000	.267	.369

Respondent No. 26

Experimental Choice Design

Set	Laptop A					Laptop B					Laptop C				
1	IBM	8MB	250MB	Mono	$2459	NEC	16MB	510MB	DualScan	$3995	Toshiba	4MB	340MB	Active	$3149
2	IBM	8MB	510MB	Mono	$3995	NEC	16MB	250MB	Active	$3149	Toshiba	4MB	340MB	DualScan	$2459
3	NEC	8MB	340MB	DualScan	$2459	IBM	16MB	510MB	Mono	$3995	Toshiba	4MB	250MB	Active	$3149
4	NEC	4MB	510MB	DualScan	$2459	IBM	8MB	250MB	Active	$3995	Toshiba	16MB	340MB	Mono	$3149
5	NEC	8MB	340MB	Active	$3995	IBM	4MB	510MB	DualScan	$3149	Toshiba	16MB	250MB	Mono	$2459
6	NEC	16MB	340MB	Mono	$3149	Toshiba	4MB	510MB	DualScan	$2459	IBM	8MB	340MB	Active	$3995
7	NEC	4MB	250MB	Active	$2459	IBM	8MB	510MB	Mono	$3149	Toshiba	16MB	510MB	DualScan	$3995
8	Toshiba	16MB	250MB	Mono	$3995	IBM	4MB	340MB	Active	$3149	NEC	8MB	340MB	DualScan	$2459
9	NEC	4MB	250MB	Mono	$3149	IBM	8MB	340MB	Active	$3149	Toshiba	16MB	510MB	DualScan	$2459
10	Toshiba	4MB	250MB	DualScan	$3995	IBM	8MB	340MB	Mono	$2459	NEC	16MB	510MB	Active	$3995
11	IBM	16MB	340MB	DualScan	$3149	Toshiba	8MB	250MB	Active	$3149	NEC	4MB	510MB	Mono	$2459
12	IBM	4MB	250MB	Active	$3995	NEC	8MB	340MB	Mono	$2459	Toshiba	16MB	510MB	DualScan	$3995
13	IBM	4MB	340MB	Active	$3149	Toshiba	8MB	510MB	DualScan	$2459	NEC	16MB	250MB	Mono	$3995
14	IBM	8MB	250MB	Active	$3995	Toshiba	16MB	340MB	Mono	$3149	NEC	4MB	510MB	DualScan	$2459
15	IBM	8MB	510MB	Mono	$3995	Toshiba	16MB	340MB	DualScan	$2459	NEC	4MB	250MB	Active	$3149
16	NEC	16MB	250MB	DualScan	$2459	Toshiba	4MB	510MB	Active	$3995	IBM	8MB	340MB	Mono	$3149
17	IBM	4MB	340MB	Active	$3995	Toshiba	8MB	250MB	DualScan	$2459	NEC	16MB	510MB	Mono	$3149
18	NEC	16MB	250MB	DualScan	$3149	NEC	4MB	510MB	Mono	$2459	IBM	8MB	340MB	Active	$3995
19	Toshiba	8MB	250MB	DualScan	$2459	IBM	16MB	510MB	Active	$3995	NEC	4MB	340MB	Mono	$3149
20	IBM	8MB	250MB	DualScan	$2459	NEC	4MB	510MB	Active	$3995	Toshiba	16MB	340MB	Mono	$3149
21	IBM	8MB	250MB	Active	$3995	NEC	16MB	340MB	DualScan	$3149	Toshiba	4MB	510MB	Mono	$2459
22	NEC	16MB	340MB	DualScan	$3149	Toshiba	4MB	250MB	Active	$2459	IBM	8MB	510MB	Mono	$3995
23	NEC	16MB	510MB	Active	$3995	Toshiba	4MB	250MB	Mono	$3149	IBM	8MB	340MB	DualScan	$2459
24	IBM	4MB	510MB	Mono	$3149	Toshiba	8MB	250MB	DualScan	$2459	NEC	16MB	340MB	Active	$3995
25	Toshiba	4MB	340MB	Mono	$2459	NEC	8MB	510MB	Active	$3995	IBM	16MB	250MB	DualScan	$3149
26	NEC	16MB	250MB	Mono	$2459	Toshiba	8MB	340MB	Active	$3995	IBM	4MB	510MB	DualScan	$3149
27	Toshiba	8MB	250MB	Mono	$2459	IBM	16MB	340MB	DualScan	$3995	NEC	4MB	510MB	Active	$3149
28	IBM	8MB	510MB	Mono	$3149	NEC	16MB	250MB	DualScan	$2459	Toshiba	4MB	340MB	Active	$3995
29	Toshiba	4MB	340MB	Active	$3149	NEC	16MB	250MB	Mono	$2459	IBM	8MB	510MB	DualScan	$3995
30	IBM	4MB	340MB	Mono	$2459	NEC	8MB	510MB	DualScan	$3149	Toshiba	16MB	250MB	Active	$3995

Partworth Values

Model	Brand Name			Memory Size				Hard Drive			Screen Type			Price Level		
	NEC	IBM	Toshiba	4MB	8MB	16MB	250MB	340MB	510MB	Mono	DualScan	Active	$3995	$3149	$2459
Self-Explicated	.000	.139	.046	.000	.108	.194	.000	.108	.194	.000	.025	.222	.000	.111	.250
Conjoint	.047	.044	.000	.000	.127	.199	.000	.136	.232	.114	.000	.212	.000	.218	.310
Choice	.172	.000	.040	.000	.214	.085	.000	.118	.050	.203	.167	.000	.000	.293	.081
Constr. Conjoint	.000	.022	.040	.000	.139	.217	.000	.149	.253	.000	.000	.169	.000	.238	.339
Constr. Choice	.000	.000	.000	.000	1.000	1.000	.000	.000	.000	.000	.000	.000	.000	.000	.000

Respondent No. 27

Experimental Choice Design

Set	Laptop A					Laptop B					Laptop C				
1	NEC	8MB	340MB	Mono	$2459	IBM	16MB	250MB	DualScan	$3995	Toshiba	4MB	510MB	Active	$3149
2	NEC	8MB	510MB	Active	$3995	Toshiba	16MB	250MB	Mono	$3149	IBM	4MB	340MB	DualScan	$2459
3	NEC	8MB	250MB	DualScan	$2459	Toshiba	16MB	510MB	Mono	$3995	IBM	4MB	340MB	Active	$3149
4	NEC	4MB	510MB	Active	$3149	IBM	8MB	250MB	Mono	$2459	Toshiba	16MB	340MB	DualScan	$3995
5	Toshiba	16MB	340MB	Mono	$3149	IBM	4MB	510MB	Active	$3995	NEC	8MB	250MB	DualScan	$2459
6	IBM	8MB	340MB	Mono	$3149	NEC	4MB	510MB	Active	$3995	Toshiba	16MB	250MB	DualScan	$2459
7	Toshiba	16MB	250MB	Active	$3995	IBM	8MB	340MB	Mono	$3149	NEC	4MB	510MB	DualScan	$2459
8	NEC	16MB	250MB	Active	$3149	Toshiba	4MB	510MB	Mono	$2459	IBM	8MB	340MB	DualScan	$3995
9	IBM	4MB	250MB	DualScan	$3995	Toshiba	8MB	340MB	Active	$3149	NEC	16MB	510MB	Mono	$2459
10	NEC	16MB	250MB	DualScan	$3149	Toshiba	4MB	340MB	Active	$2459	IBM	8MB	510MB	Mono	$3995
11	IBM	8MB	510MB	Mono	$3149	NEC	16MB	250MB	Active	$2459	Toshiba	4MB	340MB	DualScan	$3995
12	IBM	8MB	340MB	Mono	$3995	Toshiba	4MB	250MB	Active	$3149	NEC	16MB	510MB	DualScan	$2459
13	IBM	4MB	340MB	Active	$2459	Toshiba	8MB	510MB	Mono	$3995	NEC	16MB	250MB	DualScan	$3149
14	Toshiba	8MB	250MB	DualScan	$3995	NEC	16MB	340MB	Mono	$2459	IBM	4MB	510MB	Active	$3149
15	Toshiba	8MB	340MB	Active	$3995	NEC	16MB	250MB	DualScan	$3149	IBM	4MB	510MB	Mono	$2459
16	Toshiba	16MB	340MB	DualScan	$3149	NEC	4MB	250MB	Active	$2459	IBM	8MB	510MB	Mono	$3995
17	Toshiba	4MB	510MB	Mono	$2459	IBM	8MB	250MB	DualScan	$3149	NEC	16MB	340MB	Active	$3995
18	Toshiba	16MB	250MB	Mono	$2459	IBM	4MB	510MB	Active	$3995	NEC	8MB	340MB	DualScan	$3149
19	Toshiba	4MB	510MB	Mono	$3995	IBM	4MB	250MB	Active	$2459	NEC	8MB	340MB	DualScan	$3149
20	IBM	16MB	250MB	Active	$3149	NEC	4MB	340MB	DualScan	$2459	Toshiba	8MB	510MB	Mono	$3149
21	IBM	8MB	250MB	Active	$3995	NEC	16MB	340MB	Mono	$2459	Toshiba	4MB	510MB	DualScan	$3149
22	Toshiba	8MB	250MB	DualScan	$3149	NEC	4MB	340MB	Active	$2459	IBM	16MB	510MB	Mono	$3995
23	Toshiba	16MB	510MB	Active	$3995	NEC	4MB	250MB	Mono	$2459	IBM	8MB	340MB	DualScan	$3149
24	Toshiba	4MB	510MB	Mono	$2459	NEC	8MB	250MB	Active	$3149	IBM	16MB	340MB	DualScan	$3995
25	Toshiba	4MB	340MB	DualScan	$2459	NEC	8MB	510MB	Active	$3995	IBM	16MB	250MB	Mono	$3149
26	Toshiba	8MB	250MB	Mono	$2459	NEC	16MB	340MB	DualScan	$3995	IBM	4MB	510MB	Active	$3149
27	Toshiba	8MB	250MB	Mono	$2459	NEC	16MB	340MB	Active	$3995	IBM	4MB	510MB	DualScan	$3149
28	IBM	4MB	510MB	DualScan	$3149	NEC	16MB	250MB	Active	$2459	Toshiba	8MB	340MB	Active	$3995
29	Toshiba	8MB	510MB	DualScan	$3149	NEC	16MB	250MB	Mono	$2459	IBM	4MB	340MB	Mono	$3995
30	Toshiba	4MB	340MB	Mono	$3995	NEC	16MB	510MB	DualScan	$3149	IBM	8MB	250MB	Active	$2459

Partworth Values

Model	Brand Name			Memory Size			Hard Drive			Screen Type			Price Level		
	NEC	IBM	Toshiba	4MB	8MB	16MB	250MB	340MB	510MB	Mono	DualScan	Active	$3995	$3149	$2459
Self-Explicated	.000	.114	.102	.000	.222	.286	.000	.089	.200	.000	.114	.171	.000	.127	.229
Conjoint	.108	.000	.090	.000	.238	.386	.000	.064	.068	.000	.004	.141	.000	.198	.297
Choice	.109	.066	.000	.000	.239	.337	.066	.000	.001	.132	.117	.000	.000	.286	.355
Constr. Conjoint	.000	.000	.000	.000	.267	.433	.000	.071	.076	.000	.005	.158	.000	.222	.333
Constr. Choice	.000	.000	.000	.000	.376	.446	.000	.000	.126	.000	.000	.000	.000	.294	.428

Respondent No. 28

Experimental Choice Design

Set	Laptop A					Laptop B					Laptop C				
1	Toshiba	8MB	510MB	Mono	$2459	IBM	16MB	250MB	DualScan	$3995	NEC	4MB	340MB	Active	$3149
2	NEC	8MB	250MB	Active	$3995	IBM	16MB	340MB	Mono	$3149	Toshiba	4MB	510MB	DualScan	$2459
3	NEC	8MB	340MB	Active	$2459	IBM	8MB	510MB	DualScan	$3149	Toshiba	4MB	250MB	Mono	$3995
4	NEC	4MB	250MB	Active	$2459	IBM	8MB	510MB	Mono	$3995	Toshiba	16MB	340MB	DualScan	$3149
5	NEC	16MB	340MB	Mono	$3995	IBM	4MB	510MB	DualScan	$3149	Toshiba	8MB	250MB	Active	$2459
6	NEC	8MB	340MB	Mono	$3149	Toshiba	4MB	510MB	DualScan	$2459	IBM	16MB	250MB	Active	$3995
7	NEC	4MB	340MB	DualScan	$3995	IBM	8MB	510MB	Mono	$3149	Toshiba	16MB	250MB	Active	$2459
8	Toshiba	16MB	340MB	DualScan	$3149	NEC	4MB	510MB	Mono	$2459	IBM	8MB	250MB	Active	$3995
9	NEC	8MB	250MB	DualScan	$3995	IBM	4MB	340MB	Active	$3149	Toshiba	16MB	510MB	Mono	$2459
10	NEC	4MB	250MB	Mono	$2459	IBM	8MB	340MB	DualScan	$2459	Toshiba	16MB	510MB	Mono	$3995
11	IBM	8MB	340MB	DualScan	$3995	Toshiba	16MB	250MB	Active	$3149	NEC	4MB	510MB	Mono	$2459
12	IBM	4MB	510MB	DualScan	$2459	Toshiba	8MB	340MB	Active	$3149	NEC	16MB	510MB	Mono	$3995
13	IBM	4MB	340MB	Active	$3149	Toshiba	8MB	510MB	Mono	$3995	NEC	16MB	250MB	DualScan	$2459
14	IBM	8MB	250MB	Active	$3995	Toshiba	16MB	340MB	Mono	$2459	NEC	4MB	510MB	DualScan	$3149
15	IBM	8MB	340MB	DualScan	$3995	Toshiba	16MB	510MB	Mono	$3149	NEC	4MB	250MB	Active	$2459
16	IBM	4MB	340MB	DualScan	$2459	Toshiba	16MB	510MB	Mono	$2459	NEC	8MB	250MB	Active	$3995
17	IBM	8MB	510MB	Mono	$3995	Toshiba	16MB	250MB	DualScan	$3149	NEC	4MB	340MB	Active	$2459
18	IBM	16MB	250MB	Mono	$2459	NEC	4MB	340MB	DualScan	$3149	Toshiba	8MB	510MB	Active	$3995
19	IBM	4MB	510MB	Active	$3149	Toshiba	16MB	340MB	Mono	$3995	NEC	4MB	250MB	Active	$2459
20	IBM	8MB	250MB	DualScan	$3149	Toshiba	16MB	340MB	Active	$3995	NEC	8MB	510MB	Mono	$2459
21	Toshiba	16MB	340MB	Active	$3995	IBM	4MB	510MB	Mono	$2459	NEC	8MB	250MB	DualScan	$3149
22	Toshiba	8MB	510MB	Active	$3149	NEC	4MB	250MB	Mono	$2459	IBM	16MB	340MB	DualScan	$3995
23	Toshiba	16MB	510MB	DualScan	$3995	NEC	4MB	250MB	Active	$2459	IBM	8MB	340MB	Mono	$3149
24	Toshiba	16MB	510MB	Mono	$3149	IBM	8MB	250MB	DualScan	$2459	NEC	4MB	340MB	Active	$3995
25	Toshiba	8MB	340MB	DualScan	$2459	IBM	4MB	510MB	DualScan	$3995	NEC	16MB	250MB	Mono	$3149
26	IBM	8MB	250MB	Mono	$3149	Toshiba	16MB	510MB	DualScan	$3995	NEC	4MB	340MB	Active	$2459
27	IBM	8MB	250MB	Active	$3149	NEC	16MB	340MB	Mono	$3995	Toshiba	4MB	510MB	DualScan	$2459
28	Toshiba	8MB	510MB	Active	$2459	NEC	16MB	250MB	Mono	$3995	IBM	4MB	340MB	DualScan	$3149
29	NEC	4MB	340MB	DualScan	$3149	Toshiba	8MB	510MB	Active	$3995	IBM	16MB	250MB	Mono	$2459
30	Toshiba	4MB	340MB	Mono	$3995	NEC	8MB	510MB	DualScan	$3149	IBM	16MB	250MB	Active	$2459

Partworth Values

Model	Brand Name			Memory Size			Hard Drive			Screen Type			Price Level		
	NEC	IBM	Toshiba	4MB	8MB	16MB	250MB	340MB	510MB	Mono	DualScan	Active	$3995	$3149	$2459
Self-Explicated	.212	.165	.000	.000	.135	.242	.000	.118	.212	.000	.141	.182	.000	.067	.152
Conjoint	.065	.114	.000	.000	.208	.369	.000	.220	.347	.015	.089	.000	.000	.059	.081
Choice	.008	.000	.103	.000	.276	.356	.000	.097	.227	.119	.000	.062	.000	.144	.194
Constr. Conjoint	.101	.101	.000	.000	.235	.416	.000	.248	.392	.000	.000	.000	.000	.066	.091
Constr. Choice	.000	.000	.000	.000	.477	.564	.000	.082	.235	.000	.000	.012	.000	.084	.189

Appendices

Respondent No. 29

Experimental Choice Design

Set		Laptop A					Laptop B					Laptop C			
1	NEC	8MB	510MB	Mono	$3149	Toshiba	16MB	250MB	Active	$3995	IBM	4MB	340MB	DualScan	$2459
2	NEC	8MB	510MB	DualScan	$3995	IBM	16MB	250MB	Active	$3149	Toshiba	4MB	340MB	Mono	$2459
3	NEC	4MB	250MB	Active	$2459	IBM	16MB	510MB	Mono	$3149	Toshiba	8MB	340MB	DualScan	$3995
4	NEC	4MB	340MB	Active	$3995	Toshiba	16MB	250MB	Mono	$3149	IBM	8MB	510MB	DualScan	$3995
5	Toshiba	16MB	510MB	Mono	$3149	IBM	4MB	340MB	DualScan	$2459	NEC	8MB	250MB	Active	$3149
6	NEC	16MB	340MB	Active	$3995	IBM	4MB	510MB	DualScan	$2459	Toshiba	8MB	250MB	Active	$3995
7	NEC	16MB	250MB	Active	$3149	IBM	8MB	340MB	Mono	$2459	Toshiba	4MB	510MB	DualScan	$3149
8	NEC	16MB	340MB	Mono	$3995	IBM	4MB	510MB	DualScan	$2459	Toshiba	8MB	250MB	Active	$3995
9	NEC	4MB	510MB	Active	$3149	IBM	8MB	340MB	DualScan	$3149	Toshiba	8MB	250MB	Mono	$2459
10	IBM	8MB	250MB	DualScan	$3149	IBM	4MB	340MB	Active	$2459	Toshiba	16MB	510MB	Mono	$3995
11	NEC	16MB	510MB	Mono	$3149	IBM	8MB	340MB	Mono	$3995	NEC	4MB	340MB	DualScan	$2459
12	NEC	8MB	250MB	DualScan	$3149	IBM	4MB	340MB	Mono	$2459	Toshiba	16MB	510MB	Mono	$3995
13	Toshiba	4MB	510MB	Active	$3149	IBM	8MB	340MB	Mono	$3149	NEC	16MB	250MB	DualScan	$3995
14	IBM	8MB	250MB	DualScan	$2459	Toshiba	16MB	250MB	DualScan	$2459	NEC	4MB	510MB	Active	$3995
15	IBM	8MB	340MB	Active	$3995	NEC	16MB	510MB	Active	$3149	NEC	4MB	250MB	Mono	$2459
16	IBM	8MB	340MB	Mono	$2459	NEC	4MB	510MB	Active	$3149	Toshiba	16MB	250MB	DualScan	$3995
17	IBM	16MB	510MB	DualScan	$3995	IBM	8MB	340MB	Mono	$3149	Toshiba	4MB	250MB	Active	$2459
18	IBM	16MB	250MB	Mono	$2459	NEC	4MB	510MB	Active	$3995	Toshiba	8MB	510MB	DualScan	$3149
19	IBM	16MB	340MB	Active	$3995	IBM	8MB	510MB	Mono	$2459	Toshiba	4MB	250MB	DualScan	$3149
20	IBM	16MB	250MB	Active	$3149	NEC	8MB	340MB	DualScan	$3149	Toshiba	4MB	510MB	Mono	$2459
21	IBM	16MB	250MB	DualScan	$3995	NEC	4MB	340MB	Active	$3149	IBM	8MB	510MB	Mono	$2459
22	Toshiba	8MB	250MB	Active	$3995	NEC	4MB	340MB	DualScan	$2459	IBM	16MB	510MB	Mono	$3149
23	NEC	16MB	510MB	Active	$3995	NEC	4MB	250MB	Mono	$2459	IBM	8MB	340MB	DualScan	$3149
24	NEC	8MB	510MB	Mono	$3149	Toshiba	4MB	250MB	Active	$2459	IBM	16MB	340MB	DualScan	$3995
25	NEC	4MB	250MB	DualScan	$2459	IBM	8MB	510MB	Active	$2459	IBM	16MB	340MB	Mono	$3149
26	IBM	16MB	250MB	Mono	$2459	NEC	8MB	340MB	Active	$3995	Toshiba	4MB	510MB	DualScan	$3149
27	Toshiba	8MB	250MB	Mono	$2459	NEC	16MB	340MB	DualScan	$3995	IBM	4MB	510MB	Active	$3149
28	NEC	4MB	510MB	Active	$3149	Toshiba	8MB	250MB	Mono	$2459	IBM	16MB	340MB	Active	$3995
29	Toshiba	8MB	340MB	Active	$3149	NEC	16MB	510MB	Mono	$2459	IBM	4MB	250MB	DualScan	$3995
30	NEC	4MB	510MB	Mono	$3995	Toshiba	8MB	340MB	DualScan	$3149	IBM	16MB	250MB	Active	$2459

Partworth Values

Model	Brand Name			Memory Size			Hard Drive			Screen Type			Price Level		
	NEC	IBM	Toshiba	4MB	8MB	16MB	250MB	340MB	510MB	Mono	DualScan	Active	$3995	$3149	$2459
Self-Explicated	.070	.000	.105	.000	.205	.263	.000	.123	.184	.000	.164	.211	.000	.105	.237
Conjoint	.132	.018	.000	.000	.325	.375	.010	.000	.080	.000	.088	.059	.000	.193	.325
Choice	.020	.019	.000	.000	.373	.398	.000	.056	.012	.000	.166	.224	.000	.124	.303
Constr. Conjoint	.000	.000	.000	.000	.383	.442	.000	.000	.089	.000	.086	.086	.000	.227	.383
Constr. Choice	.048	.048	.000	.000	.448	.459	.000	.000	.000	.000	.167	.222	.000	.115	.271

Respondent No. 30

Experimental Choice Design

Set	Laptop A					Laptop B					Laptop C				
1	Toshiba	8MB	510MB	Mono	$3149	NEC	16MB	250MB	Active	$3995	IBM	4MB	340MB	DualScan	$2459
2	NEC	8MB	510MB	DualScan	$3995	IBM	16MB	250MB	Mono	$3149	Toshiba	4MB	340MB	Active	$2459
3	NEC	8MB	250MB	DualScan	$2459	IBM	16MB	340MB	Mono	$3995	Toshiba	4MB	510MB	Active	$3149
4	IBM	4MB	510MB	Mono	$2459	NEC	8MB	250MB	Active	$3149	Toshiba	16MB	340MB	DualScan	$3995
5	NEC	16MB	340MB	Mono	$3149	IBM	4MB	510MB	DualScan	$3995	Toshiba	8MB	250MB	Active	$2459
6	IBM	16MB	250MB	Mono	$3995	Toshiba	4MB	340MB	Active	$2459	NEC	8MB	510MB	DualScan	$3149
7	NEC	16MB	340MB	Active	$3149	IBM	8MB	340MB	Mono	$2459	Toshiba	4MB	510MB	DualScan	$3995
8	NEC	8MB	340MB	DualScan	$3149	Toshiba	4MB	510MB	Mono	$2459	IBM	16MB	250MB	Active	$3995
9	NEC	4MB	510MB	DualScan	$3149	IBM	8MB	340MB	Mono	$2459	Toshiba	16MB	250MB	Active	$2459
10	NEC	8MB	250MB	DualScan	$2459	IBM	4MB	340MB	Active	$3995	Toshiba	16MB	510MB	Mono	$3995
11	Toshiba	8MB	510MB	Mono	$3149	NEC	4MB	250MB	Active	$2459	IBM	4MB	340MB	DualScan	$2459
12	IBM	8MB	250MB	Active	$3149	NEC	16MB	340MB	DualScan	$3995	Toshiba	16MB	510MB	Mono	$3995
13	IBM	8MB	340MB	Active	$3995	Toshiba	4MB	510MB	Mono	$2459	NEC	16MB	510MB	DualScan	$3149
14	IBM	8MB	250MB	Active	$2459	Toshiba	16MB	340MB	DualScan	$3995	NEC	4MB	510MB	Mono	$3149
15	IBM	8MB	510MB	Mono	$3995	Toshiba	16MB	250MB	DualScan	$3149	NEC	4MB	340MB	Active	$2459
16	Toshiba	16MB	250MB	Active	$3149	IBM	4MB	340MB	DualScan	$3995	NEC	8MB	510MB	Mono	$2459
17	IBM	4MB	510MB	Mono	$3995	NEC	8MB	250MB	DualScan	$2459	Toshiba	16MB	340MB	Active	$3149
18	Toshiba	16MB	250MB	Mono	$3149	IBM	4MB	510MB	DualScan	$3995	NEC	8MB	340MB	Active	$2459
19	Toshiba	4MB	510MB	Active	$2459	IBM	8MB	250MB	DualScan	$3995	NEC	16MB	340MB	Mono	$3149
20	IBM	16MB	250MB	DualScan	$3995	NEC	4MB	340MB	Active	$2459	Toshiba	8MB	510MB	Mono	$3149
21	IBM	4MB	250MB	Active	$2459	NEC	16MB	340MB	Mono	$3149	Toshiba	8MB	510MB	DualScan	$3995
22	Toshiba	4MB	510MB	DualScan	$3149	NEC	8MB	250MB	Active	$2459	IBM	16MB	340MB	Mono	$3995
23	NEC	16MB	510MB	Mono	$3995	Toshiba	8MB	250MB	DualScan	$3149	IBM	4MB	340MB	Active	$2459
24	NEC	4MB	510MB	DualScan	$3149	IBM	8MB	250MB	Active	$2459	Toshiba	16MB	340MB	Mono	$3995
25	Toshiba	4MB	340MB	DualScan	$2459	NEC	8MB	510MB	Active	$2459	IBM	16MB	250MB	Mono	$3149
26	NEC	8MB	340MB	Mono	$2459	IBM	16MB	250MB	DualScan	$3995	Toshiba	4MB	510MB	Active	$3149
27	IBM	8MB	340MB	Mono	$2459	Toshiba	16MB	250MB	DualScan	$3995	NEC	4MB	510MB	Active	$3149
28	Toshiba	8MB	340MB	DualScan	$3149	NEC	16MB	510MB	Mono	$2459	IBM	4MB	510MB	Active	$3995
29	Toshiba	8MB	340MB	Active	$3149	NEC	4MB	510MB	Mono	$2459	IBM	16MB	250MB	DualScan	$3995
30	IBM	4MB	510MB	Mono	$2459	Toshiba	8MB	340MB	DualScan	$3149	NEC	16MB	250MB	Active	$3995

Partworth Values

Model	Brand Name			Memory Size				Hard Drive			Screen Type			Price Level		
	NEC	IBM	Toshiba	4MB	8MB	16MB	250MB	340MB	510MB	Mono	DualScan	Active	$3995	$3149	$2459
Self-Explicated	.009	.083	.000	.000	.130	.292	.000	.111	.250	.000	.130	.167	.000	.116	.208
Conjoint	.164	.000	.094	.023	.000	.104	.000	.036	.133	.000	.399	.454	.000	.063	.146
Choice	.040	.086	.000	.000	.102	.243	.000	.071	.136	.000	.224	.257	.000	.211	.278
Constr. Conjoint	.000	.000	.000	.000	.000	.112	.000	.043	.161	.000	.484	.550	.000	.076	.177
Constr. Choice	.040	.086	.000	.000	.102	.243	.000	.071	.136	.000	.224	.257	.000	.211	.278

Respondent No. 31

Experimental Choice Design

Set	Laptop A				Laptop B				Laptop C			
1	NEC	16MB	340MB	Mono	$2459	IBM	8MB	250MB	DualScan	$3995	Toshiba	4MB	510MB	Active	$3149
2	NEC	8MB	510MB	DualScan	$3995	IBM	16MB	250MB	Mono	$3149	Toshiba	4MB	340MB	Active	$2459
3	NEC	4MB	340MB	DualScan	$2459	IBM	16MB	510MB	Mono	$3995	Toshiba	8MB	250MB	Active	$3149
4	NEC	4MB	510MB	Active	$3149	IBM	8MB	250MB	Mono	$2459	Toshiba	16MB	340MB	DualScan	$3995
5	NEC	16MB	510MB	Mono	$3995	IBM	4MB	340MB	Active	$3149	Toshiba	8MB	250MB	DualScan	$2459
6	NEC	16MB	340MB	Mono	$2459	Toshiba	4MB	510MB	DualScan	$3995	IBM	8MB	250MB	Active	$3149
7	NEC	16MB	250MB	Active	$3995	IBM	8MB	340MB	Mono	$3149	Toshiba	4MB	510MB	DualScan	$2459
8	Toshiba	16MB	250MB	Active	$3995	IBM	4MB	510MB	Mono	$2459	NEC	8MB	340MB	DualScan	$3149
9	NEC	16MB	250MB	Active	$3995	IBM	4MB	340MB	DualScan	$3149	Toshiba	8MB	510MB	Mono	$2459
10	NEC	8MB	510MB	DualScan	$3995	IBM	4MB	340MB	Mono	$2459	Toshiba	16MB	250MB	Active	$3149
11	IBM	4MB	510MB	Active	$3995	Toshiba	16MB	250MB	DualScan	$3149	NEC	8MB	340MB	Mono	$2459
12	IBM	4MB	250MB	DualScan	$2459	Toshiba	8MB	340MB	Active	$3149	NEC	16MB	510MB	Mono	$3995
13	IBM	4MB	340MB	Active	$3149	Toshiba	8MB	510MB	Mono	$2459	NEC	16MB	250MB	DualScan	$3995
14	NEC	8MB	250MB	Active	$3149	Toshiba	16MB	340MB	Mono	$2459	IBM	4MB	510MB	DualScan	$3995
15	IBM	8MB	250MB	Active	$3995	NEC	16MB	510MB	Mono	$3149	Toshiba	4MB	340MB	DualScan	$2459
16	NEC	4MB	340MB	DualScan	$2459	Toshiba	8MB	510MB	Active	$3995	IBM	16MB	250MB	Mono	$3149
17	IBM	4MB	340MB	Active	$3995	Toshiba	8MB	250MB	DualScan	$2459	NEC	16MB	510MB	Mono	$3149
18	IBM	16MB	340MB	Mono	$3995	Toshiba	4MB	510MB	Active	$2459	NEC	8MB	250MB	DualScan	$3149
19	Toshiba	4MB	340MB	Active	$2459	IBM	16MB	510MB	Mono	$3995	NEC	8MB	250MB	DualScan	$3149
20	IBM	4MB	250MB	DualScan	$2459	Toshiba	16MB	340MB	Active	$3995	NEC	8MB	510MB	Mono	$3149
21	Toshiba	16MB	250MB	Active	$3149	NEC	4MB	510MB	Mono	$2459	IBM	8MB	340MB	DualScan	$3995
22	Toshiba	16MB	510MB	DualScan	$3995	NEC	4MB	250MB	Active	$3149	IBM	8MB	340MB	Mono	$2459
23	IBM	4MB	510MB	Active	$3995	Toshiba	16MB	250MB	Mono	$3149	NEC	8MB	340MB	DualScan	$2459
24	NEC	4MB	510MB	DualScan	$3149	IBM	8MB	250MB	Mono	$2459	Toshiba	16MB	340MB	Active	$3995
25	Toshiba	8MB	510MB	DualScan	$2459	NEC	8MB	340MB	Active	$3995	IBM	16MB	250MB	Mono	$3149
26	IBM	8MB	250MB	Mono	$2459	Toshiba	16MB	340MB	DualScan	$3995	NEC	4MB	510MB	Active	$3149
27	Toshiba	8MB	510MB	Mono	$2459	NEC	16MB	340MB	DualScan	$3995	IBM	4MB	250MB	Active	$3149
28	Toshiba	8MB	340MB	Active	$3149	NEC	16MB	250MB	Mono	$2459	IBM	4MB	510MB	DualScan	$3995
29	Toshiba	16MB	340MB	DualScan	$3149	NEC	4MB	250MB	Active	$2459	IBM	8MB	510MB	Mono	$3995
30	NEC	4MB	250MB	Active	$2459	Toshiba	8MB	510MB	DualScan	$3149	IBM	16MB	340MB	Mono	$3995

Partworth Values

Model	Brand Name			Memory Size			Hard Drive			Screen Type			Price Level		
	NEC	IBM	Toshiba	4MB	8MB	16MB	250MB	340MB	510MB	Mono	DualScan	Active	$3995	$3149	$2459
Self-Explicated	.076	.171	.000	.000	.163	.244	.000	.065	.146	.000	.171	.220	.000	.098	.220
Conjoint	.127	.050	.000	.000	.183	.320	.000	.030	.092	.000	.146	.067	.000	.125	.315
Choice	.029	.086	.000	.000	.192	.323	.000	.052	.116	.000	.143	.178	.000	.191	.298
Constr. Conjoint	.000	.000	.000	.000	.252	.439	.000	.042	.127	.000	.000	.000	.000	.172	.434
Constr. Choice	.029	.086	.000	.000	.192	.323	.000	.052	.116	.000	.143	.178	.000	.191	.298

144   Appendices

Respondent No. 32

Experimental Choice Design

Set	Laptop A					Laptop B					Laptop C				
	Brand	HD	Mem	Screen	Price	Brand	HD	Mem	Screen	Price	Brand	HD	Mem	Screen	Price
1	NEC	510MB	8MB	Mono	$2459	IBM	250MB	16MB	DualScan	$3995	Toshiba	340MB	4MB	Active	$3149
2	Toshiba	510MB	16MB	DualScan	$3995	NEC	340MB	4MB	Active	$3149	IBM	250MB	8MB	Mono	$2459
3	Toshiba	250MB	8MB	Active	$3149	IBM	510MB	16MB	Mono	$3995	NEC	340MB	4MB	DualScan	$2459
4	Toshiba	250MB	4MB	Mono	$2459	IBM	340MB	4MB	Mono	$3995	NEC	510MB	8MB	DualScan	$3149
5	Toshiba	510MB	8MB	Mono	$2459	IBM	340MB	4MB	DualScan	$3149	NEC	250MB	16MB	Active	$3995
6	NEC	510MB	16MB	Mono	$3149	Toshiba	340MB	4MB	DualScan	$2459	IBM	250MB	8MB	Active	$3995
7	NEC	250MB	4MB	Active	$2459	IBM	340MB	16MB	Mono	$3149	Toshiba	510MB	8MB	DualScan	$3995
8	NEC	340MB	8MB	Active	$3995	IBM	510MB	4MB	Mono	$2459	Toshiba	250MB	16MB	DualScan	$3149
9	IBM	250MB	8MB	Mono	$2459	NEC	340MB	4MB	Active	$3149	Toshiba	510MB	16MB	DualScan	$3995
10	Toshiba	250MB	4MB	Active	$3149	IBM	340MB	8MB	Mono	$2459	NEC	510MB	16MB	DualScan	$3995
11	IBM	510MB	4MB	DualScan	$3995	Toshiba	250MB	8MB	Active	$3149	NEC	340MB	16MB	Mono	$2459
12	IBM	250MB	4MB	DualScan	$3149	Toshiba	340MB	8MB	Active	$3995	NEC	510MB	16MB	Mono	$2459
13	IBM	250MB	4MB	Active	$3149	Toshiba	510MB	8MB	Mono	$2459	NEC	510MB	16MB	DualScan	$3995
14	NEC	250MB	8MB	Active	$3149	Toshiba	340MB	16MB	Mono	$2459	IBM	340MB	4MB	DualScan	$3995
15	Toshiba	510MB	4MB	Active	$3995	IBM	340MB	16MB	Mono	$3149	NEC	250MB	8MB	DualScan	$2459
16	Toshiba	250MB	4MB	DualScan	$2459	IBM	510MB	8MB	Mono	$3149	NEC	340MB	16MB	Active	$3995
17	IBM	340MB	4MB	Active	$3995	Toshiba	250MB	8MB	DualScan	$3149	NEC	510MB	16MB	Mono	$2459
18	Toshiba	250MB	16MB	Mono	$2459	IBM	340MB	8MB	DualScan	$3995	NEC	510MB	4MB	Active	$3149
19	IBM	510MB	4MB	Mono	$2459	Toshiba	340MB	8MB	Active	$3995	NEC	250MB	16MB	DualScan	$3149
20	Toshiba	340MB	16MB	Mono	$2459	IBM	250MB	4MB	Active	$3149	NEC	510MB	8MB	DualScan	$3995
21	Toshiba	510MB	16MB	Active	$3149	NEC	340MB	4MB	Mono	$3995	IBM	340MB	8MB	DualScan	$2459
22	IBM	510MB	8MB	DualScan	$3995	NEC	250MB	4MB	Active	$2459	IBM	340MB	16MB	Mono	$3995
23	Toshiba	250MB	16MB	Active	$3995	IBM	510MB	4MB	Mono	$2459	NEC	340MB	8MB	DualScan	$3149
24	IBM	340MB	16MB	Mono	$3149	NEC	250MB	8MB	DualScan	$2459	Toshiba	510MB	4MB	Active	$3995
25	Toshiba	340MB	4MB	DualScan	$2459	NEC	510MB	8MB	Active	$3995	IBM	250MB	16MB	Mono	$3149
26	Toshiba	250MB	4MB	DualScan	$2459	NEC	340MB	16MB	Active	$3995	IBM	510MB	8MB	Mono	$3149
27	IBM	250MB	8MB	Mono	$3149	Toshiba	340MB	16MB	DualScan	$3995	NEC	510MB	4MB	Active	$2459
28	NEC	340MB	4MB	Active	$3149	IBM	510MB	8MB	Mono	$2459	IBM	250MB	16MB	DualScan	$3995
29	Toshiba	340MB	8MB	DualScan	$3149	NEC	510MB	16MB	Mono	$2459	IBM	250MB	4MB	DualScan	$3995
30	Toshiba	510MB	8MB	Active	$3995	NEC	250MB	16MB	DualScan	$3149	IBM	340MB	4MB	Mono	$2459

Partworth Values

Model	Brand Name			Memory Size			Hard Drive			Screen Type			Price Level		
	NEC	IBM	Toshiba	4MB	8MB	16MB	250MB	340MB	510MB	Mono	DualScan	Active	$3995	$3149	$2459
Self-Explicated	.000	.152	.034	.000	.101	.182	.000	.067	.121	.000	.202	.303	.000	.108	.242
Conjoint	.146	.000	.016	.000	.046	.206	.000	.054	.014	.000	.414	.386	.000	.082	.180
Choice	.000	.016	.005	.012	.157	.000	.023	.018	.000	.000	.396	.365	.000	.408	.360
Constr. Conjoint	.000	.000	.000	.000	.058	.263	.000	.000	.000	.000	.509	.509	.000	.104	.228
Constr. Choice	.000	.105	.013	.000	.125	.125	.000	.030	.039	.000	.371	.387	.000	.320	.344

Respondent No. 33

Experimental Choice Design

Set		Laptop A					Laptop B					Laptop C			
1	NEC	510MB	8MB	Mono	$2459	IBM	250MB	16MB	DualScan	$3995	Toshiba	340MB	4MB	Active	$3149
2	NEC	510MB	8MB	DualScan	$3995	Toshiba	250MB	16MB	Active	$3149	IBM	340MB	4MB	Mono	$2459
3	Toshiba	340MB	4MB	Active	$2459	IBM	510MB	16MB	Mono	$3995	NEC	250MB	8MB	DualScan	$3149
4	NEC	510MB	4MB	Active	$3995	IBM	250MB	16MB	DualScan	$2459	Toshiba	340MB	8MB	DualScan	$3149
5	NEC	510MB	16MB	Mono	$3995	IBM	340MB	4MB	DualScan	$3149	Toshiba	250MB	8MB	Active	$2459
6	NEC	340MB	16MB	Mono	$2459	IBM	250MB	4MB	DualScan	$3149	Toshiba	510MB	8MB	Active	$3995
7	NEC	510MB	4MB	Active	$3995	IBM	340MB	16MB	Mono	$3149	Toshiba	250MB	8MB	DualScan	$2459
8	NEC	250MB	16MB	DualScan	$3995	IBM	510MB	4MB	Mono	$2459	Toshiba	340MB	8MB	DualScan	$3149
9	NEC	250MB	4MB	Mono	$2459	IBM	340MB	8MB	Active	$3149	Toshiba	510MB	16MB	DualScan	$3995
10	NEC	250MB	4MB	Active	$2459	IBM	340MB	8MB	Mono	$3149	Toshiba	510MB	16MB	DualScan	$3995
11	IBM	510MB	4MB	DualScan	$3995	Toshiba	250MB	16MB	Active	$3149	NEC	340MB	8MB	Mono	$2459
12	IBM	250MB	4MB	DualScan	$2459	Toshiba	340MB	16MB	Active	$3995	NEC	510MB	8MB	Mono	$3149
13	NEC	340MB	4MB	Active	$3149	IBM	510MB	8MB	Mono	$2459	Toshiba	250MB	16MB	DualScan	$3995
14	IBM	250MB	4MB	Mono	$3149	NEC	340MB	16MB	DualScan	$2459	Toshiba	510MB	8MB	Active	$3995
15	IBM	510MB	8MB	Mono	$3995	Toshiba	340MB	4MB	DualScan	$3149	NEC	250MB	16MB	Active	$2459
16	IBM	340MB	8MB	Mono	$2459	Toshiba	510MB	4MB	Active	$3995	NEC	250MB	16MB	DualScan	$3149
17	IBM	510MB	4MB	Mono	$2459	Toshiba	250MB	8MB	DualScan	$3149	NEC	340MB	16MB	Active	$3995
18	IBM	250MB	16MB	DualScan	$2459	NEC	340MB	4MB	Active	$3995	Toshiba	510MB	8MB	DualScan	$3149
19	Toshiba	510MB	16MB	Mono	$2459	IBM	250MB	8MB	DualScan	$3995	NEC	340MB	4MB	Active	$3149
20	IBM	250MB	16MB	Active	$3995	Toshiba	340MB	4MB	Mono	$2459	NEC	510MB	8MB	DualScan	$3149
21	NEC	340MB	16MB	DualScan	$3995	IBM	250MB	4MB	Active	$3149	Toshiba	510MB	8MB	Mono	$2459
22	NEC	510MB	16MB	Mono	$2459	Toshiba	250MB	4MB	Active	$3149	IBM	340MB	8MB	Active	$3995
23	Toshiba	510MB	16MB	DualScan	$3995	NEC	250MB	8MB	Active	$2459	IBM	340MB	8MB	Mono	$3149
24	IBM	340MB	4MB	Mono	$2459	NEC	250MB	8MB	DualScan	$3149	Toshiba	510MB	16MB	Active	$3995
25	Toshiba	250MB	4MB	Active	$2459	NEC	510MB	8MB	DualScan	$3995	IBM	340MB	16MB	Mono	$3149
26	IBM	250MB	16MB	Mono	$2459	NEC	510MB	8MB	Active	$3995	Toshiba	340MB	4MB	Mono	$3149
27	Toshiba	510MB	8MB	Mono	$3149	IBM	340MB	16MB	Active	$3995	NEC	250MB	4MB	DualScan	$3149
28	Toshiba	510MB	4MB	Active	$2459	IBM	340MB	16MB	Mono	$3149	NEC	250MB	8MB	DualScan	$3995
29	Toshiba	250MB	8MB	DualScan	$2459	IBM	510MB	16MB	Mono	$2459	IBM	340MB	4MB	Active	$3995
30	IBM	250MB	8MB	Mono	$2459	Toshiba	510MB	4MB	DualScan	$3149	NEC	340MB	16MB	Active	$3995

Partworth Values

Model	Brand Name			Memory Size			Hard Drive			Screen Type			Price Level		
	NEC	IBM	Toshiba	4MB	8MB	16MB	250MB	340MB	510MB	Mono	DualScan	Active	$3995	$3149	$2459
Self-Explicated	.070	.158	.000	.000	.123	.158	.000	.082	.184	.000	.205	.263	.000	.158	.237
Conjoint	.102	.000	.081	.044	.000	.139	.040	.000	.007	.000	.444	.562	.000	.059	.157
Choice	.000	.000	.000	.000	.000	.000	.000	.000	.000	.000	.000	1.000	.000	.000	.000
Constr. Conjoint	.000	.000	.000	.000	.000	.140	.000	.000	.000	.000	.530	.672	.000	.071	.188
Constr. Choice	.000	.000	.000	.000	.000	.000	.000	.000	.000	.000	.000	1.000	.000	.000	.000

146   *Appendices*

Respondent No. 34

Experimental Choice Design

Set			Laptop A					Laptop B					Laptop C			
1	NEC	8MB	510MB	DualScan	$2459	IBM	16MB	250MB	Mono	$3995	Toshiba	4MB	340MB	Active	$3149
2	IBM	8MB	510MB	Mono	$3149	NEC	16MB	250MB	DualScan	$3995	Toshiba	4MB	340MB	Active	$2459
3	NEC	8MB	340MB	Active	$3149	IBM	16MB	250MB	Mono	$3995	Toshiba	4MB	510MB	DualScan	$2459
4	NEC	4MB	510MB	Active	$2459	IBM	16MB	340MB	Mono	$3995	Toshiba	8MB	250MB	DualScan	$3149
5	NEC	16MB	250MB	Mono	$2459	IBM	4MB	510MB	DualScan	$3149	Toshiba	8MB	340MB	Active	$3995
6	NEC	16MB	340MB	Mono	$3149	Toshiba	4MB	510MB	DualScan	$2459	IBM	8MB	250MB	Active	$3995
7	NEC	16MB	250MB	Active	$3995	Toshiba	8MB	510MB	Mono	$3149	IBM	4MB	340MB	DualScan	$2459
8	NEC	16MB	340MB	Active	$3995	IBM	4MB	510MB	Mono	$3149	Toshiba	8MB	250MB	DualScan	$2459
9	IBM	4MB	510MB	DualScan	$3995	NEC	8MB	340MB	Active	$3149	Toshiba	16MB	250MB	Mono	$2459
10	IBM	4MB	340MB	DualScan	$2459	Toshiba	8MB	250MB	Active	$3995	NEC	16MB	510MB	Mono	$3149
11	IBM	4MB	510MB	DualScan	$2459	Toshiba	16MB	250MB	Mono	$3995	NEC	8MB	340MB	Active	$3149
12	IBM	8MB	510MB	Mono	$3995	Toshiba	4MB	340MB	Active	$3149	NEC	16MB	250MB	DualScan	$2459
13	IBM	4MB	340MB	Active	$3995	Toshiba	8MB	510MB	Mono	$2459	NEC	16MB	250MB	DualScan	$3149
14	Toshiba	8MB	250MB	Active	$3149	IBM	4MB	510MB	Mono	$2459	NEC	16MB	340MB	DualScan	$3995
15	IBM	16MB	340MB	Mono	$3995	Toshiba	4MB	510MB	DualScan	$3149	NEC	8MB	250MB	Active	$2459
16	Toshiba	16MB	340MB	DualScan	$3995	IBM	4MB	510MB	Active	$2459	NEC	8MB	250MB	Mono	$3149
17	IBM	4MB	510MB	Active	$3995	Toshiba	8MB	250MB	DualScan	$3149	NEC	16MB	340MB	Mono	$2459
18	Toshiba	16MB	250MB	Mono	$2459	IBM	4MB	340MB	DualScan	$3149	NEC	8MB	510MB	Active	$3995
19	NEC	16MB	340MB	Mono	$2459	IBM	4MB	510MB	Active	$2459	Toshiba	8MB	250MB	DualScan	$3995
20	Toshiba	8MB	250MB	DualScan	$2459	IBM	4MB	340MB	Active	$3995	NEC	16MB	510MB	Mono	$3149
21	Toshiba	16MB	340MB	Active	$3995	NEC	4MB	510MB	Mono	$3149	IBM	8MB	340MB	DualScan	$2459
22	Toshiba	4MB	510MB	DualScan	$3149	NEC	16MB	250MB	Active	$3995	IBM	8MB	340MB	Mono	$2459
23	Toshiba	16MB	510MB	DualScan	$3995	NEC	4MB	250MB	Mono	$3149	IBM	8MB	340MB	Active	$2459
24	IBM	4MB	510MB	Mono	$2459	NEC	16MB	250MB	DualScan	$3149	Toshiba	8MB	340MB	Active	$3995
25	Toshiba	4MB	340MB	DualScan	$2459	NEC	8MB	510MB	Active	$3995	IBM	16MB	250MB	Mono	$3149
26	Toshiba	8MB	510MB	Mono	$2459	NEC	16MB	340MB	DualScan	$3995	IBM	4MB	250MB	Active	$3149
27	IBM	4MB	340MB	Mono	$3149	NEC	16MB	250MB	DualScan	$2459	Toshiba	4MB	510MB	Active	$3995
28	Toshiba	4MB	250MB	Active	$2459	NEC	16MB	510MB	DualScan	$3149	IBM	8MB	340MB	Mono	$3995
29	IBM	8MB	250MB	DualScan	$3149	NEC	4MB	510MB	Active	$2459	Toshiba	16MB	340MB	Mono	$3995
30	Toshiba	16MB	340MB	Mono	$3995	NEC	8MB	510MB	DualScan	$3149	IBM	4MB	250MB	Active	$2459

Partworth Values

Model	Brand Name			Memory Size				Hard Drive			Screen Type			Price Level		
	NEC	IBM	Toshiba	4MB	8MB	16MB	250MB	340MB	510MB	Mono	DualScan	Active	$3995	$3149	$2459
Self-Explicated	.000	.187	.146	.000	.139	.313	.000	.069	.156	.000	.146	.219	.000	.097	.125
Conjoint	.000	.256	.232	.000	.227	.448	.097	.002	.000	.036	.023	.000	.163	.079	.000
Choice	.000	.152	.158	.000	.530	.577	.000	.019	.061	.000	.091	.175	.010	.000	.029
Constr. Conjoint	.000	.364	.329	.000	.322	.636	.000	.000	.000	.000	.000	.000	.000	.000	.000
Constr. Choice	.000	.157	.157	.000	.513	.569	.000	.022	.067	.000	.095	.182	.000	.000	.025

Appendices   147

Respondent No. 35

Experimental Choice Design

Set	Laptop A					Laptop B					Laptop C				
1	NEC	8MB	510MB	Mono	$3149	IBM	16MB	250MB	DualScan	$3995	Toshiba	4MB	340MB	Active	$2459
2	NEC	8MB	510MB	DualScan	$3995	IBM	16MB	250MB	Mono	$2459	Toshiba	4MB	340MB	Active	$3149
3	NEC	8MB	250MB	Active	$2459	Toshiba	16MB	340MB	DualScan	$3995	IBM	4MB	510MB	Mono	$3149
4	NEC	4MB	510MB	Active	$3995	IBM	16MB	250MB	Mono	$2459	Toshiba	8MB	340MB	DualScan	$3149
5	NEC	16MB	340MB	Mono	$3149	IBM	4MB	510MB	Active	$3995	Toshiba	8MB	250MB	DualScan	$2459
6	NEC	16MB	340MB	Mono	$3995	Toshiba	16MB	510MB	DualScan	$2459	IBM	8MB	250MB	Active	$3149
7	Toshiba	16MB	250MB	Active	$3149	IBM	8MB	340MB	Mono	$3149	NEC	4MB	510MB	DualScan	$3995
8	NEC	16MB	340MB	DualScan	$3995	IBM	4MB	510MB	Mono	$2459	Toshiba	8MB	250MB	Active	$2459
9	NEC	16MB	340MB	DualScan	$3995	IBM	8MB	340MB	Active	$3149	Toshiba	4MB	510MB	Mono	$2459
10	NEC	4MB	250MB	DualScan	$3995	Toshiba	8MB	340MB	Active	$2459	IBM	16MB	510MB	Mono	$3149
11	NEC	8MB	510MB	DualScan	$3149	NEC	16MB	340MB	Active	$2459	Toshiba	16MB	250MB	Mono	$3995
12	IBM	4MB	510MB	DualScan	$3995	Toshiba	16MB	250MB	Active	$3149	NEC	8MB	340MB	Mono	$2459
13	IBM	8MB	250MB	DualScan	$2459	Toshiba	4MB	340MB	Active	$3149	NEC	16MB	510MB	Mono	$3995
14	IBM	4MB	340MB	Active	$3149	Toshiba	8MB	510MB	Mono	$3995	NEC	16MB	250MB	DualScan	$2459
15	IBM	8MB	250MB	Active	$3995	NEC	16MB	340MB	Mono	$2459	Toshiba	4MB	510MB	DualScan	$2459
16	IBM	8MB	510MB	Mono	$3995	Toshiba	16MB	250MB	DualScan	$3149	NEC	4MB	340MB	Active	$2459
17	IBM	16MB	250MB	Active	$2459	Toshiba	8MB	510MB	DualScan	$3995	NEC	4MB	340MB	Active	$3149
18	NEC	4MB	510MB	Mono	$3995	IBM	8MB	250MB	DualScan	$3995	Toshiba	16MB	340MB	Active	$3149
19	Toshiba	16MB	250MB	Mono	$2459	IBM	16MB	340MB	Active	$2459	NEC	4MB	510MB	DualScan	$3149
20	IBM	4MB	510MB	DualScan	$3149	NEC	4MB	340MB	Active	$3149	Toshiba	8MB	340MB	Mono	$3995
21	IBM	16MB	250MB	Active	$3995	NEC	8MB	340MB	Mono	$2459	Toshiba	4MB	340MB	DualScan	$2459
22	Toshiba	4MB	510MB	DualScan	$2459	NEC	8MB	250MB	Active	$3149	IBM	16MB	340MB	Mono	$3995
23	Toshiba	8MB	510MB	Active	$2459	NEC	4MB	250MB	Mono	$3995	IBM	16MB	340MB	DualScan	$2459
24	IBM	8MB	510MB	Mono	$3149	NEC	4MB	250MB	Active	$2459	Toshiba	16MB	340MB	DualScan	$2459
25	Toshiba	4MB	510MB	Mono	$2459	NEC	8MB	340MB	DualScan	$3995	IBM	16MB	250MB	DualScan	$3995
26	IBM	8MB	250MB	Mono	$2459	Toshiba	16MB	340MB	DualScan	$3995	NEC	4MB	510MB	Active	$3149
27	Toshiba	8MB	250MB	DualScan	$2459	NEC	16MB	510MB	Mono	$3995	IBM	4MB	340MB	Active	$3149
28	IBM	8MB	340MB	Mono	$3149	NEC	16MB	250MB	Active	$2459	IBM	4MB	510MB	DualScan	$3995
29	Toshiba	8MB	340MB	Mono	$2459	NEC	16MB	250MB	Active	$3149	IBM	4MB	510MB	DualScan	$3995
30	IBM	4MB	340MB	Mono	$3995	NEC	8MB	510MB	DualScan	$2459	Toshiba	16MB	250MB	Active	$3149

Partworth Values

Model	Brand Name			Memory Size			Hard Drive			Screen Type			Price Level		
	NEC	IBM	Toshiba	4MB	8MB	16MB	250MB	340MB	510MB	Mono	DualScan	Active	$3995	$3149	$2459
Self-Explicated	.000	.118	.078	.000	.176	.265	.000	.147	.265	.000	.092	.206	.000	.098	.147
Conjoint	.095	.030	.000	.000	.420	.353	.000	.096	.222	.000	.058	.109	.000	.060	.155
Choice	.134	.000	.023	.000	.292	.321	.000	.147	.108	.139	.167	.000	.000	.079	.231
Constr. Conjoint	.000	.000	.000	.000	.443	.443	.000	.110	.255	.000	.067	.125	.000	.069	.177
Constr. Choice	.000	.000	.000	.000	.389	.442	.000	.184	.240	.000	.063	.080	.000	.148	.238

Respondent No. 36

Experimental Choice Design

Set	Laptop A					Laptop B					Laptop C				
1	NEC	8MB	510MB	Mono	$2459	IBM	16MB	250MB	DualScan	$3995	Toshiba	4MB	340MB	Active	$3149
2	NEC	8MB	340MB	DualScan	$3995	IBM	16MB	250MB	Active	$3149	Toshiba	4MB	510MB	Mono	$2459
3	IBM	4MB	340MB	Active	$2459	Toshiba	8MB	510MB	Mono	$3995	NEC	16MB	250MB	DualScan	$3149
4	NEC	4MB	510MB	Active	$2459	Toshiba	8MB	340MB	Mono	$3149	IBM	16MB	250MB	DualScan	$3995
5	NEC	4MB	340MB	Mono	$3995	IBM	4MB	510MB	DualScan	$3149	Toshiba	8MB	250MB	Active	$2459
6	NEC	16MB	340MB	Mono	$3995	IBM	8MB	510MB	DualScan	$2459	Toshiba	8MB	250MB	Active	$3149
7	NEC	16MB	250MB	Active	$3995	IBM	8MB	340MB	Mono	$2459	Toshiba	4MB	510MB	DualScan	$3149
8	NEC	16MB	250MB	Active	$3149	Toshiba	4MB	340MB	DualScan	$2459	IBM	8MB	510MB	Mono	$3995
9	IBM	4MB	250MB	Active	$2459	NEC	8MB	340MB	DualScan	$3149	Toshiba	16MB	510MB	Mono	$3149
10	Toshiba	4MB	510MB	Active	$3995	IBM	8MB	250MB	DualScan	$2459	NEC	16MB	340MB	Mono	$3149
11	NEC	4MB	510MB	DualScan	$3995	IBM	8MB	340MB	Mono	$2459	Toshiba	4MB	340MB	Active	$3149
12	Toshiba	4MB	250MB	Active	$2459	IBM	16MB	340MB	DualScan	$3995	NEC	16MB	510MB	Mono	$3149
13	NEC	4MB	340MB	Active	$2459	Toshiba	8MB	510MB	Mono	$3995	IBM	16MB	250MB	DualScan	$3149
14	Toshiba	8MB	250MB	Active	$3149	IBM	16MB	340MB	Mono	$3995	NEC	4MB	510MB	DualScan	$2459
15	Toshiba	8MB	340MB	Mono	$3995	IBM	16MB	250MB	DualScan	$3149	NEC	4MB	510MB	Active	$2459
16	IBM	8MB	250MB	DualScan	$2459	Toshiba	4MB	510MB	Active	$3995	NEC	16MB	340MB	Mono	$3149
17	NEC	16MB	510MB	Mono	$3995	Toshiba	8MB	250MB	DualScan	$3149	IBM	4MB	340MB	Active	$2459
18	NEC	16MB	250MB	Mono	$2459	NEC	8MB	340MB	DualScan	$3149	IBM	4MB	510MB	Active	$3995
19	IBM	4MB	510MB	Active	$3149	Toshiba	16MB	250MB	Mono	$2459	NEC	8MB	340MB	DualScan	$3995
20	NEC	16MB	250MB	Active	$3995	Toshiba	4MB	340MB	DualScan	$2459	IBM	8MB	510MB	Mono	$3149
21	Toshiba	16MB	250MB	DualScan	$3149	NEC	8MB	510MB	Mono	$2459	IBM	4MB	340MB	Active	$3995
22	Toshiba	8MB	250MB	Active	$3149	NEC	4MB	510MB	DualScan	$2459	IBM	8MB	340MB	Mono	$3995
23	NEC	16MB	510MB	Active	$3995	IBM	8MB	250MB	Mono	$3149	Toshiba	8MB	340MB	DualScan	$2459
24	Toshiba	4MB	510MB	DualScan	$3149	NEC	8MB	250MB	Active	$2459	IBM	16MB	340MB	Mono	$3995
25	Toshiba	4MB	340MB	DualScan	$2459	NEC	8MB	510MB	Mono	$3149	IBM	16MB	250MB	Active	$3995
26	Toshiba	4MB	250MB	Mono	$2459	NEC	8MB	340MB	Active	$3995	IBM	16MB	250MB	DualScan	$3149
27	IBM	16MB	250MB	Mono	$2459	NEC	8MB	510MB	DualScan	$3995	Toshiba	4MB	340MB	Active	$3149
28	IBM	8MB	510MB	Mono	$3149	NEC	16MB	250MB	DualScan	$2459	Toshiba	4MB	340MB	Active	$3995
29	Toshiba	16MB	340MB	DualScan	$3149	IBM	8MB	510MB	Active	$2459	NEC	4MB	250MB	Mono	$3995
30	NEC	4MB	510MB	DualScan	$2459	IBM	8MB	340MB	Mono	$3149	Toshiba	16MB	250MB	Active	$3995

Partworth Values

Model	Brand Name			Memory Size			Hard Drive			Screen Type			Price Level		
	NEC	IBM	Toshiba	4MB	8MB	16MB	250MB	340MB	510MB	Mono	DualScan	Active	$3995	$3149	$2459
Self-Explicated	.000	.054	.097	.000	.215	.323	.000	.201	.258	.000	.151	.194	.000	.057	.129
Conjoint	.201	.000	.060	.000	.223	.284	.000	.131	.072	.000	.131	.222	.009	.000	.163
Choice	.000	.064	.038	.000	.354	.413	.000	.098	.124	.000	.170	.218	.000	.182	.170
Constr. Conjoint	.000	.000	.000	.000	.292	.371	.000	.132	.132	.000	.171	.290	.000	.000	.207
Constr. Choice	.000	.064	.038	.000	.354	.413	.000	.098	.124	.000	.170	.218	.000	.182	.170

Appendices

Respondent No. 37

Experimental Choice Design

Set	Laptop A				Laptop B				Laptop C			
1	NEC	510MB	8MB	Mono	$2459	Toshiba	250MB	16MB	DualScan	$3149	IBM	340MB	4MB	Active	$3995
2	NEC	510MB	8MB	DualScan	$3995	Toshiba	340MB	16MB	Mono	$3149	IBM	250MB	4MB	Active	$2459
3	NEC	250MB	8MB	Active	$2459	IBM	340MB	16MB	Mono	$3995	Toshiba	510MB	4MB	DualScan	$3149
4	IBM	340MB	4MB	Active	$2459	NEC	510MB	8MB	Mono	$3149	Toshiba	250MB	16MB	DualScan	$3995
5	NEC	340MB	16MB	Mono	$3995	NEC	510MB	4MB	DualScan	$3149	IBM	250MB	8MB	Active	$2459
6	Toshiba	340MB	16MB	Mono	$3995	NEC	510MB	4MB	DualScan	$2459	IBM	250MB	8MB	Active	$3149
7	NEC	250MB	16MB	Active	$3995	IBM	340MB	8MB	Mono	$2459	Toshiba	510MB	4MB	DualScan	$3149
8	NEC	340MB	8MB	Active	$3149	IBM	510MB	4MB	Active	$3149	Toshiba	250MB	16MB	DualScan	$3995
9	NEC	510MB	8MB	DualScan	$3995	IBM	340MB	4MB	DualScan	$2459	Toshiba	250MB	16MB	Mono	$3995
10	NEC	250MB	16MB	Active	$3149	Toshiba	340MB	8MB	Mono	$2459	IBM	510MB	4MB	Mono	$2459
11	NEC	510MB	8MB	DualScan	$3995	Toshiba	340MB	16MB	DualScan	$2459	IBM	250MB	4MB	Active	$3995
12	Toshiba	340MB	4MB	Active	$3149	IBM	340MB	8MB	Mono	$2459	NEC	510MB	16MB	Mono	$3995
13	IBM	340MB	4MB	DualScan	$2459	NEC	250MB	8MB	DualScan	$3149	Toshiba	510MB	16MB	DualScan	$2459
14	IBM	250MB	8MB	Active	$3149	NEC	340MB	16MB	Mono	$3995	Toshiba	510MB	4MB	Mono	$3149
15	IBM	340MB	8MB	Active	$3995	IBM	250MB	16MB	DualScan	$2459	NEC	510MB	4MB	Mono	$3149
16	Toshiba	250MB	16MB	DualScan	$3995	IBM	340MB	4MB	Active	$3149	NEC	510MB	8MB	Mono	$3149
17	Toshiba	510MB	4MB	Mono	$3995	IBM	340MB	8MB	DualScan	$2459	NEC	510MB	16MB	Active	$3995
18	IBM	250MB	16MB	Active	$2459	Toshiba	340MB	8MB	DualScan	$3149	NEC	510MB	4MB	DualScan	$3149
19	Toshiba	510MB	8MB	Active	$3995	IBM	250MB	4MB	Mono	$2459	NEC	340MB	16MB	DualScan	$2459
20	IBM	250MB	16MB	DualScan	$3995	NEC	340MB	4MB	Active	$2459	Toshiba	510MB	8MB	Mono	$3149
21	Toshiba	340MB	8MB	Active	$3995	IBM	250MB	16MB	Mono	$3149	NEC	510MB	4MB	DualScan	$2459
22	IBM	250MB	16MB	DualScan	$3995	NEC	340MB	4MB	Active	$2459	Toshiba	510MB	8MB	Mono	$3149
23	IBM	250MB	16MB	DualScan	$3995	IBM	510MB	8MB	Mono	$3149	Toshiba	340MB	4MB	Active	$2459
24	Toshiba	510MB	4MB	DualScan	$3149	NEC	250MB	8MB	Active	$2459	IBM	340MB	16MB	Mono	$3995
25	NEC	340MB	4MB	Active	$2459	IBM	510MB	8MB	DualScan	$3995	IBM	250MB	16MB	Mono	$3149
26	Toshiba	250MB	8MB	Mono	$2459	NEC	340MB	16MB	DualScan	$3995	IBM	510MB	4MB	Active	$3149
27	Toshiba	250MB	8MB	Active	$2459	NEC	340MB	16MB	Mono	$3149	IBM	510MB	4MB	DualScan	$3995
28	Toshiba	340MB	8MB	DualScan	$3149	NEC	250MB	16MB	Mono	$2459	IBM	510MB	4MB	Active	$3995
29	IBM	340MB	8MB	DualScan	$3149	IBM	510MB	4MB	Mono	$3995	NEC	250MB	16MB	Mono	$2459
30	IBM	340MB	8MB	DualScan	$3995	NEC	4MB	510MB	Active	$3149	Toshiba	250MB	16MB	Mono	$2459

Partworth Values

Model	Brand Name			Memory Size			Hard Drive			Screen Type			Price Level		
	NEC	IBM	Toshiba	4MB	8MB	16MB	250MB	340MB	510MB	Mono	DualScan	Active	$3995	$3149	$2459
Self-Explicated	.000	.065	.036	.000	.143	.323	.000	.115	.258	.000	.129	.194	.000	.072	.161
Conjoint	.047	.059	.000	.000	.338	.605	.000	.065	.158	.000	.095	.106	.000	.029	.072
Choice	.015	.030	.000	.000	.254	.441	.000	.145	.160	.000	.128	.190	.000	.091	.179
Constr. Conjoint	.000	.036	.000	.000	.346	.619	.000	.066	.162	.000	.097	.108	.000	.029	.074
Constr. Choice	.000	.000	.000	.000	.482	.716	.000	.000	.000	.000	.080	.243	.000	.041	.041

Respondent No. 38

Experimental Choice Design

Set	Laptop A				Laptop B				Laptop C			
1	Toshiba	8MB	510MB	Mono	$3995	IBM	16MB	250MB	DualScan	$3149	NEC	4MB	340MB	Active	$2459
2	NEC	8MB	510MB	DualScan	$3995	Toshiba	16MB	340MB	Mono	$3149	IBM	4MB	250MB	Active	$2459
3	IBM	4MB	340MB	Active	$2459	NEC	8MB	510MB	Mono	$3995	Toshiba	16MB	250MB	DualScan	$3149
4	NEC	4MB	250MB	Active	$2459	Toshiba	16MB	510MB	Mono	$3995	IBM	8MB	340MB	DualScan	$3149
5	IBM	16MB	340MB	Mono	$3995	NEC	4MB	510MB	Active	$3149	Toshiba	8MB	250MB	DualScan	$2459
6	NEC	8MB	510MB	Mono	$3995	Toshiba	4MB	340MB	DualScan	$2459	IBM	16MB	250MB	Active	$3995
7	IBM	16MB	250MB	Active	$3995	Toshiba	8MB	510MB	Mono	$3149	NEC	4MB	340MB	DualScan	$2459
8	NEC	4MB	340MB	DualScan	$3149	IBM	8MB	340MB	Mono	$2459	Toshiba	4MB	250MB	Active	$3995
9	NEC	16MB	510MB	DualScan	$3149	Toshiba	8MB	340MB	Active	$3995	IBM	16MB	250MB	Mono	$2459
10	NEC	16MB	250MB	DualScan	$3149	IBM	4MB	340MB	Mono	$2459	Toshiba	8MB	510MB	Mono	$2459
11	Toshiba	8MB	250MB	Active	$3995	NEC	16MB	250MB	Mono	$3149	IBM	4MB	340MB	DualScan	$3995
12	NEC	8MB	510MB	Active	$3149	Toshiba	4MB	340MB	DualScan	$2459	IBM	16MB	510MB	Mono	$3995
13	NEC	4MB	510MB	Active	$3149	Toshiba	8MB	250MB	DualScan	$2459	IBM	16MB	340MB	Mono	$3995
14	IBM	8MB	250MB	Active	$3149	Toshiba	16MB	340MB	DualScan	$3995	NEC	4MB	510MB	Mono	$2459
15	NEC	4MB	510MB	Active	$3149	Toshiba	16MB	340MB	Mono	$3995	IBM	8MB	250MB	DualScan	$2459
16	Toshiba	16MB	340MB	DualScan	$3995	NEC	4MB	250MB	Active	$2459	IBM	8MB	510MB	Mono	$3149
17	IBM	16MB	510MB	Mono	$3995	NEC	8MB	250MB	DualScan	$3149	Toshiba	4MB	340MB	Active	$2459
18	IBM	16MB	250MB	Mono	$3149	NEC	4MB	340MB	Active	$2459	Toshiba	8MB	510MB	DualScan	$3995
19	IBM	4MB	510MB	DualScan	$2459	Toshiba	16MB	250MB	Active	$3995	NEC	8MB	340MB	Mono	$3149
20	Toshiba	16MB	250MB	Active	$3995	IBM	4MB	510MB	DualScan	$2459	NEC	8MB	340MB	Mono	$3149
21	IBM	16MB	250MB	Active	$3995	Toshiba	8MB	340MB	DualScan	$3149	NEC	4MB	510MB	Mono	$2459
22	Toshiba	8MB	510MB	Active	$3995	NEC	4MB	340MB	DualScan	$2459	NEC	16MB	340MB	Mono	$3149
23	IBM	8MB	510MB	DualScan	$3995	Toshiba	16MB	250MB	Active	$3149	NEC	4MB	340MB	Mono	$2459
24	IBM	4MB	510MB	Active	$3149	NEC	8MB	250MB	Mono	$2459	Toshiba	16MB	340MB	DualScan	$3995
25	Toshiba	4MB	510MB	Active	$2459	NEC	8MB	340MB	Active	$3995	IBM	16MB	250MB	DualScan	$3149
26	NEC	8MB	250MB	Mono	$2459	IBM	16MB	340MB	DualScan	$3995	Toshiba	4MB	510MB	Active	$3149
27	Toshiba	8MB	250MB	Mono	$2459	NEC	16MB	340MB	DualScan	$3995	IBM	4MB	510MB	Active	$3149
28	Toshiba	8MB	340MB	DualScan	$3149	NEC	16MB	250MB	Mono	$2459	IBM	4MB	510MB	Active	$3995
29	IBM	8MB	340MB	Mono	$3149	Toshiba	4MB	510MB	DualScan	$2459	NEC	16MB	250MB	Active	$3995
30	IBM	8MB	340MB	Active	$3995	NEC	4MB	510MB	DualScan	$2459	Toshiba	16MB	250MB	Mono	$3149

Partworth Values

Model	Brand Name			Memory Size			Hard Drive			Screen Type			Price Level		
	NEC	IBM	Toshiba	4MB	8MB	16MB	250MB	340MB	510MB	Mono	DualScan	Active	$3995	$3149	$2459
Self-Explicated	.033	.022	.000	.000	.222	.333	.000	.133	.200	.000	.093	.167	.000	.119	.267
Conjoint	.136	.006	.000	.000	.411	.578	.018	.011	.000	.008	.000	.079	.000	.130	.190
Choice	.039	.000	.013	.000	.318	.450	.000	.087	.096	.000	.015	.126	.000	.146	.288
Constr. Conjoint	.139	.006	.000	.000	.421	.591	.000	.000	.000	.000	.000	.076	.000	.133	.194
Constr. Choice	.031	.000	.000	.000	.285	.440	.000	.074	.099	.000	.031	.111	.000	.161	.319

Respondent No. 39

Experimental Choice Design

Set	Laptop A					Laptop B					Laptop C				
1	NEC	8MB	510MB	Mono	$3149	Toshiba	16MB	250MB	DualScan	$3995	IBM	4MB	340MB	Active	$2459
2	NEC	16MB	510MB	DualScan	$3995	IBM	8MB	250MB	Active	$3149	Toshiba	4MB	340MB	Mono	$2459
3	NEC	8MB	340MB	DualScan	$3149	IBM	16MB	510MB	Mono	$3995	Toshiba	4MB	250MB	Active	$2459
4	NEC	4MB	510MB	Active	$3149	Toshiba	8MB	250MB	Mono	$2459	IBM	16MB	340MB	DualScan	$3995
5	NEC	16MB	340MB	Mono	$3995	IBM	4MB	510MB	Mono	$3149	Toshiba	8MB	250MB	DualScan	$2459
6	NEC	16MB	340MB	Active	$3149	IBM	4MB	510MB	DualScan	$2459	Toshiba	8MB	250MB	Active	$3995
7	Toshiba	16MB	250MB	Active	$3995	IBM	8MB	340MB	Mono	$3149	NEC	4MB	510MB	DualScan	$2459
8	NEC	16MB	340MB	Mono	$3995	IBM	4MB	510MB	Mono	$3149	IBM	8MB	250MB	DualScan	$2459
9	NEC	4MB	250MB	Mono	$3995	Toshiba	8MB	510MB	Active	$2459	Toshiba	16MB	340MB	DualScan	$3149
10	Toshiba	4MB	510MB	Mono	$3149	NEC	8MB	340MB	DualScan	$2459	IBM	16MB	250MB	Active	$3995
11	Toshiba	8MB	510MB	DualScan	$3995	IBM	16MB	250MB	Mono	$2459	NEC	4MB	340MB	Active	$3149
12	NEC	16MB	250MB	Active	$3149	Toshiba	4MB	340MB	Mono	$2459	IBM	8MB	510MB	DualScan	$3995
13	IBM	4MB	340MB	Active	$3149	Toshiba	8MB	510MB	Mono	$3995	NEC	16MB	250MB	DualScan	$2459
14	IBM	8MB	250MB	Active	$3149	Toshiba	16MB	340MB	Mono	$3995	NEC	4MB	510MB	DualScan	$2459
15	IBM	8MB	340MB	Mono	$3149	Toshiba	4MB	250MB	Active	$3995	NEC	8MB	510MB	DualScan	$2459
16	IBM	16MB	250MB	DualScan	$3149	Toshiba	4MB	510MB	Active	$3995	NEC	8MB	340MB	Mono	$2459
17	IBM	4MB	510MB	Mono	$2459	Toshiba	8MB	250MB	DualScan	$3149	NEC	16MB	340MB	Active	$3995
18	NEC	16MB	250MB	Mono	$2459	Toshiba	4MB	340MB	DualScan	$3149	IBM	8MB	510MB	Active	$3995
19	IBM	4MB	510MB	Mono	$2459	Toshiba	16MB	250MB	Active	$3995	NEC	8MB	340MB	DualScan	$3149
20	IBM	16MB	250MB	DualScan	$3149	Toshiba	8MB	340MB	Active	$3995	NEC	4MB	510MB	Mono	$2459
21	Toshiba	16MB	250MB	Active	$3149	NEC	4MB	510MB	Mono	$3995	IBM	8MB	510MB	DualScan	$2459
22	Toshiba	8MB	250MB	DualScan	$3995	NEC	4MB	340MB	Active	$2459	IBM	16MB	510MB	Mono	$3149
23	IBM	16MB	250MB	DualScan	$3149	Toshiba	4MB	340MB	Active	$2459	NEC	8MB	510MB	Mono	$3995
24	IBM	4MB	340MB	DualScan	$3995	NEC	16MB	250MB	Active	$2459	Toshiba	8MB	510MB	Mono	$3149
25	Toshiba	4MB	340MB	Mono	$2459	IBM	8MB	510MB	Active	$3995	NEC	16MB	250MB	DualScan	$3149
26	Toshiba	8MB	250MB	DualScan	$2459	IBM	16MB	340MB	DualScan	$3995	NEC	4MB	510MB	Active	$3149
27	Toshiba	8MB	250MB	DualScan	$2459	IBM	16MB	340MB	Mono	$3995	NEC	4MB	510MB	Active	$3149
28	IBM	8MB	510MB	Mono	$3995	NEC	16MB	250MB	Mono	$2459	Toshiba	4MB	340MB	Active	$3149
29	IBM	8MB	340MB	DualScan	$2459	NEC	16MB	510MB	DualScan	$3149	Toshiba	4MB	250MB	Mono	$3995
30	Toshiba	4MB	510MB	Active	$3995	NEC	8MB	340MB	DualScan	$3149	IBM	16MB	250MB	Mono	$2459

Partworth Values

Model	Brand Name			Memory Size			Hard Drive			Screen Type			Price Level		
	NEC	IBM	Toshiba	4MB	8MB	16MB	250MB	340MB	510MB	Mono	DualScan	Active	$3995	$3149	$2459
Self-Explicated	.000	.082	.147	.000	.147	.265	.000	.157	.235	.000	.052	.118	.000	.183	.235
Conjoint	.024	.000	.143	.000	.165	.320	.000	.022	.106	.048	.155	.000	.000	.070	.275
Choice	.000	.000	.005	.000	.267	.444	.046	.000	.006	.042	.036	.000	.000	.464	.435
Constr. Conjoint	.000	.000	.158	.000	.198	.385	.000	.026	.127	.000	.000	.000	.000	.084	.330
Constr. Choice	.000	.011	.036	.000	.280	.477	.000	.002	.020	.000	.000	.000	.000	.468	.468

Respondent No. 40

Experimental Choice Design

Set	Laptop A					Laptop B					Laptop C				
1	NEC	8MB	510MB	Mono	$2459	Toshiba	16MB	340MB	DualScan	$3995	IBM	4MB	250MB	Active	$3149
2	NEC	8MB	510MB	DualScan	$3995	IBM	4MB	250MB	Active	$3149	Toshiba	16MB	340MB	Mono	$2459
3	NEC	8MB	250MB	Active	$3149	IBM	16MB	510MB	Mono	$2459	Toshiba	4MB	340MB	DualScan	$2459
4	NEC	4MB	250MB	Active	$3149	IBM	8MB	510MB	Mono	$2459	Toshiba	16MB	340MB	DualScan	$3995
5	IBM	8MB	340MB	Mono	$2459	NEC	4MB	510MB	DualScan	$3149	Toshiba	16MB	250MB	Active	$3995
6	IBM	16MB	340MB	Mono	$3149	NEC	4MB	250MB	DualScan	$2459	Toshiba	8MB	510MB	Active	$3995
7	IBM	8MB	340MB	Active	$3995	Toshiba	16MB	510MB	Mono	$3149	NEC	4MB	250MB	DualScan	$2459
8	NEC	16MB	340MB	Active	$3149	Toshiba	8MB	510MB	DualScan	$2459	IBM	4MB	250MB	Mono	$3995
9	IBM	4MB	510MB	DualScan	$3149	NEC	8MB	340MB	Active	$3995	Toshiba	16MB	250MB	Mono	$2459
10	IBM	4MB	510MB	DualScan	$3149	IBM	8MB	250MB	Active	$2459	NEC	16MB	340MB	Mono	$2459
11	IBM	8MB	510MB	DualScan	$3995	Toshiba	4MB	250MB	Active	$2459	NEC	16MB	340MB	Mono	$3149
12	NEC	4MB	340MB	DualScan	$2459	Toshiba	8MB	250MB	Active	$3149	IBM	16MB	510MB	Mono	$3995
13	IBM	4MB	340MB	Active	$3149	Toshiba	8MB	510MB	Mono	$2459	NEC	16MB	250MB	DualScan	$3995
14	NEC	8MB	340MB	DualScan	$3149	Toshiba	16MB	250MB	Mono	$2459	IBM	4MB	510MB	Active	$3995
15	IBM	8MB	340MB	Mono	$2459	Toshiba	16MB	250MB	DualScan	$3149	NEC	4MB	510MB	Active	$3995
16	IBM	16MB	250MB	Active	$2459	Toshiba	8MB	510MB	DualScan	$3995	NEC	4MB	340MB	Mono	$3149
17	NEC	4MB	510MB	Active	$3995	IBM	8MB	250MB	DualScan	$3149	Toshiba	16MB	340MB	Mono	$2459
18	Toshiba	16MB	250MB	Mono	$2459	IBM	4MB	510MB	DualScan	$3149	NEC	8MB	340MB	Active	$3995
19	NEC	16MB	510MB	Active	$3149	IBM	4MB	340MB	DualScan	$2459	Toshiba	8MB	250MB	Mono	$3995
20	Toshiba	4MB	250MB	Active	$2459	IBM	8MB	340MB	DualScan	$3995	NEC	16MB	510MB	Mono	$3149
21	Toshiba	16MB	250MB	Active	$3995	NEC	4MB	340MB	DualScan	$3149	IBM	8MB	510MB	Mono	$2459
22	Toshiba	8MB	510MB	DualScan	$3149	NEC	4MB	250MB	Mono	$3149	IBM	16MB	340MB	Active	$3995
23	Toshiba	16MB	510MB	Active	$3995	NEC	4MB	340MB	Mono	$2459	IBM	8MB	250MB	DualScan	$2459
24	Toshiba	4MB	510MB	Mono	$3149	NEC	8MB	250MB	DualScan	$3149	IBM	16MB	340MB	Active	$3995
25	Toshiba	4MB	340MB	DualScan	$2459	NEC	8MB	250MB	Active	$2459	IBM	16MB	510MB	Mono	$3149
26	IBM	8MB	340MB	Mono	$2459	NEC	16MB	250MB	DualScan	$3995	Toshiba	4MB	510MB	Active	$3149
27	IBM	8MB	250MB	Mono	$2459	NEC	16MB	340MB	DualScan	$3995	Toshiba	4MB	510MB	Active	$3149
28	Toshiba	8MB	340MB	Active	$3149	NEC	16MB	250MB	Mono	$2459	IBM	4MB	510MB	DualScan	$3995
29	Toshiba	8MB	340MB	DualScan	$3149	NEC	16MB	250MB	Mono	$2459	IBM	4MB	510MB	Active	$3995
30	NEC	4MB	510MB	Mono	$3995	Toshiba	8MB	340MB	Active	$2459	IBM	16MB	250MB	DualScan	$3149

Partworth Values

Model	Brand Name			Memory Size			Hard Drive			Screen Type			Price Level		
	NEC	IBM	Toshiba	4MB	8MB	16MB	250MB	340MB	510MB	Mono	DualScan	Active	$3995	$3149	$2459
Self-Explicated	.061	.091	.000	.000	.108	.242	.000	.040	.121	.000	.236	.303	.000	.108	.242
Conjoint	.057	.094	.000	.000	.189	.348	.010	.000	.000	.000	.395	.423	.030	.000	.125
Choice	.018	.050	.000	.000	.156	.245	.000	.025	.089	.000	.274	.377	.000	.103	.238
Constr. Conjoint	.058	.096	.000	.000	.194	.357	.000	.000	.000	.000	.405	.434	.000	.000	.113
Constr. Choice	.018	.050	.000	.000	.156	.245	.000	.025	.089	.000	.274	.377	.000	.103	.238

Respondent No. 41

Experimental Choice Design

Set	Laptop A					Laptop B					Laptop C				
1	IBM	16MB	250MB	Mono	$2459	NEC	8MB	510MB	DualScan	$3995	Toshiba	4MB	340MB	Active	$3149
2	NEC	8MB	510MB	DualScan	$3995	IBM	16MB	250MB	Active	$3149	Toshiba	4MB	340MB	Mono	$2459
3	IBM	8MB	340MB	Active	$3995	NEC	16MB	510MB	Mono	$3149	Toshiba	4MB	250MB	DualScan	$2459
4	Toshiba	4MB	510MB	Mono	$2459	IBM	8MB	340MB	Active	$3995	NEC	16MB	250MB	DualScan	$2459
5	IBM	16MB	510MB	Mono	$3995	NEC	4MB	340MB	Active	$3149	Toshiba	8MB	250MB	DualScan	$2459
6	IBM	8MB	510MB	Mono	$3149	NEC	4MB	340MB	DualScan	$2459	Toshiba	16MB	340MB	Active	$3995
7	NEC	16MB	250MB	DualScan	$3149	IBM	8MB	340MB	Mono	$2459	Toshiba	4MB	510MB	Active	$3995
8	IBM	8MB	250MB	Active	$3149	Toshiba	4MB	510MB	Mono	$3149	NEC	16MB	340MB	DualScan	$3995
9	NEC	4MB	510MB	Active	$3995	IBM	16MB	340MB	Mono	$2459	Toshiba	8MB	250MB	DualScan	$2459
10	IBM	16MB	250MB	DualScan	$3149	NEC	8MB	340MB	Mono	$2459	Toshiba	4MB	510MB	Active	$3995
11	IBM	8MB	510MB	DualScan	$3995	Toshiba	16MB	250MB	Active	$3149	NEC	4MB	340MB	Mono	$2459
12	Toshiba	4MB	250MB	Active	$2459	NEC	16MB	340MB	DualScan	$3995	IBM	8MB	510MB	Mono	$3149
13	IBM	4MB	340MB	DualScan	$3149	Toshiba	8MB	510MB	Mono	$2459	NEC	16MB	250MB	Active	$3995
14	IBM	8MB	250MB	Active	$3149	Toshiba	16MB	340MB	Mono	$2459	NEC	4MB	510MB	DualScan	$3995
15	NEC	16MB	510MB	Mono	$3995	Toshiba	8MB	340MB	Active	$3149	IBM	4MB	250MB	DualScan	$2459
16	NEC	16MB	340MB	Mono	$2459	IBM	4MB	510MB	DualScan	$3149	Toshiba	8MB	250MB	Active	$3149
17	IBM	4MB	510MB	Active	$3995	Toshiba	8MB	340MB	DualScan	$3149	NEC	16MB	250MB	Mono	$2459
18	IBM	16MB	250MB	Mono	$2459	NEC	8MB	340MB	DualScan	$3149	Toshiba	4MB	510MB	Active	$3995
19	IBM	16MB	340MB	DualScan	$3995	NEC	4MB	510MB	Mono	$2459	Toshiba	8MB	250MB	Active	$3149
20	IBM	4MB	250MB	DualScan	$2459	Toshiba	16MB	340MB	Active	$3995	NEC	8MB	510MB	Mono	$3149
21	Toshiba	16MB	510MB	DualScan	$3995	IBM	4MB	340MB	Mono	$2459	NEC	8MB	250MB	Active	$3149
22	IBM	8MB	510MB	Mono	$3149	Toshiba	4MB	250MB	Active	$2459	NEC	16MB	340MB	DualScan	$3995
23	IBM	4MB	510MB	Active	$3995	NEC	16MB	250MB	DualScan	$3149	Toshiba	8MB	340MB	Mono	$2459
24	IBM	16MB	510MB	Mono	$3149	NEC	4MB	250MB	DualScan	$2459	Toshiba	8MB	340MB	Active	$3995
25	Toshiba	4MB	340MB	DualScan	$2459	NEC	16MB	510MB	Active	$3995	IBM	8MB	250MB	Mono	$3149
26	IBM	16MB	250MB	Mono	$2459	Toshiba	8MB	510MB	DualScan	$3995	NEC	4MB	340MB	Active	$3149
27	IBM	16MB	250MB	Mono	$2459	NEC	8MB	340MB	Active	$3995	Toshiba	4MB	510MB	DualScan	$3149
28	Toshiba	8MB	340MB	Active	$3995	IBM	16MB	250MB	Mono	$3149	NEC	4MB	340MB	DualScan	$3149
29	NEC	4MB	340MB	Active	$2459	IBM	16MB	510MB	DualScan	$3149	Toshiba	8MB	250MB	Mono	$3995
30	Toshiba	4MB	340MB	Mono	$3995	NEC	8MB	510MB	DualScan	$3149	IBM	16MB	250MB	Active	$2459

Partworth Values

Model	Brand Name			Memory Size			Hard Drive			Screen Type			Price Level		
	NEC	IBM	Toshiba	4MB	8MB	16MB	250MB	340MB	510MB	Mono	DualScan	Active	$3995	$3149	$2459
Self-Explicated	.054	.061	.000	.000	.081	.121	.000	.135	.242	.000	.212	.273	.000	.135	.303
Conjoint	.119	.000	.012	.023	.000	.002	.000	.143	.097	.000	.117	.333	.000	.217	.383
Choice	.058	.000	.053	.000	.165	.356	.000	.039	.049	.000	.115	.148	.000	.388	.301
Constr. Conjoint	.000	.000	.000	.000	.000	.000	.000	.143	.143	.000	.141	.399	.000	.259	.458
Constr. Choice	.066	.066	.000	.000	.641	.825	.000	.000	.047	.000	.000	.062	.000	.000	.000

Respondent No. 42

Experimental Choice Design

Set	Laptop A				Laptop B				Laptop C			
1	Toshiba	8MB	510MB	Mono	$3995	IBM	16MB	250MB	DualScan	$3149	NEC	4MB	340MB	Active	$2459
2	NEC	8MB	510MB	DualScan	$3995	IBM	16MB	250MB	Active	$3149	Toshiba	4MB	340MB	Mono	$2459
3	Toshiba	4MB	510MB	DualScan	$2459	IBM	16MB	340MB	Mono	$3995	NEC	8MB	250MB	Active	$3149
4	Toshiba	4MB	510MB	Active	$3149	IBM	8MB	340MB	DualScan	$3995	NEC	16MB	250MB	Mono	$2459
5	NEC	16MB	340MB	Mono	$3995	IBM	4MB	510MB	DualScan	$3149	Toshiba	8MB	250MB	Active	$2459
6	NEC	16MB	340MB	Mono	$3995	IBM	4MB	510MB	Active	$2459	Toshiba	8MB	250MB	DualScan	$3149
7	Toshiba	16MB	250MB	Active	$3995	IBM	8MB	340MB	Mono	$3149	NEC	4MB	510MB	DualScan	$2459
8	NEC	16MB	250MB	Mono	$3149	IBM	4MB	510MB	Active	$2459	Toshiba	8MB	340MB	DualScan	$3995
9	Toshiba	4MB	250MB	DualScan	$3995	IBM	8MB	510MB	Active	$3149	NEC	16MB	340MB	Mono	$2459
10	NEC	8MB	250MB	DualScan	$3149	Toshiba	4MB	340MB	Active	$2459	IBM	16MB	510MB	Mono	$3995
11	IBM	8MB	510MB	DualScan	$3995	Toshiba	16MB	250MB	Active	$3149	NEC	4MB	340MB	Mono	$2459
12	NEC	4MB	510MB	DualScan	$3149	Toshiba	8MB	250MB	Active	$2459	IBM	16MB	340MB	Mono	$3995
13	Toshiba	4MB	250MB	DualScan	$3149	IBM	8MB	340MB	Mono	$2459	NEC	16MB	510MB	Active	$3995
14	IBM	8MB	250MB	DualScan	$2459	Toshiba	16MB	340MB	Mono	$3995	NEC	4MB	510MB	Active	$3149
15	IBM	16MB	340MB	Mono	$3995	NEC	8MB	250MB	Active	$3149	Toshiba	4MB	510MB	DualScan	$2459
16	IBM	16MB	250MB	DualScan	$2459	NEC	4MB	510MB	Active	$3995	Toshiba	8MB	340MB	Mono	$3149
17	IBM	8MB	510MB	Mono	$3995	Toshiba	16MB	250MB	DualScan	$3149	NEC	4MB	340MB	Active	$2459
18	IBM	16MB	250MB	Mono	$2459	Toshiba	8MB	340MB	Active	$3995	NEC	4MB	510MB	DualScan	$3149
19	NEC	8MB	510MB	Mono	$2459	Toshiba	4MB	250MB	Active	$3995	IBM	16MB	340MB	DualScan	$3149
20	NEC	4MB	250MB	Active	$2459	Toshiba	16MB	340MB	DualScan	$3995	IBM	8MB	510MB	Mono	$3149
21	NEC	16MB	250MB	Active	$3995	IBM	8MB	340MB	Mono	$3149	Toshiba	4MB	510MB	DualScan	$2459
22	IBM	16MB	250MB	DualScan	$3149	NEC	4MB	340MB	Active	$2459	Toshiba	8MB	510MB	Mono	$3995
23	Toshiba	16MB	510MB	Active	$3995	NEC	8MB	250MB	Mono	$3149	IBM	4MB	340MB	DualScan	$2459
24	Toshiba	4MB	510MB	DualScan	$3149	IBM	8MB	250MB	Active	$2459	NEC	16MB	340MB	Mono	$3995
25	Toshiba	4MB	340MB	Active	$2459	IBM	8MB	510MB	DualScan	$3995	NEC	16MB	250MB	Mono	$3149
26	Toshiba	16MB	250MB	Mono	$2459	NEC	8MB	510MB	DualScan	$3995	IBM	4MB	340MB	Active	$3149
27	NEC	8MB	250MB	Mono	$2459	Toshiba	16MB	340MB	DualScan	$3149	IBM	4MB	510MB	Active	$3995
28	NEC	4MB	510MB	DualScan	$3149	Toshiba	16MB	250MB	Mono	$2459	IBM	8MB	340MB	Active	$3995
29	Toshiba	8MB	340MB	Mono	$3149	NEC	16MB	250MB	Active	$3995	IBM	4MB	510MB	DualScan	$2459
30	NEC	16MB	340MB	Active	$3995	Toshiba	8MB	510MB	Mono	$3149	IBM	4MB	250MB	DualScan	$2459

Partworth Values

Model	Brand Name			Memory Size			Hard Drive			Screen Type			Price Level		
	NEC	IBM	Toshiba	4MB	8MB	16MB	250MB	340MB	510MB	Mono	DualScan	Active	$3995	$3149	$2459
Self-Explicated	.037	.000	.016	.000	.288	.370	.000	.202	.259	.000	.086	.111	.000	.173	.222
Conjoint	.129	.013	.000	.000	.190	.368	.009	.000	.086	.000	.086	.051	.000	.039	.331
Choice	.026	.019	.000	.000	.298	.429	.000	.049	.012	.000	.054	.016	.000	.417	.443
Constr. Conjoint	.126	.000	.000	.000	.196	.379	.000	.000	.084	.000	.071	.071	.000	.040	.340
Constr. Choice	.000	.000	.000	.000	.293	.499	.000	.000	.000	.000	.000	.000	.000	.493	.501

Appendices 155

Respondent No. 43

Experimental Choice Design

Set	Laptop A					Laptop B					Laptop C				
1	NEC	8MB	510MB	Mono	$2459	IBM	16MB	250MB	DualScan	$3995	Toshiba	4MB	340MB	Active	$3149
2	NEC	8MB	340MB	DualScan	$3149	IBM	16MB	250MB	Active	$3995	Toshiba	4MB	510MB	Mono	$2459
3	NEC	8MB	340MB	DualScan	$2459	IBM	16MB	510MB	Mono	$3995	Toshiba	4MB	250MB	Active	$3149
4	NEC	4MB	510MB	DualScan	$2459	IBM	16MB	250MB	DualScan	$3149	Toshiba	8MB	340MB	Active	$3995
5	IBM	16MB	250MB	Mono	$2459	NEC	4MB	510MB	DualScan	$3149	Toshiba	8MB	340MB	Active	$3995
6	NEC	16MB	340MB	Mono	$3149	IBM	4MB	510MB	DualScan	$2459	Toshiba	8MB	250MB	Active	$3995
7	NEC	16MB	250MB	Active	$3995	IBM	8MB	340MB	DualScan	$2459	Toshiba	4MB	510MB	DualScan	$3149
8	NEC	16MB	340MB	DualScan	$3149	IBM	4MB	510MB	Mono	$2459	Toshiba	8MB	250MB	Active	$3995
9	NEC	4MB	250MB	DualScan	$3995	IBM	8MB	340MB	Active	$2459	Toshiba	16MB	510MB	Mono	$3149
10	NEC	8MB	250MB	Active	$3149	IBM	4MB	340MB	DualScan	$2459	Toshiba	16MB	510MB	Mono	$3995
11	IBM	8MB	510MB	DualScan	$3995	Toshiba	16MB	250MB	Mono	$3149	NEC	4MB	340MB	Active	$2459
12	Toshiba	4MB	340MB	DualScan	$3149	NEC	8MB	250MB	Active	$2459	IBM	16MB	510MB	Mono	$3995
13	IBM	4MB	340MB	Active	$3149	NEC	8MB	510MB	Mono	$2459	Toshiba	16MB	250MB	DualScan	$3995
14	IBM	8MB	250MB	Active	$3149	NEC	16MB	340MB	Mono	$3995	Toshiba	4MB	510MB	DualScan	$2459
15	IBM	16MB	510MB	Mono	$3995	Toshiba	8MB	250MB	DualScan	$3149	NEC	4MB	340MB	Active	$2459
16	IBM	8MB	340MB	Mono	$2459	Toshiba	4MB	510MB	Active	$3995	NEC	16MB	250MB	DualScan	$3149
17	IBM	16MB	510MB	Mono	$3995	Toshiba	8MB	250MB	DualScan	$3149	NEC	4MB	340MB	Active	$2459
18	IBM	16MB	250MB	Mono	$2459	Toshiba	4MB	340MB	DualScan	$3149	NEC	8MB	510MB	Active	$3995
19	Toshiba	4MB	510MB	Active	$2459	IBM	8MB	250MB	Mono	$3995	NEC	16MB	340MB	DualScan	$3149
20	IBM	16MB	250MB	DualScan	$3149	Toshiba	4MB	340MB	Mono	$2459	NEC	8MB	510MB	Active	$3995
21	NEC	16MB	250MB	Active	$3995	Toshiba	4MB	340MB	Mono	$2459	IBM	8MB	510MB	DualScan	$3149
22	IBM	16MB	250MB	DualScan	$3995	NEC	4MB	510MB	Active	$2459	Toshiba	8MB	340MB	Mono	$3149
23	Toshiba	16MB	340MB	Mono	$3995	NEC	4MB	510MB	Active	$3149	IBM	8MB	250MB	DualScan	$2459
24	IBM	4MB	510MB	Mono	$2459	Toshiba	8MB	250MB	DualScan	$3149	NEC	16MB	340MB	Active	$3995
25	Toshiba	4MB	340MB	DualScan	$2459	NEC	8MB	250MB	Active	$3995	IBM	16MB	510MB	Mono	$3149
26	Toshiba	8MB	250MB	Mono	$2459	NEC	16MB	510MB	DualScan	$3149	IBM	4MB	340MB	Active	$3995
27	Toshiba	8MB	340MB	Mono	$2459	NEC	16MB	250MB	Active	$3995	IBM	4MB	510MB	DualScan	$3149
28	Toshiba	8MB	510MB	DualScan	$3995	NEC	16MB	250MB	Active	$2459	IBM	4MB	340MB	Active	$3149
29	IBM	8MB	340MB	DualScan	$3149	NEC	16MB	510MB	Mono	$3995	Toshiba	4MB	250MB	Active	$2459
30	NEC	16MB	340MB	DualScan	$3995	IBM	8MB	510MB	Mono	$3149	Toshiba	4MB	250MB	Active	$2459

Partworth Values

Model	Brand Name			Memory Size			Hard Drive			Screen Type			Price Level		
	NEC	IBM	Toshiba	4MB	8MB	16MB	250MB	340MB	510MB	Mono	DualScan	Active	$3995	$3149	$2459
Self-Explicated	.000	.078	.118	.000	.131	.294	.000	.098	.176	.000	.137	.206	.000	.160	.206
Conjoint	.000	.036	.029	.000	.202	.360	.000	.045	.135	.000	.229	.207	.000	.240	.213
Choice	.000	.027	.062	.000	.236	.452	.018	.000	.066	.000	.119	.120	.000	.126	.300
Constr. Conjoint	.000	.034	.034	.000	.208	.370	.000	.047	.138	.000	.225	.225	.000	.233	.233
Constr. Choice	.000	.032	.081	.000	.208	.424	.000	.000	.083	.000	.121	.135	.000	.139	.277

Respondent No. 44

Experimental Choice Design

Set	Laptop A					Laptop B					Laptop C				
1	IBM	8MB	510MB	Mono	$2459	NEC	16MB	250MB	Active	$3995	Toshiba	4MB	340MB	DualScan	$3149
2	Toshiba	16MB	340MB	DualScan	$3995	IBM	8MB	250MB	Active	$3149	NEC	4MB	510MB	Mono	$2459
3	NEC	8MB	340MB	Active	$3995	IBM	16MB	510MB	Mono	$2459	Toshiba	4MB	250MB	DualScan	$3149
4	NEC	4MB	510MB	Active	$2459	IBM	16MB	340MB	DualScan	$3995	Toshiba	8MB	250MB	Mono	$3149
5	NEC	8MB	340MB	Active	$3995	IBM	4MB	510MB	DualScan	$2459	Toshiba	16MB	250MB	Mono	$3149
6	Toshiba	8MB	340MB	Mono	$3149	NEC	4MB	510MB	DualScan	$2459	IBM	16MB	250MB	Active	$3995
7	IBM	4MB	250MB	Active	$3995	NEC	8MB	340MB	DualScan	$2459	Toshiba	16MB	510MB	Mono	$3149
8	NEC	4MB	510MB	Active	$3149	Toshiba	16MB	250MB	Mono	$2459	IBM	8MB	340MB	DualScan	$3995
9	NEC	4MB	340MB	DualScan	$3995	IBM	8MB	250MB	Active	$3149	Toshiba	16MB	510MB	Mono	$2459
10	NEC	8MB	340MB	DualScan	$3149	IBM	4MB	250MB	Mono	$2459	Toshiba	16MB	510MB	Active	$3995
11	IBM	8MB	510MB	DualScan	$3995	Toshiba	16MB	250MB	Active	$3149	NEC	4MB	510MB	Mono	$2459
12	IBM	16MB	250MB	DualScan	$3149	Toshiba	4MB	340MB	Mono	$2459	NEC	8MB	340MB	Active	$3995
13	IBM	4MB	340MB	DualScan	$3995	Toshiba	8MB	250MB	Active	$2459	NEC	4MB	510MB	Mono	$3149
14	IBM	8MB	250MB	Active	$3995	Toshiba	16MB	340MB	Mono	$3149	NEC	4MB	510MB	DualScan	$2459
15	IBM	8MB	340MB	Active	$3995	Toshiba	16MB	250MB	DualScan	$3149	NEC	4MB	510MB	Mono	$2459
16	IBM	16MB	340MB	Active	$2459	NEC	4MB	510MB	Active	$3995	Toshiba	8MB	250MB	Mono	$3149
17	IBM	4MB	250MB	Mono	$3149	Toshiba	8MB	510MB	DualScan	$3995	NEC	16MB	340MB	DualScan	$2459
18	IBM	16MB	340MB	Mono	$2459	Toshiba	4MB	250MB	DualScan	$3149	NEC	8MB	510MB	Active	$3995
19	IBM	8MB	510MB	Mono	$2459	Toshiba	4MB	340MB	Active	$3995	NEC	16MB	250MB	DualScan	$3149
20	NEC	8MB	250MB	DualScan	$2459	Toshiba	4MB	340MB	Active	$3995	IBM	16MB	510MB	Mono	$3149
21	Toshiba	16MB	250MB	Active	$3995	NEC	4MB	510MB	Mono	$3149	IBM	8MB	340MB	DualScan	$2459
22	NEC	16MB	250MB	DualScan	$3149	IBM	4MB	510MB	Active	$3995	Toshiba	8MB	340MB	Mono	$2459
23	Toshiba	8MB	250MB	DualScan	$3995	IBM	4MB	510MB	Mono	$2459	NEC	16MB	340MB	Active	$3149
24	Toshiba	4MB	510MB	Mono	$3149	NEC	8MB	250MB	DualScan	$2459	IBM	16MB	340MB	Active	$3995
25	Toshiba	4MB	250MB	DualScan	$2459	NEC	8MB	510MB	Active	$3995	IBM	16MB	340MB	Mono	$3149
26	Toshiba	8MB	250MB	Mono	$2459	NEC	16MB	340MB	Active	$3995	IBM	4MB	510MB	Active	$3149
27	Toshiba	8MB	250MB	Mono	$3149	NEC	16MB	340MB	DualScan	$3995	IBM	4MB	510MB	Active	$2459
28	Toshiba	8MB	340MB	Mono	$3149	NEC	16MB	510MB	DualScan	$3995	IBM	4MB	250MB	Active	$2459
29	Toshiba	8MB	340MB	DualScan	$3149	IBM	16MB	510MB	Active	$2459	NEC	4MB	250MB	Mono	$3995
30	Toshiba	4MB	250MB	Mono	$3995	NEC	8MB	510MB	Active	$3149	IBM	16MB	340MB	DualScan	$2459

Partworth Values

Model	Brand Name			Memory Size				Hard Drive			Screen Type			Price Level	
	NEC	IBM	Toshiba	4MB	8MB	16MB	250MB	340MB	510MB	Mono	DualScan	Active	$3995	$3149	$2459
Self-Explicated	.000	.069	.206	.000	.209	.235	.000	.039	.088	.000	.229	.294	.000	.137	.176
Conjoint	.000	.081	.156	.000	.305	.315	.155	.000	.047	.000	.282	.232	.092	.000	.070
Choice	.012	.000	.002	.000	.376	.356	.008	.000	.103	.000	.284	.408	.101	.091	.000
Constr. Conjoint	.000	.108	.208	.000	.406	.419	.000	.000	.000	.000	.341	.341	.000	.000	.033
Constr. Choice	.000	.006	.067	.000	.407	.407	.000	.000	.120	.000	.276	.407	.000	.000	.000

Respondent No. 45

Experimental Choice Design

Set	Laptop A				Laptop B				Laptop C			
1	NEC	16MB	250MB	Mono	$2459	Toshiba	8MB	340MB	DualScan	$3149	IBM	4MB	510MB	Active	$3995
2	NEC	16MB	510MB	DualScan	$3149	IBM	8MB	340MB	Active	$3995	Toshiba	4MB	250MB	Mono	$2459
3	NEC	8MB	250MB	Active	$2459	Toshiba	16MB	510MB	DualScan	$3995	IBM	4MB	340MB	Mono	$3149
4	NEC	4MB	510MB	Active	$2459	IBM	16MB	250MB	DualScan	$3995	Toshiba	8MB	340MB	Mono	$3149
5	Toshiba	16MB	340MB	Active	$3995	IBM	4MB	510MB	DualScan	$3149	NEC	8MB	250MB	Mono	$2459
6	Toshiba	8MB	340MB	Mono	$3149	IBM	4MB	250MB	DualScan	$2459	NEC	16MB	510MB	Active	$3995
7	IBM	8MB	340MB	DualScan	$3995	Toshiba	16MB	250MB	Mono	$2459	NEC	4MB	510MB	Active	$2459
8	NEC	16MB	340MB	DualScan	$3149	Toshiba	4MB	510MB	Mono	$2459	IBM	8MB	250MB	Active	$3995
9	NEC	4MB	510MB	Active	$3995	IBM	16MB	340MB	Mono	$3149	Toshiba	8MB	250MB	DualScan	$2459
10	IBM	4MB	250MB	Mono	$2459	NEC	8MB	340MB	Active	$3149	Toshiba	16MB	510MB	DualScan	$3995
11	IBM	8MB	340MB	Mono	$3995	Toshiba	16MB	250MB	Active	$3149	NEC	4MB	510MB	DualScan	$2459
12	IBM	16MB	250MB	Active	$3995	Toshiba	4MB	340MB	Mono	$2459	NEC	8MB	510MB	DualScan	$3149
13	IBM	4MB	340MB	Active	$3149	Toshiba	16MB	510MB	DualScan	$3149	NEC	8MB	250MB	Mono	$2459
14	IBM	8MB	250MB	Active	$3149	NEC	16MB	340MB	DualScan	$3995	Toshiba	4MB	510MB	Mono	$2459
15	IBM	8MB	510MB	Mono	$3995	NEC	16MB	340MB	Active	$2459	Toshiba	4MB	250MB	DualScan	$3149
16	IBM	8MB	340MB	DualScan	$3995	Toshiba	4MB	250MB	Active	$2459	NEC	16MB	510MB	Mono	$3149
17	IBM	8MB	340MB	Mono	$3995	Toshiba	16MB	250MB	DualScan	$3149	NEC	4MB	510MB	Active	$2459
18	Toshiba	4MB	250MB	Active	$2459	IBM	16MB	340MB	Mono	$3149	NEC	8MB	510MB	DualScan	$3149
19	NEC	16MB	340MB	Active	$3995	Toshiba	4MB	250MB	Mono	$2459	IBM	8MB	510MB	DualScan	$3149
20	IBM	4MB	250MB	Mono	$2459	Toshiba	16MB	340MB	Active	$3995	NEC	8MB	510MB	DualScan	$3149
21	Toshiba	8MB	510MB	Active	$3995	IBM	4MB	340MB	Mono	$3149	NEC	16MB	250MB	DualScan	$2459
22	NEC	16MB	510MB	Active	$3149	Toshiba	4MB	250MB	DualScan	$2459	IBM	8MB	340MB	Mono	$3995
23	Toshiba	8MB	510MB	Mono	$3995	IBM	4MB	250MB	DualScan	$2459	NEC	16MB	340MB	Mono	$3149
24	IBM	4MB	510MB	Mono	$3149	NEC	8MB	250MB	DualScan	$2459	Toshiba	16MB	340MB	Active	$3995
25	Toshiba	4MB	340MB	DualScan	$2459	NEC	16MB	510MB	Active	$3995	IBM	8MB	250MB	Mono	$3149
26	NEC	16MB	250MB	Mono	$2459	Toshiba	8MB	510MB	Active	$3995	IBM	4MB	340MB	DualScan	$3149
27	NEC	8MB	250MB	DualScan	$2459	Toshiba	16MB	340MB	Mono	$3995	IBM	4MB	510MB	Active	$3149
28	Toshiba	16MB	510MB	Active	$3995	NEC	8MB	250MB	Mono	$2459	IBM	4MB	340MB	DualScan	$3149
29	Toshiba	8MB	250MB	DualScan	$3149	NEC	4MB	340MB	Active	$2459	IBM	16MB	510MB	Mono	$3995
30	Toshiba	4MB	340MB	Mono	$2459	NEC	8MB	510MB	Active	$3149	IBM	16MB	250MB	DualScan	$3995

Partworth Values

Model	Brand Name			Memory Size			Hard Drive			Screen Type			Price Level		
	NEC	IBM	Toshiba	4MB	8MB	16MB	250MB	340MB	510MB	Mono	DualScan	Active	$3995	$3149	$2459
Self-Explicated	.000	.233	.130	.000	.207	.233	.000	.104	.133	.000	.037	.067	.000	.148	.333
Conjoint	.018	.008	.000	.000	.755	.776	.000	.015	.065	.000	.034	.055	.000	.045	.087
Choice	.100	.000	.065	.000	.433	.434	.045	.015	.000	.027	.010	.000	.000	.253	.395
Constr. Conjoint	.000	.000	.000	.000	.768	.790	.000	.015	.066	.000	.034	.056	.000	.046	.089
Constr. Choice	.000	.000	.000	.000	.480	.494	.000	.005	.008	.000	.007	.007	.000	.282	.491

Respondent No. 46

Experimental Choice Design

Set	Laptop A				Laptop B				Laptop C			
1	NEC	4MB	510MB	DualScan	$3149	IBM	16MB	250MB	Mono	$3995	Toshiba	8MB	340MB	Active	$2459
2	Toshiba	4MB	510MB	DualScan	$3149	NEC	16MB	250MB	Active	$3995	IBM	8MB	340MB	Mono	$2459
3	Toshiba	8MB	340MB	Active	$2459	IBM	4MB	510MB	Mono	$3995	NEC	16MB	250MB	DualScan	$3149
4	NEC	4MB	510MB	Active	$2459	Toshiba	16MB	250MB	Mono	$2459	IBM	8MB	340MB	DualScan	$3149
5	NEC	4MB	340MB	Mono	$3995	Toshiba	4MB	510MB	DualScan	$2459	IBM	8MB	250MB	Active	$3149
6	NEC	16MB	340MB	Mono	$3149	IBM	4MB	340MB	DualScan	$2459	Toshiba	8MB	510MB	Active	$3995
7	NEC	16MB	250MB	Active	$3995	IBM	8MB	340MB	DualScan	$3149	Toshiba	4MB	510MB	Mono	$2459
8	NEC	16MB	340MB	DualScan	$3995	Toshiba	4MB	510MB	Mono	$2459	IBM	8MB	250MB	Active	$3149
9	NEC	16MB	340MB	DualScan	$3995	IBM	4MB	250MB	Active	$2459	Toshiba	4MB	510MB	Mono	$3149
10	IBM	8MB	510MB	DualScan	$3995	Toshiba	8MB	340MB	Mono	$3149	NEC	16MB	250MB	Active	$2459
11	IBM	8MB	340MB	Mono	$3995	IBM	4MB	250MB	Active	$2459	Toshiba	8MB	340MB	DualScan	$3149
12	IBM	4MB	510MB	DualScan	$3995	NEC	16MB	250MB	Active	$3149	NEC	16MB	250MB	Mono	$2459
13	IBM	4MB	340MB	Active	$3149	Toshiba	8MB	510MB	Mono	$2459	NEC	16MB	340MB	DualScan	$3995
14	IBM	8MB	340MB	Mono	$3995	Toshiba	8MB	510MB	DualScan	$3149	NEC	16MB	250MB	Active	$2459
15	IBM	8MB	340MB	Active	$2459	Toshiba	16MB	250MB	DualScan	$3995	NEC	4MB	510MB	Mono	$3149
16	IBM	4MB	340MB	DualScan	$3995	Toshiba	8MB	510MB	Active	$3149	NEC	16MB	250MB	Mono	$2459
17	Toshiba	4MB	510MB	Active	$3995	NEC	16MB	250MB	Mono	$2459	IBM	8MB	340MB	DualScan	$3149
18	Toshiba	16MB	250MB	Mono	$3149	IBM	4MB	340MB	Active	$3995	NEC	8MB	510MB	DualScan	$2459
19	IBM	4MB	510MB	Mono	$3995	NEC	8MB	340MB	Active	$3995	NEC	16MB	250MB	DualScan	$3149
20	IBM	16MB	250MB	Mono	$3995	Toshiba	4MB	340MB	Active	$2459	NEC	8MB	510MB	DualScan	$3149
21	Toshiba	16MB	250MB	Active	$3995	IBM	4MB	340MB	Mono	$3149	NEC	8MB	510MB	DualScan	$2459
22	Toshiba	16MB	250MB	DualScan	$3995	NEC	4MB	510MB	Active	$2459	IBM	8MB	340MB	Mono	$3149
23	Toshiba	8MB	510MB	DualScan	$3995	NEC	16MB	250MB	Active	$3149	IBM	4MB	340MB	Mono	$2459
24	Toshiba	8MB	510MB	Mono	$3149	NEC	16MB	250MB	DualScan	$2459	IBM	4MB	340MB	Active	$3995
25	IBM	4MB	340MB	DualScan	$2459	NEC	8MB	510MB	Active	$3149	Toshiba	16MB	250MB	DualScan	$3995
26	Toshiba	4MB	510MB	DualScan	$3149	NEC	16MB	340MB	Mono	$3995	IBM	8MB	250MB	Active	$2459
27	NEC	8MB	510MB	Mono	$2459	IBM	16MB	250MB	DualScan	$3995	IBM	4MB	340MB	Active	$3149
28	Toshiba	8MB	510MB	Mono	$3149	NEC	16MB	250MB	DualScan	$2459	IBM	4MB	340MB	Active	$3995
29	IBM	4MB	250MB	Active	$2459	IBM	8MB	510MB	DualScan	$3149	Toshiba	16MB	340MB	Mono	$3995
30	NEC	16MB	340MB	DualScan	$3995	Toshiba	4MB	510MB	Mono	$3149	IBM	8MB	250MB	Active	$2459

Partworth Values

Model	Brand Name			Memory Size			Hard Drive			Screen Type			Price Level		
	NEC	IBM	Toshiba	4MB	8MB	16MB	250MB	340MB	510MB	Mono	DualScan	Active	$3995	$3149	$2459
Self-Explicated	.000	.194	.086	.000	.036	.323	.000	.115	.258	.000	.043	.097	.000	.086	.129
Conjoint	.008	.000	.015	.000	.171	.801	.000	.074	.097	.059	.038	.000	.000	.028	.025
Choice	.000	.000	.000	.000	.000	.999	.000	.000	.000	.000	.000	.000	.000	.000	.000
Constr. Conjoint	.000	.000	.000	.000	.185	.866	.000	.080	.105	.000	.000	.000	.000	.029	.029
Constr. Choice	.000	.000	.000	.000	.000	1.000	.000	.000	.000	.000	.000	.000	.000	.000	.000

Respondent No. 47

Experimental Choice Design

Set	Laptop A					Laptop B					Laptop C				
1	NEC	8MB	510MB	Mono	$2459	IBM	16MB	340MB	DualScan	$3995	Toshiba	4MB	250MB	Active	$3149
2	NEC	8MB	340MB	Active	$3995	Toshiba	16MB	250MB	DualScan	$3149	IBM	4MB	510MB	Mono	$2459
3	NEC	16MB	340MB	Mono	$2459	Toshiba	8MB	510MB	DualScan	$3149	IBM	4MB	250MB	Active	$3995
4	NEC	4MB	510MB	Active	$3995	IBM	8MB	250MB	Mono	$2459	Toshiba	16MB	340MB	DualScan	$3149
5	NEC	16MB	250MB	Mono	$2459	Toshiba	8MB	510MB	DualScan	$3149	IBM	4MB	340MB	Active	$3995
6	Toshiba	16MB	510MB	Mono	$3149	IBM	8MB	340MB	DualScan	$2459	NEC	4MB	250MB	Active	$3995
7	Toshiba	8MB	250MB	Active	$3995	IBM	16MB	510MB	DualScan	$2459	NEC	4MB	340MB	Active	$3149
8	NEC	16MB	340MB	DualScan	$3149	Toshiba	8MB	510MB	Mono	$2459	IBM	4MB	250MB	DualScan	$3995
9	IBM	8MB	340MB	DualScan	$3149	NEC	4MB	340MB	Active	$3995	IBM	4MB	250MB	Active	$2459
10	NEC	4MB	250MB	Active	$3995	Toshiba	8MB	340MB	Mono	$2459	IBM	16MB	250MB	Mono	$3995
11	IBM	16MB	510MB	DualScan	$2459	NEC	4MB	250MB	Active	$3149	Toshiba	8MB	340MB	DualScan	$2459
12	IBM	4MB	340MB	Active	$3995	NEC	8MB	250MB	DualScan	$3149	Toshiba	16MB	510MB	Mono	$2459
13	Toshiba	8MB	340MB	Active	$3995	IBM	4MB	510MB	Mono	$2459	NEC	16MB	510MB	Mono	$3149
14	IBM	8MB	510MB	DualScan	$3149	NEC	16MB	340MB	Mono	$2459	Toshiba	4MB	250MB	DualScan	$3995
15	IBM	8MB	250MB	Mono	$2459	IBM	16MB	510MB	DualScan	$3995	NEC	4MB	340MB	Active	$3149
16	IBM	16MB	340MB	Mono	$3149	Toshiba	4MB	510MB	Active	$3995	NEC	8MB	250MB	DualScan	$2459
17	IBM	4MB	510MB	Active	$3995	Toshiba	8MB	250MB	Mono	$2459	NEC	16MB	340MB	DualScan	$3149
18	IBM	16MB	510MB	Mono	$3149	Toshiba	4MB	340MB	DualScan	$2459	NEC	8MB	250MB	Active	$3995
19	NEC	16MB	510MB	DualScan	$2459	Toshiba	4MB	250MB	Mono	$3995	IBM	8MB	340MB	Active	$3149
20	IBM	16MB	250MB	DualScan	$3149	Toshiba	4MB	340MB	Active	$3995	NEC	8MB	510MB	Mono	$2459
21	Toshiba	16MB	250MB	Active	$3995	NEC	4MB	340MB	Mono	$3149	IBM	8MB	510MB	DualScan	$2459
22	Toshiba	16MB	510MB	DualScan	$3995	NEC	4MB	250MB	Active	$3149	IBM	8MB	340MB	Mono	$2459
23	Toshiba	16MB	340MB	DualScan	$3995	NEC	4MB	510MB	Active	$3149	IBM	8MB	250MB	Mono	$2459
24	Toshiba	16MB	340MB	Mono	$3149	NEC	4MB	510MB	DualScan	$2459	IBM	8MB	250MB	Active	$3995
25	Toshiba	4MB	340MB	DualScan	$2459	NEC	8MB	510MB	Active	$3995	IBM	16MB	250MB	Mono	$3149
26	NEC	8MB	510MB	Mono	$3995	IBM	16MB	340MB	DualScan	$3995	Toshiba	4MB	250MB	Active	$3149
27	Toshiba	8MB	340MB	Mono	$2459	IBM	16MB	510MB	DualScan	$3995	NEC	4MB	250MB	Active	$3149
28	Toshiba	8MB	250MB	DualScan	$3149	NEC	16MB	510MB	DualScan	$3995	IBM	4MB	340MB	Active	$3149
29	NEC	16MB	250MB	DualScan	$3149	IBM	8MB	340MB	Mono	$2459	Toshiba	4MB	510MB	Active	$3995
30	IBM	16MB	510MB	Mono	$3149	NEC	8MB	340MB	Active	$3995	Toshiba	4MB	250MB	DualScan	$2459

Partworth Values

Model	Brand Name			Memory Size			Hard Drive			Screen Type			Price Level		
	NEC	IBM	Toshiba	4MB	8MB	16MB	250MB	340MB	510MB	Mono	DualScan	Active	$3995	$3149	$2459
Self-Explicated	.000	.071	.040	.000	.095	.214	.000	.032	.071	.000	.119	.357	.000	.127	.286
Conjoint	.065	.029	.000	.000	.096	.244	.025	.000	.061	.000	.065	.350	.172	.000	.280
Choice	.084	.008	.000	.000	.094	.021	.049	.063	.000	.000	.403	.434	.000	.130	.324
Constr. Conjoint	.000	.000	.000	.000	.114	.292	.000	.000	.058	.000	.078	.418	.000	.000	.232
Constr. Choice	.084	.008	.000	.000	.094	.021	.049	.063	.000	.000	.403	.434	.000	.130	.324

Respondent No. 48

Experimental Choice Design

Set	Laptop A						Laptop B						Laptop C					
1	NEC	8MB	510MB	Mono	$2459	IBM	16MB	250MB	DualScan	$3995	Toshiba	4MB	340MB	Active	$3149
2	NEC	8MB	510MB	DualScan	$3995	Toshiba	4MB	250MB	Active	$3149	IBM	16MB	340MB	Mono	$2459
3	IBM	4MB	340MB	Active	$3149	NEC	16MB	510MB	Mono	$3995	Toshiba	8MB	250MB	DualScan	$2459
4	NEC	4MB	510MB	Active	$2459	IBM	8MB	250MB	Mono	$3995	Toshiba	16MB	340MB	DualScan	$3149
5	NEC	8MB	340MB	Mono	$3995	IBM	4MB	510MB	DualScan	$3149	Toshiba	16MB	250MB	Active	$3149
6	Toshiba	16MB	510MB	Mono	$3995	IBM	4MB	340MB	DualScan	$2459	NEC	8MB	250MB	Active	$3149
7	IBM	8MB	250MB	Active	$3995	NEC	16MB	510MB	Mono	$3149	Toshiba	4MB	340MB	DualScan	$2459
8	NEC	16MB	250MB	DualScan	$3149	IBM	4MB	510MB	Mono	$2459	Toshiba	8MB	340MB	Active	$3995
9	Toshiba	4MB	250MB	DualScan	$3995	IBM	8MB	340MB	Active	$3149	NEC	16MB	510MB	Mono	$2459
10	Toshiba	16MB	250MB	DualScan	$3149	NEC	8MB	510MB	Mono	$2459	IBM	4MB	340MB	Active	$2459
11	IBM	8MB	510MB	DualScan	$3995	NEC	16MB	340MB	Active	$3149	NEC	4MB	340MB	Mono	$2459
12	IBM	8MB	340MB	DualScan	$3995	Toshiba	16MB	250MB	Mono	$2459	IBM	4MB	510MB	Active	$3149
13	IBM	4MB	340MB	Active	$3149	NEC	4MB	510MB	Active	$2459	Toshiba	16MB	510MB	Mono	$3995
14	IBM	8MB	250MB	Active	$3149	Toshiba	8MB	510MB	Mono	$3149	NEC	16MB	250MB	DualScan	$3995
15	Toshiba	8MB	340MB	DualScan	$3995	Toshiba	16MB	340MB	Mono	$2459	NEC	4MB	510MB	Active	$2459
16	NEC	16MB	340MB	Mono	$2459	Toshiba	4MB	510MB	Active	$3149	IBM	8MB	250MB	DualScan	$3149
17	IBM	16MB	510MB	Mono	$3995	Toshiba	8MB	250MB	Active	$2459	NEC	4MB	340MB	DualScan	$2459
18	IBM	16MB	250MB	Mono	$2459	Toshiba	8MB	340MB	Active	$3995	NEC	4MB	510MB	DualScan	$3149
19	IBM	8MB	340MB	Mono	$2459	Toshiba	4MB	510MB	Active	$3995	NEC	4MB	250MB	DualScan	$3149
20	Toshiba	16MB	250MB	Active	$3995	IBM	4MB	340MB	DualScan	$2459	NEC	8MB	510MB	Mono	$3149
21	NEC	16MB	250MB	Active	$3149	Toshiba	4MB	510MB	DualScan	$2459	IBM	8MB	340MB	Mono	$2459
22	NEC	16MB	340MB	Mono	$3149	IBM	4MB	250MB	Active	$2459	Toshiba	8MB	510MB	DualScan	$3995
23	Toshiba	16MB	510MB	Active	$3995	IBM	4MB	250MB	Mono	$3149	NEC	8MB	340MB	DualScan	$2459
24	IBM	16MB	510MB	Mono	$2459	Toshiba	8MB	250MB	DualScan	$2459	NEC	4MB	340MB	Active	$3995
25	Toshiba	4MB	340MB	DualScan	$3995	IBM	16MB	250MB	Active	$3995	NEC	8MB	510MB	Mono	$3149
26	Toshiba	8MB	250MB	Mono	$2459	NEC	16MB	340MB	DualScan	$3149	IBM	4MB	510MB	Active	$3149
27	IBM	8MB	510MB	Mono	$2459	NEC	16MB	340MB	DualScan	$3995	Toshiba	4MB	250MB	Active	$3149
28	Toshiba	4MB	510MB	Active	$3149	IBM	16MB	250MB	DualScan	$2459	IBM	8MB	340MB	DualScan	$3995
29	NEC	8MB	250MB	DualScan	$3149	Toshiba	16MB	340MB	Mono	$2459	IBM	4MB	510MB	Active	$3995
30	Toshiba	4MB	510MB	Mono	$3995	NEC	8MB	340MB	Active	$3149	IBM	16MB	250MB	DualScan	$2459

Partworth Values

Model	Brand Name			Memory Size			Hard Drive			Screen Type			Price Level		
	NEC	IBM	Toshiba	4MB	8MB	16MB	250MB	340MB	510MB	Mono	DualScan	Active	$3995	$3149	$2459
Self-Explicated	.013	.029	.000	.000	.176	.265	.000	.114	.206	.000	.229	.294	.000	.092	.206
Conjoint	.115	.014	.000	.000	.207	.252	.000	.007	.000	.000	.390	.492	.000	.000	.134
Choice	.020	.002	.000	.000	.129	.263	.000	.096	.097	.000	.428	.458	.000	.157	.161
Constr. Conjoint	.000	.000	.000	.000	.236	.287	.000	.000	.000	.000	.445	.560	.000	.000	.152
Constr. Choice	.000	.000	.000	.000	.132	.268	.000	.093	.096	.000	.438	.468	.000	.163	.169

Appendices

Respondent No. 49

Experimental Choice Design

Set	Laptop A					Laptop B					Laptop C				
1	NEC	8MB	340MB	Mono	$2459	Toshiba	4MB	510MB	Active	$3995	IBM	16MB	250MB	DualScan	$3149
2	NEC	4MB	510MB	Active	$3995	IBM	16MB	250MB	DualScan	$3149	Toshiba	8MB	340MB	Mono	$2459
3	IBM	8MB	340MB	Active	$3995	Toshiba	4MB	510MB	Mono	$2459	NEC	16MB	250MB	DualScan	$3149
4	IBM	4MB	510MB	Active	$2459	NEC	16MB	250MB	Mono	$3995	Toshiba	8MB	510MB	DualScan	$3149
5	NEC	16MB	510MB	Mono	$3995	IBM	4MB	340MB	DualScan	$2459	Toshiba	8MB	250MB	Active	$3149
6	NEC	8MB	510MB	Mono	$3149	IBM	4MB	340MB	DualScan	$2459	Toshiba	16MB	250MB	Active	$3995
7	NEC	4MB	250MB	Active	$2459	IBM	16MB	340MB	Mono	$3149	Toshiba	8MB	250MB	DualScan	$3995
8	Toshiba	4MB	340MB	Active	$3149	IBM	8MB	510MB	Mono	$3995	NEC	16MB	250MB	DualScan	$2459
9	Toshiba	4MB	250MB	DualScan	$3995	IBM	8MB	340MB	Active	$3149	NEC	16MB	510MB	Mono	$2459
10	NEC	4MB	510MB	DualScan	$3149	IBM	8MB	340MB	Active	$2459	Toshiba	16MB	250MB	Mono	$3995
11	IBM	8MB	510MB	DualScan	$3995	Toshiba	16MB	250MB	Active	$3149	NEC	4MB	340MB	Mono	$2459
12	IBM	4MB	250MB	Active	$2459	Toshiba	8MB	510MB	DualScan	$3995	NEC	16MB	340MB	Mono	$3149
13	Toshiba	4MB	340MB	DualScan	$3149	IBM	8MB	510MB	Mono	$2459	NEC	16MB	250MB	Active	$3995
14	IBM	8MB	250MB	Active	$3149	Toshiba	16MB	340MB	Mono	$2459	NEC	4MB	510MB	DualScan	$3995
15	IBM	8MB	340MB	Active	$3995	NEC	4MB	510MB	Mono	$3149	Toshiba	16MB	250MB	DualScan	$2459
16	IBM	16MB	340MB	Mono	$2459	NEC	16MB	510MB	Active	$3995	Toshiba	4MB	250MB	DualScan	$3149
17	NEC	4MB	510MB	Active	$3995	Toshiba	16MB	250MB	Mono	$3149	IBM	8MB	340MB	DualScan	$3149
18	IBM	16MB	510MB	DualScan	$3995	Toshiba	4MB	340MB	Mono	$2459	NEC	8MB	250MB	Active	$3149
19	Toshiba	8MB	250MB	Active	$2459	Toshiba	4MB	510MB	Mono	$3995	NEC	8MB	340MB	DualScan	$3149
20	IBM	8MB	250MB	DualScan	$2459	NEC	4MB	340MB	Active	$3995	Toshiba	16MB	510MB	Mono	$3149
21	NEC	16MB	250MB	Active	$3995	Toshiba	4MB	510MB	DualScan	$3149	IBM	8MB	340MB	Mono	$2459
22	Toshiba	16MB	510MB	Mono	$3149	NEC	4MB	250MB	Active	$2459	IBM	8MB	340MB	DualScan	$3995
23	Toshiba	16MB	510MB	Active	$3995	IBM	4MB	250MB	Mono	$2459	NEC	8MB	340MB	DualScan	$3149
24	NEC	8MB	510MB	Mono	$3149	Toshiba	4MB	250MB	Active	$2459	IBM	16MB	340MB	DualScan	$3995
25	Toshiba	4MB	510MB	DualScan	$2459	NEC	16MB	340MB	Active	$3149	IBM	8MB	250MB	Mono	$3995
26	Toshiba	16MB	250MB	Mono	$2459	NEC	8MB	340MB	DualScan	$3995	IBM	4MB	510MB	Active	$3149
27	NEC	8MB	250MB	Mono	$2459	Toshiba	16MB	340MB	DualScan	$3995	IBM	4MB	510MB	Active	$3149
28	NEC	4MB	510MB	Active	$3149	Toshiba	16MB	250MB	Mono	$2459	IBM	8MB	510MB	DualScan	$3995
29	Toshiba	8MB	340MB	DualScan	$2459	IBM	16MB	510MB	Active	$3149	NEC	4MB	250MB	Mono	$3995
30	Toshiba	4MB	510MB	Mono	$3995	NEC	8MB	340MB	DualScan	$3149	IBM	16MB	250MB	Active	$2459

Partworth Values

Model	Brand Name			Memory Size			Hard Drive			Screen Type			Price Level		
	NEC	IBM	Toshiba	4MB	8MB	16MB	250MB	340MB	510MB	Mono	DualScan	Active	$3995	$3149	$2459
Self-Explicated	.059	.000	.026	.000	.160	.206	.000	.160	.206	.000	.229	.294	.000	.105	.235
Conjoint	.288	.000	.014	.160	.000	.087	.086	.039	.000	.000	.267	.406	.006	.000	.060
Choice	.000	.137	.088	.000	.090	.097	.065	.032	.000	.000	.304	.403	.000	.276	.299
Constr. Conjoint	.380	.000	.018	.000	.000	.010	.000	.000	.000	.000	.352	.535	.000	.000	.076
Constr. Choice	.000	.000	.000	.000	.102	.102	.000	.000	.000	.000	.321	.506	.000	.307	.392

Respondent No. 50

Experimental Choice Design

Set	Laptop A				Laptop B				Laptop C			
1	NEC	8MB	510MB	Mono	$2459	IBM	16MB	250MB	DualScan	$3995	Toshiba	4MB	340MB	Active	$3149
2	NEC	16MB	510MB	Mono	$3149	IBM	8MB	250MB	Active	$3995	Toshiba	4MB	340MB	DualScan	$2459
3	NEC	8MB	250MB	Active	$2459	IBM	16MB	340MB	Mono	$3995	Toshiba	4MB	510MB	DualScan	$3149
4	NEC	4MB	340MB	Active	$2459	IBM	8MB	510MB	Mono	$3995	Toshiba	16MB	250MB	DualScan	$3149
5	Toshiba	16MB	250MB	Active	$3995	IBM	4MB	510MB	Mono	$3149	NEC	8MB	340MB	DualScan	$2459
6	NEC	16MB	340MB	DualScan	$3149	IBM	4MB	250MB	Mono	$2459	Toshiba	8MB	510MB	Active	$3995
7	Toshiba	4MB	250MB	Active	$2459	IBM	8MB	340MB	Mono	$3149	NEC	16MB	510MB	DualScan	$3995
8	NEC	8MB	340MB	Active	$3149	IBM	4MB	250MB	Mono	$2459	Toshiba	16MB	510MB	DualScan	$3995
9	NEC	4MB	250MB	DualScan	$3995	IBM	8MB	340MB	Active	$3149	Toshiba	16MB	510MB	Mono	$2459
10	NEC	8MB	250MB	DualScan	$3149	IBM	4MB	340MB	Active	$2459	Toshiba	16MB	510MB	Mono	$3995
11	IBM	8MB	250MB	DualScan	$3149	NEC	16MB	250MB	Active	$3149	Toshiba	8MB	340MB	Mono	$2459
12	IBM	4MB	510MB	Active	$3995	Toshiba	8MB	340MB	Mono	$3149	NEC	16MB	510MB	DualScan	$3995
13	IBM	4MB	250MB	DualScan	$3149	NEC	8MB	510MB	Mono	$2459	Toshiba	16MB	250MB	Active	$3995
14	IBM	4MB	340MB	Active	$3149	Toshiba	8MB	510MB	Mono	$2459	NEC	16MB	510MB	Active	$3995
15	IBM	8MB	250MB	Mono	$3149	NEC	4MB	340MB	DualScan	$2459	Toshiba	16MB	340MB	Active	$2459
16	IBM	8MB	510MB	Mono	$3995	Toshiba	4MB	250MB	DualScan	$2459	NEC	4MB	250MB	Active	$3149
17	NEC	16MB	340MB	DualScan	$2459	Toshiba	8MB	510MB	Active	$3149	IBM	4MB	340MB	Mono	$3149
18	IBM	4MB	250MB	Active	$3995	Toshiba	16MB	340MB	Mono	$2459	NEC	8MB	510MB	DualScan	$3149
19	IBM	16MB	510MB	DualScan	$3995	Toshiba	4MB	250MB	Mono	$3995	NEC	8MB	340MB	Active	$3149
20	NEC	4MB	250MB	DualScan	$2459	Toshiba	16MB	340MB	Active	$3995	IBM	8MB	510MB	Mono	$3149
21	Toshiba	16MB	510MB	Active	$3995	NEC	4MB	340MB	Mono	$3149	IBM	8MB	250MB	DualScan	$2459
22	Toshiba	4MB	510MB	DualScan	$3149	NEC	8MB	250MB	Active	$2459	IBM	16MB	340MB	Mono	$3995
23	Toshiba	8MB	250MB	Active	$3149	NEC	4MB	510MB	Mono	$2459	IBM	16MB	340MB	DualScan	$3995
24	Toshiba	4MB	510MB	Mono	$3149	NEC	16MB	250MB	DualScan	$2459	IBM	8MB	340MB	Active	$3149
25	NEC	8MB	340MB	DualScan	$2459	Toshiba	4MB	510MB	Active	$3995	IBM	16MB	250MB	Mono	$3149
26	Toshiba	8MB	250MB	DualScan	$2459	IBM	16MB	340MB	Active	$3995	NEC	4MB	510MB	Mono	$3149
27	Toshiba	8MB	250MB	DualScan	$2459	IBM	16MB	340MB	Mono	$3995	NEC	4MB	510MB	Active	$3149
28	NEC	16MB	250MB	Active	$3149	Toshiba	8MB	340MB	Mono	$3995	IBM	4MB	510MB	DualScan	$2459
29	Toshiba	8MB	340MB	DualScan	$3149	NEC	16MB	510MB	Active	$2459	IBM	4MB	250MB	Mono	$3995
30	Toshiba	4MB	340MB	Mono	$2459	NEC	8MB	510MB	DualScan	$3149	IBM	16MB	250MB	Active	$3995

Partworth Values

Model	Brand Name			Memory Size			Hard Drive			Screen Type			Price Level		
	NEC	IBM	Toshiba	4MB	8MB	16MB	250MB	340MB	510MB	Mono	DualScan	Active	$3995	$3149	$2459
Self-Explicated	.000	.229	.102	.000	.076	.171	.000	.089	.200	.000	.063	.143	.000	.143	.257
Conjoint	.000	.202	.146	.000	.020	.056	.000	.371	.494	.035	.146	.000	.000	.102	.053
Choice	.000	.096	.049	.000	.075	.178	.000	.329	.444	.000	.073	.066	.000	.183	.209
Constr. Conjoint	.000	.243	.176	.000	.025	.067	.000	.448	.596	.000	.000	.000	.000	.093	.093
Constr. Choice	.000	.100	.052	.000	.076	.178	.000	.324	.439	.000	.072	.072	.000	.182	.210

References

Addelman, Sidney (1962), "Symmetrical and Asymmetrical Fractional Factorial Plans," *Technometrics*, 4, 47-58.

Allenby, Greg M. and Peter E. Rossi (1991), "There is No Aggregate Bias: Why Macro Logit Models Work," *Journal of Business and Economic Statistics*, 9 (January), 1-14.

_____ and James L. Ginter (1995), "Using Extremes to Design Products and Segment Markets," *Journal of Marketing Research*, 32 (November), 392-403.

_____, Neeraj Arora, and James L. Ginter (1995), "Incorporating Prior Knowledge into the Design and Analysis of Conjoint Studies," *Journal of Marketing Research*, 17, 152-62.

Amemiya, T. (1981), "Qualitative Response Models: A Survey," *Journal of Economic Literature*, 19, 1438-536.

Anderson, Don A. and James B. Wiley (1992), "Efficient Choice Set Designs for Estimating Cross-Effects Models," *Marketing Letters*, 3, 357-70.

_____, Aloys Borgers, Dick Ettema, and Harry Timmermans (1992a), "Estimating Availability Effects in Travel Choice Modeling: A Stated Choice Approach," *Transportation Research Record* 1357, 51-65.

Anderson, Simon P., Andre de Palma, and Jaques-Francois Thisse (1992b), *Discrete Choice Theory of Product Differentiation*, Mass. MIT Press.

Batsell, Richard R. (1980), "Consumer Resource Allocation Models at the Individual Level," *Journal of Consumer Research*, 7, 78-87.

_____ and L. Lodish (1981), "A Model and Measurement Methodology for Predicting Individual Consumer Choice," *Journal of Marketing Research*, 18, 1-12.

_____ and Jordan J. Louviere (1991), "Experimental Choice Analysis," *Marketing Letters*, 2, 199-214.

_____ and John Polking (1985), "A New Class of Market Share Models," *Marketing Science*, Vol. 4, No. 3, 177-198.

Bauer, Hans H., Andreas Herrmann, and Andreas Mengen (1994), "Eine Methode zur gewinnmaximalen Produktgestaltung auf der Basis des Conjoint Measurement," *Zeitschrift für Betriebswirtschaft*, 64. Jahrgang, Heft 1, 81-94.

Ben-Akiva, Moshe and Steven Lerman (1985), *Discrete Choice Analysis*, Mass. MIT Press.

_____ and Takayuki Morikawa (1990), "Estimation of Travel Demand Models From Multiple Data Sources," in *Transportation and Traffic Theory*, M. Koshi, ed. New York: Elsevier, 461-76.

Bettman, J. R. (1979), *An Information Processing Theory of Consumer Choice*, Addison-Wesley, Reading, MA.

Block, H. D. and J. Marschak (1960), "Random Orderings and Stochastic Theories of Response," in I. Olkin (eds.), *Contributions to Probability and Statistics*, Stanford: Stanford University Press, 97-132.

Bose, R. C. (1947), "Mathematical Theory of the symmetrical factorial design," *Sankhya*, 8, 107-66.

_____ and Kishen, K. (1940), "On the Problem of Confounding in General Symmetrical Factorial Design, *Sankhya*, 5, 21-36.

Bunch, David S., Jordan J. Louviere, and Don Anderson (1996), "A Comparison of Experimental Design Strategies for Multinomial Logit Models: The Case of Generic Attributes," *Working Paper*, Graduate School of Management, University of California at Davis.

_____ and Richard R. Batsell (1989), "A Monte Carlo Comparison of Estimators for the Multinomial Logit Model," Journal of Marketing Research, 26 (February), 56-68.

Carmone, Frank J., Paul E. Green, and Arun K. Jain (1978), "Robustness of Conjoint Analysis: Some Monte Carlo Results," *Journal of Marketing Research*, Vol. 15, 300-3.

Carroll, J. Douglas and Paul E. Green (1995), "Psychometric Methods in Marketing Research: Part I, Conjoint Analysis", *Journal of Marketing Research*, 32 (November), 385-91.

Carson, Richard T., Jordan J. Louviere, Don A. Anderson, Phipps Arabie, David S. Bunch, David A. Hensher, Richard M. Johnson, Warren F. Kuhfeld, Dan

Steinberg, Joffrey Swait, Harry Timmermans, and James B. Wiley (1994), "Experimental Analysis of Choice," *Marketing Letters*, 5.4 (October), 351-67.

Cattin, Philippe and Friedhelm Bliemel (1978), "Metric vs. Nonmetric Procedures for Multiattribute Modeling: Some Simulation Results," *Decision Sciences*, Vol. 9, 472-9.

Chapman, R. G. (1984), "An Approach to Estimating Logit Models of a Single Decision Maker's Choice Behavior," *Advances in Consumer Research*, 11, 656-61.

Chintagunta, P. K. (1992), "Estimating a Multinomial Probit Model of Brand Choice using the Method of Simulated Moments," *Marketing Science*, 11, 4, 386-407.

Currim, I. S. (1982), "Predictive Testing of Consumer Choice Models Not Subject to Independence of Irrelevant Alternatives," *Journal of Marketing Research*, 19, 208-22.

Daganzo, C. F. (1979), *Multinomial Probit: The Theory and Its Applications to Demand Forecasting*. New York: Academic Press.

Debreu, G. (1960), "Review of R. D. Luce, Individual Choice Behavior: A Theoretical Analysis," *American Economic Review*, 50, 186-8.

DeSarbo, Wayne, Venkatram Ramaswamy, and Steven H. Cohen (1995), "Market Segmentation with Choice-Based Conjoint Analysis," *Marketing Letters*, 6:2, 137-47.

Dey, Aloke (1985), *Orthogonal Fractional Factorial Designs*, New York: John Wiley & Sons.

Einhorn, Hillel J. (1970), "The Use of Nonlinear, Noncompensatory Models in Decision Making," *Psychological Bulletin*, 73, 221-30.

Eliashberg J. and G. L. Lilien (1993), *Marketing: Handbooks in Operations Research and Management Science*, Vol. 5, North-Holland: Elsevier Science Publishers B. V.

Elrod, T. and M. P. Keane (1995), "A Factor-Analytic Probit Model for Representing the Market Structures in Panel Data," *Journal of Marketing Research*, 32, 1, 1-16.

_____, Jordan J. Louviere, and Krishnakumar S. Davey (1992), "An Empirical Comparison of Ratings-Based and Choice-Based Conjoint Models," *Journal of Marketing Research*, 26, 368-77.

Fishbein, Martin (1967), "A Behavior Theory Approach to the Relations between Beliefs about an Object and the Attitude towards the Object," in *Readings in Attitude and Theory Measurement*, ed. M. Fishbein, New York: John Wiley & Sons, Inc., 389-99.

Fisher, R. A. (1926), "The Arrangement of Field Experiments", *Journal of Min. Agriculture,* 33, 503-13.

Foekens, Eijte W., Peter S. H. Leefang, and Dick R. Wittink (1994), "A Comparison and an Exploration of the Forecasting Accuracy of a Loglinear Model at Different Levels of Aggregation," *International Journal of Forecasting*, 10 (September), 245-61.

Ford, Ian, D. M. Titterington, and Christos P. Kitsos (1989), "Recent Advances in Nonlinear Experimental Design," *Technometrics*, Vol. 31 (February), No. 1, 49-60.

Gaul, Wolfgang, Eberhard Aust, and Daniel Baier (1995), "Gewinnorientierte Produktliniengestaltung unter Berücksichtigung des Kundennutzens," *Zeitschrift für Betriebswirtschaft*, 65. Jahrgang, Heft 8, 835-55.

Gelfand, Alan E. and Adrian F. M. Smith (1990), "Sampling-Based Approaches to Calculating Marginal Densities," *Journal of the American Statistical Association*, 85, 398-409.

Green, P. E. (1974), "On the Design of Choice Experiments involving Multifactor Alternatives," *Journal of Consumer Research*, 1, 61-8.

_____ (1984), "Hybrid Models for Conjoint Analysis: An Expository Review," *Journal of Marketing Research*, 21, 155-69.

_____, J. Douglas Carroll, and Frank J. Carmone (1978), "Some New Types of Fractional Factorial Designs for Marketing Experiments," *Research in Marketing*, Vol. 1, 99-122.

_____ and Abba M. Krieger (1988), "Choice Rules and Sensitivity Analysis in Conjoint Simulators," *Journal of the Academy of Marketing Science*, 16, 114-27.

_____ and _____ (1995), "Attribute Importance Weights Modification in Assessing a Brand's Competitive Potential," *Marketing Science*, 14, No. 3 Part 1 of 2, 253-70.

_____ and _____ (1996), "Individualized Hybrid Models for Conjoint Analysis," *Management Science*, Vol. 42 (June), No. 6, 850-67.

_____ and Vithala R. Rao (1971), "Conjoint Measurement for Quantifying Judgmental Data," *Journal of Marketing Research*, 13, 355-63.

_____ and V. Srinivasan (1978), "Conjoint Analysis in Consumer Research: Issues and Outlook," *Journal of Marketing Research*, 5, 103-23.

_____ and _____ (1990), "Conjoint Analysis in Marketing: New Developments with Implications for Research and Practice," *Journal of Marketing Research*, 54, 3-19.

Hagerty, M. R. (1985), "Improving the Predictive Power of Conjoint Analysis: The Use of Factor Analysis and Cluster Analysis," *Journal of Marketing Research*, 22, 168-84.

_____ (1986), "The Cost of Simplifying Preference Models," *Marketing Science*, 5, 298-319.

Hartmann, Wolfgang M., Minbo Kim, and Ying C. So (1995), Technical Report: *Applications of Nonlinear Optimization Using PROC NLP and SAS/IML Software*, Cary, NC: SAS Institute Inc.

Hausman, J. A. and D. McFadden (1984), "Specification Tests for the Multinomial Logit Model," *Econometrica*, 52, 1219-40.

_____ and D. A. Wise (1978), "A Conditional Probit Model for Qualitative Choice: Discrete Decisions Recognizing Interdependence and Heterogeneous Preferences," *Econometrica*, 46, 403-26.

Huber, Joel and Klaus Zwerina (1996), "The Importance of Utility Balance in Efficient Choice Designs," *Journal of Marketing Research*, 33, 307-17.

_____, _____, and Jonathan Pinnell (1996), "Are Utility Balanced Choice Designs Really More Efficient?" presented at *Marketing Science Conference*, Gainesville (FL), March.

_____, Dick R. Wittink, John A. Fiedler, and Richard Miller (1993), "The Effectiveness of Alternative Preference Elicitation Procedures in Predicting Choice," *Journal of Marketing Research*, 30, 105-14.

Jain, Arun K., Franklin Acito, Naresh K. Malhotra, and Vijay Mahajan (1979), "A Comparison of the Internal Validity of Alternative Parameter Estimation Methods in Decompositional Multiattribute Preference Models," *Journal of Marketing Research*, Vol. 16, 313-22.

Johnson, Richard M. and Bryan K. Orme (1996), "How Many Questions should you ask in Choice-Based Conjoint Studies?" *Presented at the Seventh ART Forum*, Beaver Creek, CO.

Kamakura, Wagner and Gary J. Russell (1989), "A Probabilistic Choice Model for Market Segmentation and Elasticity Structure," *Journal of Marketing Research*, 16, 379-90.

Keller, Kevin Lane and Richard Staelin (1987), "Effects of Quality and Quantity of Information on Decision Effectiveness," *Journal of Consumer Research*, 14, 200-13.

Kirk, Roger E. (1995), *Experimental Design: Procedures for the Behavioral Science*, 3rd ed., New York: Brooks/Cole Publishing Company.

Kotler, Philip (1997), *Marketing Management. Analysis, Planning, Implementation, and Control*, 9th ed., Prentice Hall, New Jersey.

_____ and Friedhelm Bliemel (1996), *Marketing-Management. Analyse, Planung, Umsetzung und Steuerung*, 8. Auflage, Stuttgart: Poeschel-Verlag.

Krieger, Abba B. and Paul E. Green (1991), "Designing Pareto Optimal Stimuli for Multiattribute Choice Experiments," *Marketing Letters*, 2, 337-48.

Kruskal, Joseph B. (1965), "Analysis of Factorial Experiments by Estimating Monotone Transformations of the Data," *Journal of the Royal Statistical Society*, Series B, 27, 251-63.

Kuehn, A. A. and R. L. Day (1962), "Strategy of Product Quality," *Harvard Business Review*, 40, 100-10.

Kuhfeld, Warren F., Randall D. Tobias, and Mark Garratt (1994), "Efficient Experimental Design with Marketing Research Applications," *Journal of Marketing Research*, Vol. 31 (Nov.), 545-557.

Lazari, Andreas G. and Don A. Anderson (1994), "Designs of Discrete Choice Experiments for Estimating Both Attribute and Availability Cross Effects," *Journal of Marketing Research*, 31 (August), 375-83.

Lenk, Peter J., Wayne S. DeSarbo, Paul E. Green, and Martin R. Young (1996), "Hierarchical Bayes Conjoint Analysis: Recovery of Partworth Heterogeneity form Reduced Experimental Designs," *Marketing Science*, Vol. 15, No. 2, 173-91.

Louviere, Jordan J. (1986), "A Conjoint Model for Analyzing New Product Positions in a Differentiated Market with Price Competition," *Advances in Consumer Research*, 13, 375-80.

_____ (1988), "Analyzing Decision Making: Metric Conjoint Analysis," *Sage University Paper Series on Quantitative Applications in the Social Sciences*, No. 67. Newbury Park, CA: Sage Publications.

_____ and George Woodworth (1983), "Design and Analysis of Simulated Consumer Choice of Allocation Experiments: A Method Based on Aggregate Data," *Journal of Marketing Research*, 20 (November), 350-67.

Luce, R. (1959) *Individual Choice Behavior: A Theoretical Analysis*. Wiley, New York.

_____ and John W. Tukey (1964), "Simultaneous Conjoint Measurement: A New Type of Fundamental Measurement," *Journal of Mathematical Psychology*, 1, 1-27.

Madalla, G. S. (1983), *Limited Dependent and Qualitative Variables in Econometrics*, NY, Cambridge University Press.

Manski, C. F. (1977), "The Structure of Random Utility Models," *Theory and Decision*, 8, 229-54.

McAlister, Leigh, Rajendra Srivastava, Joel Horowitz, Morgan Jones, Wagner Kamakura, Jack Kulchitsky, Brian Ratchford, Gary Russell, Fareena Sultan, Tetsuo Yai, Doyle Weiss and Russ Winer (1991), "Incorporating Choice Dynamics in Models of Consumer Behavior," *Marketing Letters*, 2 (3), 241-52.

McFadden, Daniel (1974), "Conditional Logit Analysis of Qualitative Choice Behavior," in *Frontiers in Econometrics*, P. Zarembka, ed., New York: Academic Press, 105-42.

_____ (1975), "On Independence, Structure and Simultaneity in Transportation Demand Analysis," *Working Paper* No. 7511, Urban Travel

Demand Forecasting Project, Institute of Transportation Studies, University of California, Berkeley.

_____ (1976), "Quantal Choice Analysis: A Survey," *Annals of Economic and Social Measurement*, 5/6, 363-90.

_____ (1978), "Modeling the Choice of Residential Location," in A. Karlvist, L. Lundqvist, F. Snickars, and J. Weibull (eds.), *Spatial Interaction Theory and Planning Models*, Amsterdam: North-Holland, pp. 75-96.

_____ (1981), "Econometric Models of Probabilistic Choice," in C. F. Manski and D. McFadden (eds.), *Structural Analysis of Discrete Data with Econometric Applications*, Cambridge: MIT Press, 198-272.

_____ (1986), "The Choice Theory Approach to Market Research," *Marketing Science*, Vol. 5, No. 4 (Fall), 275-97.

_____ (1987), "Regression Based Specification Tests for the Multinomial Logit Model," *Journal of Econometrics*, 34, 63-82.

_____ (1989), "A Method of Simulated Moments of Discrete Response Models without Numerical Integration," *Econometrica*, 57, 995-1026.

_____, Tye, W., and Train K. (1977), "An Application of Diagnostic Tests for the Irrelevant Alternatives Property of the Multinomial Logit Model," *Transportation Research Record* 637, 39-46.

Meyer, Robert and Eric J. Johnson (1989), "Information Overload and the Nonrobustness of Linear Models: A Comment on Keller and Staelin," *Journal of Consumer Research*, 15, 498-503.

Meyer, Robert and Eric J. Johnson (1995), "Empirical Generalizations in the Modeling of Consumer Choice," *Marketing Science*, Vol. 14, No. 3, Part 2 of 2, 180-9.

Montgomery, Henry, Marcus Selart, Tommy Garling, and Eric Lindberg (1994), "The Judgment-Choice Discrepancy: Noncompatibility or Restructuring," *Journal of Behavioral Decision Making*, 7, 145-55.

Moore, L. William (1980), "Levels of Aggregation in Conjoint Analysis: An Empirical Comparison," *Journal of Marketing Research*, 17 (November), 516-23.

_____ and D. R. Lehmann (1989), "A Paired Comparison Nested Logit Model of Individual Preference Structures," *Journal of Marketing Research*, 26, 420-8.

Payne, John W. (1976), "Task Complexity and Contingent Processing in Decision-Making: An Information Search and Protocol Analysis," *Organizational Behavior and Human Performance*, 16, 366-87.

Raktoe, B. L., A. Hedayat, and W. T. Federer (1981), *Factorial Designs*, New York: John Wiley & Sons.

Rosenberg, Milton J. (1956), "Cognitive Structure and Attitudinal Affect," *Journal of Abnormal and Social Psychology*, 53, 367-72.

Rossi, E. Peter and Greg M. Allenby (1993), "A Bayesian Approach to Estimating Household Parameters," *Journal of Marketing Research*, 30 (May), 171-82.

Rotondo, John (1986), "Price as an Aspect of Choice in EBA," Marketing Science, Vol. 5, No. 4 (Fall), 391-402.

SAS Institute Inc. (1995), *SAS/QC Software: Usage and Reference, Version 6, First Edition, Volume 1*, Cary, NC: SAS Institute Inc.

Sawtooth Software (1993), *The CBC System for Choice-Based Conjoint Analysis*. Ketchum Idaho: ID Sawtooth Software.

Schweikl, H. (1985), *Computergestütze Präferenzanalyse mit individuell wichtigen Produktmerkmalen*, Berlin: Duncker & Humbolt Verlag.

Simon, Hermann (1992), "Pricing Opportunities - And How to Exploit Them," *Sloan Management Review*, 33, 55-65.

_____ and Eckhard Kucher (1988), "Die Bestimmung empirischer Preisabsatzfunktionen: Methoden, Befunde, Erfahrungen," *Zeitschrift für Betriebswirtschaft*, 58. Jahrgang, Heft 1, 171-83.

Srinivasan, V. (1988), "A Conjunctive-Compensatory Approach to the Self-Explication of Multiattributed Preference," *Decision Sciences*, 19, 295-305.

_____ and Chan Su Park (1995), "Surprising Robustness of the Self-Explicated Approach to Customer Preference Structure Measurement," *Working Paper*, Graduate School of Business, Stanford University.

_____ and Allan D. Shocker (1973), "Linear Programming Techniques for Multidimensional Analysis of Preferences," *Psychometrika*, 38, 337-69.

_____, Arun K. Jain, and Naresh K. Malhotra (1983), "Improving the Predictive Power of Conjoint Analysis by Constrained Parameter Estimation," *Journal of Marketing Research*, 20, 433-8.

Swait, Joffre and Jordan J. Louviere (1993), "The Role of the Scale Parameter in the Estimation and Use of Generalized Extreme Utility Models," *Journal of Marketing Research*, 30 (August), 305-14.

_____, Tulin Erdem, Jordan J. Louviere, and Chris Dubelaar (1993), "The Equilibration Price: A Measure of Consumer-perceived Brand Equity," *International Journal of Research in Marketing*, 10, 23-45.

Thomas, Lutz (1979), "Conjoint Measurement als Instument der Absatzforschung," *Zeitschrift für Betriebswirtschaft*, 49. Jahrgang, Heft 3, 199-210.

Thurstone, L. L. (1927), "A Law of Comparative Judgment," *Psychological Review*, 34, 273-86.

Timmermans, Harry, Aloys Borgers, and Peter van der Waerden (1992), "Mother Logit Analysis of Substitution Effects in Consumer Shopping Destination Choice," *Journal of Business Research*, 24, 177-89.

Tversky, A. (1972), "Elimination by Aspects: A Theory of Choice," *Psychological Review*, 79, 281-99.

_____ and S. Sattath (1979), "Preference Trees," *Psychological Review*, 86 542-73.

van der Lans, Ivo A. and Willem H. Heiser (1992), "Constrained Part-Worth Estimation in Conjoint Analysis Using the Self-Explicated Utility Model," *International Journal of Research in Marketing*, 9, 325-44.

Wedel, Michel and Wayne DeSarbo (1993), "A Latent Binomial Logit Methodology for the Analysis of Paired Comparison Choice Data," *Decision Sciences*, 24, 1157-70.

Winer, B. J., Donald R. Brown, and Kenneth M. Michels (1991), *Statistical Principles in Experimental Design*, 3rd ed., New York: McGraw-Hill, Inc.

Wittink, Dick and Philippe Cattin (1989), "Commercial Use of Conjoint Analysis: An Update," *Journal of Marketing*, 53, 91-6.

_____, Marco Vriens, and Wim Burhenne (1994), "Commercial Use of Conjoint Analysis in Europe: Results and Critical Reflections," *International Journal of Research in Marketing*, 11, 41-52.

Yates, F. (1935), "Complex Experiments," *Journal of the Royal Statistical Society*, Supplement, 2, 181-247.

_____ (1937), "The Design and Analysis of Factorial Experiments," *Imperial Bureau au Soil Science Tech. Comm.* No. 35.

Zwerina, Klaus and Joel Huber (1996), "Deriving Individual Preference Structures from Practical Choice Experiments," *Working Paper*, The Fuqua School of Business, Duke University.

_____ and _____ (1996), "The Role of a Default Alternative in Efficient Choice Experiments," *Working Paper*, The Fuqua School of Business, Duke University.

_____, _____, and Warren Kuhfeld (1996), "A General Method for Constructing Efficient Choice Designs," *Working Paper*, The Fuqua School of Business, Duke University.

Printed by Printforce, the Netherlands